# The Death and Life of Speculative Theology

# The Death and Life of Speculative Theology

## A Lonergan Idea

Ryan Hemmer

LEXINGTON BOOKS/FORTRESS ACADEMIC
*Lanham • Boulder • New York • London*

Published by Lexington Books/Fortress Academic
Lexington Books is an imprint of The Rowman & Littlefield Publishing Group, Inc.
4501 Forbes Boulevard, Suite 200, Lanham, Maryland 20706
www.rowman.com

86-90 Paul Street, London EC2A 4NE, United Kingdom

Copyright © 2023 by The Rowman & Littlefield Publishing Group, Inc.

Scripture quotations are from the New Revised Standard Version of the Bible, copyright © 1989 National Council of the Churches of Christ in the United States of America. Used by permission. All rights reserved.

Portions of chapter 4 were adapted from "Systems and Sequences: The Renewal of Theological Understanding and the Problem of Speculative Pluralism," in Joseph Ogbonnaya and Gerard Whelan, SJ, eds., *Intellect, Affect, and God: The Trinity, History, and the Life of Grace: Essays in Honor of Robert M. Doran, SJ*. Milwaukee: Marquette University Press, 2021. Used by permission.

Portions of chapter 5 were adapted from "Censorial Liberation and Speculative Method," in Joseph Ogbonnaya, ed., *Perspectives on Psychic Conversion*. Milwaukee: Marquette University Press, forthcoming. Used by permission.

*All rights reserved.* No part of this book may be reproduced in any form or by any electronic or mechanical means, including information storage and retrieval systems, without written permission from the publisher, except by a reviewer who may quote passages in a review.

British Library Cataloguing in Publication Information Available

**Library of Congress Cataloging-in-Publication Data**

Names: Hemmer, Ryan, 1987– author.
Title: The death and life of speculative theology : a Lonergan idea / Ryan Hemmer.
Description: Lanham : Lexington Books/Fortress Academic, [2023] | Includes bibliographical references and index. | Summary: "Drawing on the thought of Bernard Lonergan, The Death and Life of Speculative Theology narrates the rise and fall of speculative theology, retrieves and transposes its central achievements, and shows how it might be renewed as a modern science for a modern culture"— Provided by publisher.
Identifiers: LCCN 2023017987 (print) | LCCN 2023017988 (ebook) | ISBN 9781978715271 (cloth) | ISBN 9781978715288 (epub)
Subjects: LCSH: Catholic Church—Doctrines. | Theology, Doctrinal—History. | Lonergan, Bernard J. F.—Influence.
Classification: LCC BX1751.3 .H466 2023  (print) | LCC BX1751.3  (ebook) | DDC 230/.2—dc23/eng/20230530
LC record available at https://lccn.loc.gov/2023017987
LC ebook record available at https://lccn.loc.gov/2023017988

∞™ The paper used in this publication meets the minimum requirements of American National Standard for Information Sciences—Permanence of Paper for Printed Library Materials, ANSI/NISO Z39.48-1992.

*For Kate*

# Contents

| | |
|---|---|
| Acknowledgments | ix |
| Introduction | 1 |
| Chapter 1: Forgetting and Misremembering | 5 |
| Chapter 2: Form and Action | 19 |
| Chapter 3: Why Speculative Theology Failed | 55 |
| Chapter 4: Repurposing Royal Ruins | 89 |
| Chapter 5: Speculation, Procession, Collaboration | 123 |
| Conclusion | 159 |
| Bibliography | 163 |
| Subject Index | 179 |
| Name Index | 183 |
| About the Author | 185 |

# Acknowledgments

My life in books is not lived in public. I work behind the scenes, helping authors find their voices and refine their words. I ask them to write with the confidence that expertise promises but more often quells. What follows reflects my desire to practice what I preach to others, to find, refine, and speak in my own voice—and to refute the old adage concerning those that can't, do.

This book's first incarnation was a doctoral dissertation, written under the supervision of Robert ("Bob") Doran, SJ. He died mere months after I defended it. Bob was one of the last true masters of the intellectual tradition and practitioners of the speculative craft. His genius, though, did not come at the expense of his compassion, which he offered with an open hand to both students and strangers. I am confident about what I have written in this book because Bob was confident in me. May he rest in peace.

While Doran was, as my footnotes attest, my living master, I've spent most of my adult life apprenticing to two others whom I never got to meet: Bernard Lonergan and Jane Jacobs. Though Lonergan's name appears on almost every page of this book, Jacobs is its moral and intellectual center (and the inspiration for its title).

If doctors make the worst patients, then editors must make the worst authors. My thanks then to my editor, Gayla Freeman, for her professionalism and forbearance. Thanks, too, to my peer reviewer, whom the reader can thank for the finished text's more Latin-restricted diet and more full-throated political voice, and to the book's endorsers for their attention and care.

I am grateful, too, for my friends who have accompanied me through many difficult years spent thinking and writing about speculative method, especially Jon Heaps, whose intellectual prowess is surpassed only by his immense talent for friendship. And Robyn Boeré, who effortlessly embodies all the practical and intellectual virtues and shares their fruits recklessly with others—even with me.

My deepest, most abiding gratitude is reserved for Kate, Emilia, and the life we share together.

# Introduction

The queen's rule has ended. Her abdication was uncoerced. For seven centuries, theology stood atop the topography of human knowledge and organized it into an ordered whole. It disclosed that knowledge's divine origin and beatific end. *Science* was the certain knowledge of things through their causes, while *theological* science expressed the ground of all causality and the goal of all things. But theology's regency is over. It is no longer *regina scientiarum*—no longer queen of the sciences. Many would argue that it is no longer a science at all.

Theology today is a set of practices, a body of doctrine, a library of texts, or a sociology of religious symbols, rituals, and experiences. In each case (and some cases are mutually opposed), theology is an "already-out-there-now" or an "already-in-here-now" real. Its concern is with contents, with things—with books, beliefs, believers, and with pushing around the phantasms of the past. But theologians themselves have little time for analyzing the nature or structure of their own concerning, their own believing, or their own knowing.

Modern theology's antimodernists lionize invulnerable theological products that enjoy timeless authority, while its postmodernists (a by now wretched, *almost* meaningless term) retreat from those same products for political, ethical, and even pious reasons. But Jane Jacobs describes a different habit of thought. She "does not focus on 'things' and expect them to explain themselves" but instead affirms that "processes are always of the essence" and that "things have significances as participants in processes, for better or worse."[1] Orders and relations, in other words, precede things. And thinking is an order, a process, a way—a method.

Yet, few matters in contemporary theology invite such ecumenical condemnation as theological method. Modern Protestants, Catholics, and Orthodox may not agree on much (including the question of whether they are obligated to agree at all), but their leading intellectual lights speak as one of method's venal legacy. Antagonists in the decline narratives vary—Schleiermacherian pietism, Kantian idealism, or secular scientism—but the moral of the story remains the same: method is the cause of theology's modern irrelevance and a hindrance to its renewal. This book adopts, advances, and defends the unfashionable opinion that speculative theological method is no mere artifact of a fallen Catholic cultural hegemony, no vain attempt to chase the cultural and institutional capital of an ascendent natural science, but is instead an essential element of theological rationality—one only heightened by the vagaries of the moment.

But before the reader mistake this work for another tiresome repristination project—a pitiful longing for the empire, the commonwealth, or Walsh's "thirteenth, greatest of centuries"—allow me to state in indicative terms that theology is not a science of nostalgia. Repristination is erudite obfuscation. And one need look no further than the ongoing romance between postliberals and their authoritarian patrons for corroborating evidence to support this indictment. Theologians should not rule the world, and neither should kings or bishops. Virtue is not impressed by coercion—even when the coercers dress up in cassocks and crowns and cite Augustine and Aquinas while on the stump.

Various geopolitical developments in recent years rightfully raise suspicions that even casual celebrations of Catholic cultural or intellectual patrimony are thinly veiled social wedges meant to obscure the racial, religious, and sexual agendas of antiliberal Christian nationalism. All of us should sit for a while at the business end of those suspicions. But the revolutionary imagination that longs to purify the present by setting a refiner's fire to the past consigns to the conflagration tools and materials with which a better world might be made. Only prudence can discern the difference between the failure of nerve—cowardice—that fears to relinquish its ill-begotten gains, and the dialectical process of *ressourcement*, which advances what is good in the inherited past while reversing what is evil. The judgment of one from the other is a wager that retrospect alone can evaluate. Only fortitude can put one intellectual and moral foot in front of the other in the face of that wager's odds.

It is my belief that the speculative tradition, despite the serious accusations with which it is charged, plays a role in the intellectual life that cannot be set aside. If it must be abandoned, it must also be replaced. I have elected to pursue the liberal preference for revisions and iterations to revolutions and blank slates. Thus, the sources, arguments, and—perhaps—conclusions presented in this work may conform to the jaded expectations of more revolutionary spirits. Maybe they are right. If they are, what follows will fail to persuade. But perhaps, at the margin, a benighted soul tempted by today's Thomistic marketing of revanchist snake oil may find in these pages some integral reasons for rejecting reactionary fantasies.

*The Death and Life of Speculative Theology* provides a retrospective of theology's regnant past, a diagnosis of its confused present, and a wager on its cosmopolitan future. It invites readers first to remember theological science's crowning achievement: speculative method—the intellectual procedure by which analogy and dialectic worked to resolve stubborn ambiguities and seeming contradictions in the deposit of faith. Speculative method, at its high medieval apex, secured theology's regency by creating and applying the philosophical, analogical, and intellectual tools with which all forms of human knowledge secure themselves and their subjects by assimilating and accommodating their unique objects of abstractive inquiry. But this intellectual order was built upon a nexus of cultural and civilizational circumstances that set the limits of scientific, philosophical, and social possibility. Within this order, culture is the social objectification of the human soul, its expression in the world of cooperation. As the soul is what remains when all manner of material, spatial, and temporal determinations have been bracketed from the question of being, so this classical notion of culture is eternal, spiritual, and universal. Where classicist culture prevails, philosophy is *philosophia perennis*, science is the certain knowledge of things through their causes, and social, civil, and ecclesial relations mirror the hierarchical geographies of the heavens. Styles of living that fail to conform are, by definition, uncultured—even barbaric.

Classicism was the superstructure within which speculative theology developed and thrived. But it is now infertile soil. Modern science has abandoned the Aristotelian ideal of eternal law and replaced it with the canons of empirical analysis. Modern philosophy has subordinated metaphysics to cognitional theory. And modern anthropology has discovered that culture is not a permanent achievement but a set of meanings and values that inform shared styles of life. Theology was queen because classicist culture was king. But classicism is dead, and we have killed it—with modern science, modern philosophy, and the modern notion of culture.

Catholics cope with classicism's death in both diverging and converging ways. Until recently, postliberals lionized "optional" polities of Christian community. Members of these alternative structures of social cooperation were meant to exist amidst their secular neighbors, witnessing to the rule of God by rejecting the worldly quest for political power. But in today's reactionary consolidation, many postliberals have been swallowed up by more ambitious revanchists, who seek the coercive, political means to restore classicism to power in the hope that cultural hegemony (and the instruments of the administrative state) will once again secure theology's rule over knowledge, and, more importantly, the classicist's rule over the masses. Revolutionaries, for their part, dance on classicism's grave. But they must build a new world without knowing in advance if the new will prove more durably just than the old. But there remains a liberal alternative to these dominant approaches. *The Death and Life of Speculative Theology* argues that speculative method can be decoupled from classicism; transformed through modern science, philosophy, and culture; and made useful for addressing some of the many problems facing this cosmopolitan age. The same forces that led to the queen's abdication can help her abandon monarchical ambition and embrace democratic process.

A renewed speculative theology can provoke, organize, regulate, and invigorate intellectual pluralism and thereby contribute to the greater work of making the world a home for the human spirit.[2] But speculative theology is not a panacea. Modern challenges are legion. No single science can resolve them all. So, one might as well begin with those problems closest to hand, in the hope that their solutions will accumulate to serve the larger project of social, cultural, and personal renewal. Thus, this book narrates the rise and fall of speculative theology, anticipates how it might be renewed, repurposes some of its forgotten achievements, and applies its democratically reformed method to specific contemporary problems to show that modern theology can be a modern science for a modern culture. Modernity is not "late." It is not "post." Modernity is just getting started. What it will be depends upon what we make of it. Drawing upon and advancing the prodigious work and enduring ideas of Bernard Lonergan, this book argues that speculative method can be part of that making.

## NOTES

1. Jane Jacobs, *The Death and Life of Great American Cities*, Modern Library edition (New York: Modern Library, 1993), xvii.

2. I adopt this turn of phrase from Robert Doran. In my view, the phrase itself is a Doranian gloss on the Ignatian notion of *magis*.

*Chapter 1*

# Forgetting and Misremembering

Theology was once divided into two parts. The first concerned itself with the past. It sought harmony between the material and cultural diversity of divine revelation in history and the Church's expression of that revelation in its dogmatic teaching. Theologians of the first part evolved to utilize the methods, tools, and techniques of modern historical study to accomplish this lofty task. And their successes provisioned their counterparts with the raw materials for an ensuing set of theological assignments. The second part of theology engaged the present. It labored to understand the Church's doctrines and the nexus between them through the application of theology's handmaid, philosophy—and its techniques of theory, dialectic, and analogy. This theological domain required faith's illumination of reason, and reason's earnest, pious, and calm advance. The result, with divine aid, was some imperfect, but highly fruitful understanding of the mysteries made known in revelation and expressed in the Church's confession.

The first part of theology, the part concerned with historical revelation and the development of doctrine, was called "positive theology." The second part, with its sanctified reason and search for faith's understanding was designated "speculative theology." The working arrangement between these twin labors persisted from the sixteenth century through much of the twentieth.[1] But in the reorganization of institutions and institutional forms of knowledge in the wake of the Second Vatican Council, the positive/speculative division declined, and the historical/systematic division ascended.

The Council vindicated certain lines of revision and renewal that had been steadily, if also controversially, developing in Catholic Europe throughout the pre- and post-War periods. Yves Congar, Henri de Lubac, and their associated *nouvelle théologie* luminaries—first Dominicans, then Jesuits—had for decades committed themselves to a renewed positive theology, to what Charles Péguy called a *ressourcement* of the biblical, patristic, and liturgical sources of faith and doctrine, augmenting classical methods with modern analysis.[2] The priority the *nouvelle théologie* assigned to positive theology was not without justification. As Jürgen Mettepenningen writes, "The representatives of the *nouvelle théologie* attached the same importance to this positive theological method as to the speculative theological method. In their opinion, all-embracing speculative theology had lost contact with (the) reality (of faith) to such a degree that a corrective manoeuvre had become necessary."[3]

The coupling of positive method with modern historiographical research yielded undeniably progressive results. In patristics, generations of researchers have been aided by the production of critical texts of the Church Fathers published in the *Sources Chrétiennes* series, founded under the editorial leadership of de Lubac and his Jesuit confrères Jean Daniélou and Claude Mondésert, while the early monographs of Hans Urs von Balthasar catalyzed decades of renewed scholarly attention to Greek theologians like Gregory of Nyssa and Maximus the Confessor.[4]

Early and mid-century reform movements both in Europe and North America sought to recover more ancient forms of liturgical practice. These efforts culminated in 1963 with the promulgation of *Sancrosanctum concilium* at the conclusion of Vatican II's second session.[5] The controversial use of historical-critical methods in the study of sacred scripture, vehemently critiqued in Leo XIII's 1893 encyclical, *Providentissimus Deus*, was vindicated in Vatican II's *Dei verbum* (1965).[6] And the renewed dedication to the study of Thomas Aquinas in the wake of Leo's *Aeterni patris* (1879) reached new levels of historical, methodological, and theological rigor in the Thomistic studies of Marie-Dominique Chenu, Henri Bouillard, and Bernard Lonergan.[7]

The enriching effects of positive theology's renewal in the twentieth century are numerous, and they continue to reverberate in Catholic theology almost sixty years after the conclusion of the council. At the same time, however, positive theology's transformation and ascendence in modern Catholic thought has coincided with—and even been purchased by—speculative theology's relative decline.[8] Speculative method today is a forgotten part of theology, a creature of the preconciliar age. There are multiple modern ideological constituencies—both conservative and radical—that prefer the continuance of this speculative amnesia. But there exist others who see in the speculative tradition (and especially in the medieval cultural and political conditions that gave it life) an aesthetic by which to rend away power and influence from an illegitimate secular, liberal order. If Vatican II sought to "open the windows" to the fresh air of the modern world, these ostensible champions of the speculative tradition seek the means to slam them shut. But their ambition does not end with hermetically sealing Catholicism from the risk of worldly contaminants. Their goal is rule—over church, over culture, and over civilization itself.

Today there exist twin trends that respond to speculative method and its classicist superstructure, a tendency to forget and a tendency to misremember. The former is exemplified in the postconciliar rejection of speculation's intention, while the latter appears in the no less postconciliar enthusiasm for weaponizing past speculation's culture to claim dominion over the future. I have often remarked to friends that negative partisanship can be measured by which extremes one finds silly and which ones one finds dangerous. My own negative partisanship will no doubt be on display in these pages. For while I dissent from what Sarah Coakley calls the modern forms of resistance to speculative theology that one finds in many departments of religion, my grievances with them are intellectual. I simply dispute the facts in evidence. And while I would not characterize those impulses as silly, I would assert the other extreme as dangerous. I will thus devote more space in this chapter to critiquing speculation's false friends, those who find in the speculative tradition and especially in the classicist culture that gave it life, the styles, moods, and sensibilities that can give historical, intellectual, and religious cover to the most Nietzschean elements of modern reactionism.

## FORGETTING SPECULATION'S INTENT

In a telling concession to the audaciousness of her decision to write a systematic theology in the dominant intellectual and religious climate, Sarah Coakley identifies three "forms of resistance" to speculative or systematic theology that should, at first glance, render her project (along with any other speculative endeavor) untenable. These resisters belong to disparate ideological factions and pursue distinct moral ends—ranging from progressive social liberation to pious mystical silence. But each represents a challenge to the possibility of speculative method.

The first is a philosophical critique emerging from Martin Heidegger's adaptation of what Immanuel Kant termed "ontotheology." This form of resistance "claims that systematic theology falsely, and idolatrously, turns God into an object of human knowledge."[9] Because God is not a thing within a world, he is not proportionate to any act of human knowing, for all such acts are circumscribed by being in the world. Theology must, accordingly, be an un-knowing, a negativity or *apophasis*, and so a work of intellect only by way of remotion.[10]

For those whose theological utterances have not yet completed their purgative course, the question of God is a question of identity. Katherine Sonderegger suggests that "such compression and assimilation of *quiddity* into identity seeks to head off what many modern theologians consider to be a foreign invader: 'substance metaphysics.'"[11] For those convinced of this latter risk and committed to this former compression, theology is encounter, and the job of dogmatics (over against systematics) is volitional submission to what is audibly received. But for all its ostensible passivity and emphasis on hearing, theologians of encounter have much to say. "From this," Sonderegger writes, "spring the marvelous dynamism and singularity of Karl Barth's doctrine of God."[12] But, as Sonderegger demonstrates so vividly, *what?* and *who?* are questions not so easily sublimated. Not everything, she avers, is Christology.[13] Insofar as Christocentrism has become the first principle of post-Rahnerian Catholic systematics and post-Barthian Protestant dogmatics, speculations about divine aseity have been rendered useless at best and dangerous at worst.

A second form of resistance, Coakley observes, is political. It is organized around the Marxist critique of hegemony, casting "systematic theology (amongst other discourses that provide any purportedly complete vision of an intellectual landscape), as inappropriately totalizing, and thereby necessarily suppressive of the voices and perspectives of marginalized people."[14] To grasp a whole from within the multiplicities of experience, culture, and power is to privilege as universal the individual theologian's experiential and cultural horizon. Such privileging is also an exclusion of the theologian's experiential and cultural others, rendering these others' lives and perspectives subtheological. Speculators are agents of capital, managers of the pains and privations of labor, doling out opiates of intellectual amusement to suppress revolutionary praxis.

Psychoanalytic and feminist critique, a third form of resistance, "accuses systematic thinking (of any sort) of being 'phallocentric,' that is, ordered according to the 'symbolic,' 'male' mode of thinking which seeks to clarify, control, and master. It is thereby repressive of creative materials culturally associated with 'femininity' and the female body, which are characteristically pushed into the unconscious."[15] If patriarchy is expressed not just in systematic structures or speculative articulations, but in the noetic acts that have such structures and articulations as their term, then there can be no moral therapy for the products of those acts. The well is already poisoned before any water is brought to the surface. Only a radically distinct noetic order, differing in both intention and execution from that of the old masculine regime, can cultivate liberated noematic fruit.

It would be both intellectually dishonest and morally culpable to dismiss these critiques out of hand. Data corroborating them are not difficult to find. There is no denying that certain strands of speculative theology proffer a univocal, self-caused God whose existence is only first among many within a single entitative order. Other strands foolishly attempt to take leave of creaturely concreteness in pursuit of pure reason, one that rises above differences in subjectivity, assumes a universal perspective, and utters a universal word. And a simple glance at any speculative bibliography exposes a tradition composed almost entirely of male voices, who rarely reflect on the gendered quality of speculation, even as they exclude female perspectives.

For practitioners of the modern forms of resistance, speculative theology is best forgotten. Yet, there can be a totalizing tendency to such critiques of totalization. The speculative tradition is not monolithic, and its exemplars are not so easily targeted by these critiques. Even the criticisms themselves are not beyond dispute.[16] More to the point, only puritanical moralities are compelled to sideline thinkers and ways of thinking whose all too human garments feature spots and wrinkles. If, however, one's moral imagination anticipates the wheat and tares of the past to grow up together, one can approach a tradition with dialectical sensitivity, advancing what is good and true, reversing what is evil and false, while risking the intellectual and moral fallibility of those judgments and trusting them to the care of future inquirers.

## MISREMEMBERING SPECULATION'S CULTURE

In an infamous passage in the preface to his celebrated book, *The Liberal Imagination*, Lionel Trilling characterized liberalism as America's "sole intellectual tradition." This verdict reflected not a rose-colored view of the postwar consensus, but a recognition of conservatism's absence among "ideas in general circulation" in mid-century American life. He characterized conservatism as an impulse, a set of sensibilities that do not "express themselves in ideas but only in action or in irritable mental gestures which seek to resemble ideas."[17] Richard Hofstadter called this irritability "the paranoid style in American politics," a style which made political life "an arena for uncommonly angry minds."[18] When writing those words in 1965, Hofstadter was witnessing liberalism's triumph—in popularity, in power, and in concrete policy achievements. Even the fear elicited by populist enthusiasm for Barry Goldwater seemed overwrought in the face of his electoral wipeout in the 1964 presidential election. But just five years later, Garry Wills would write of a liberalism "coming apart at the seams" and of Richard Nixon as the "last liberal," the self-made man who tried to revive the liberal creed but who instead "reduced it to absurdity."[19]

While Trilling's assessment of liberalism's vitality seemed laughable by the end of Nixon's first term, his assessment of conservatives, classicists, and reactionaries (at times distinct personalities and at others functional synonyms) is another matter. Tempting as his characterization might be for conservatism's enemies to embrace, Mark Lilla insists that "it is nothing but a prejudice to assume that revolutionaries think while reactionaries only react."[20] Political, social, and religious reaction is not an autonomic reflex. It is an intellectual project. Conservatism, argues Corey Robin, is "ideas-driven praxis, and no amount of preening from the right or polemic from the left can reduce or efface the catalog of mind one finds there."[21]

That catalog, the intellectual apparatus by which classicism mounts its counterrevolutionary charge, has, for all its variation, a variable: loss and its reasons. The loss is felt. The reasons are argued—often through narratives of decline, genealogies of corruption, and other erudite accounts of culture's fall from grace. This Edenic two-step from classicist culture to modernist barbarism has countless antecedents, but perhaps none more potent than Nietzsche himself. Alasdair MacIntyre argues that, for Nietzsche, "the specific task of the genealogist of morality was to trace both socially and conceptually how rancor and resentment on the part of the inferior destroyed the aristocratic nobility of archaic heroes and substituted a priestly set of values in which a concern for purity and impurity provided a disguise for malice and hate."[22] Nietzsche explains his culture's decline as the conquest of the glories of classical Rome by the poverty of the church. Today's genealogists, seeking their own story to explicate the decline of Christian culture, employ strikingly similar arguments to explain away new moral grammars of liberation and the new priestly caste that stands in judgment of (social) sins.

But the reactionary penchant for genealogy is bigger than its generic resemblance to late-nineteenth-century moral philosophy. Its exulted forms wind through Eric Voegelin's history of the gnostic immanentizing of the eschaton and include Leo Strauss's championing of philosophical reading as intellectual politics. They take on more pointed forms in today's reactionary accounts of modernity's genesis, its destruction of Christian civilization, and its legacy of corruption that ostensibly explains the moral, intellectual, and social woes of today. Historical pivot points vary, but common antagonists include the late medieval rise of nominalist notions of being in the Franciscan schools of William of Ockham and John Duns Scotus, the Reformation's rejection of hierarchy, Descartes's *cogito*, or Kant's demotion of the knowledge of God from pure to practical reason. (And often these are episodes of a single story.) All versions depict a decisive moment or series of moments in which the decisions of an elite few determined the destiny of the many. When compared to the piety, probity, and intellectual acuity of high medieval culture, these tales assert, modern culture is low indeed.

"It's a compelling story," writes Lilla, but "it is nothing but a myth—not a lie, just an imaginative assemblage of past events and ideas and present hopes and fears."[23] We tell ourselves such stories, cribbing Joan Didion, in order to live—not just to live in a culture we deem hostile to our interests, but to live with ourselves. "We want the comfort," Lilla writes, "however cold, of thinking that we understand the present, while at the same time escaping full responsibility for the future."[24] Mytho-historical decline narratives resemble nothing so much as what MacIntyre calls "unmasking," the process of laying bare modernity's pretense and exposing its true face. But, as MacIntyre argues, "*Unmasking* the unacknowledged motives of arbitrary will and desire which sustain the moral masks of modernity is itself one of the most characteristically modern of activities."[25] As intellectual praxis, unmasking is counterrevolution; and counterrevolution "is one of the ways in which the conservative makes feudalism fresh and medievalism modern."[26] Unmasking admits of no Burkean pretense. It is of radical provenance. It is what Sam Tanenhaus calls conservatism's "adversary culture," and it is why, in his view, conservatives (or, in my usage, classicists) are ideologues rather than realists.[27]

If unmasking is no more than intellectual therapy to cope with classicist culture's demise, it can provide both comfort for the convinced and challenge for the skeptical. But once unmasking becomes a political project, its entire moral calculus changes. Genealogies begin to "feed a more insidious dream: that political action might help us find our way back to the Road Not Taken."[28] If the journey to our modern cultural catastrophe began with a single deliberative step, a step that need not and should not have been taken, then we can, through political will, find our way back to the path's divergence and make a different choice. When intellectuals go public, we must ask, "What are they seeking in politics?"[29]

According to Rémi Brague, a return to the past is inevitable. So incoherent is the weight of modernity's contradictions, that nothing short of cultural suicide lies ahead. Self-preservation dictates a new course. "One way or another," he writes, "our culture will have to make a step backward to *some* Middle Ages."[30] Because this return is unavoidable, the only question, for Brague, is to what kind of Middle Ages we return. Will we choose its humane franchise or its barbarous one? Surveying emerging political and social trends in Europe and North America, R. R. Reno suggests that we are witnessing the "return of the strong gods," that is, the rejection of the weak, procedural, contractual forms of human belonging expressed in liberal internationalism, technocracy, and the open society, in favor of stronger forms of solidarity like nationalism, populism, and confessional community. Like Brague, Reno deems the strong gods' return as inevitable. The question is what theophany we want. For like Brague's barbarous form of the Middle Ages, the strong gods, too, have dark mirrors: militarism, fascism, communism, racism, and anti-Semitism.[31] Such "dark gods" rise up from below in response to "the chthonian preoccupation with race and sex that dominates in so many progressive circles."[32] According to Reno, "open-society therapies of weakening" are not only powerless to overcome "the perverse gods of blood, soil, and identity" but actually encourage their growing power.[33] Absent the call to multiculturalism, the dark gods remain submerged. But, now unleashed, only a "new metaphysical dream," a new "we," possesses the nobility of spirit necessary to hold off the dark gods' return. To avoid the dangers of the ideological passions they inspire, "we need to nurture two primeval sources of solidarity that limit the claims of the civic 'we': the domestic society of marriage and the supernatural community of the church, synagogue, and other communities of transcendence."[34] A distinctive feature of such sources of solidarity, according to Sohrab Ahmari, is their involuntary nature. Sacrifice and the freedom by which it is offered are meaningful only insofar as they are "sustained by the authority of tradition and religion," the "vast range of ties that bound traditional peoples," including "folkways and folk wisdom, family loyalty, unchosen religious obligations such as baptism and circumcision, rule-bound forms of worship, and, above all, submission to moral and spiritual authorities."[35] The past, in other words, is the means by which "we can retrace a path out of the current chaos and confusion."[36] By restoring the kinetic power of what was—the "humane" Middle Ages, the strong gods of solidarity, and the authority of tradition—we can be saved from what is.

But how many times can Napoleon return from Elba's exile? By what power are tradition and traditional communities restored? Is that power spiritual or political? And if liberalism has rendered all forms of spiritual association voluntary, how will spiritual authority procure the coercive means to create, sustain, and enforce domestic society and transcendent community? Few modern commentators are as brilliant or as bold in their answers to such questions as Adrian Vermeule. A widely regarded scholar of administrative law and self-proclaimed integralist, he argues for a "common good constitutionalism" that both overturns the liberal order and embodies the truer expression of the jurisprudential tradition that liberalism claims as its own. In Vermeule's society, "rights very much exist, but are grounded and justified in a different way than under standard autonomy-based liberal theories." For Vermeule, liberty is "a bad master" but "a good servant." To realize the common good-based society he champions requires, by his own analogy, a "reorientation of thought, and on a large scale," an overturning of "recent deviant precedent," and a reversion to an older, "better justified" nexus of notions, rules, and orders.[37] This philosophy of law is insurgent. It would, like William and the Norman invaders of medieval England, overturn the established order by asserting its integral right to rule. Common good constitutionalism is not, according to Vermeule, a departure from the canons of western legal theory, but its ground and goal—the foundation and finality from which postwar liberal jurisprudence is a temporary and unfortunate detour.

At its core, common good constitutional order lionizes more than just the superiority of the natural law as a philosophical ground for political and legal judgment. It "draws upon natural law both to construe the civil law and to justify action for the common good on the part of the political authority."[38]

By prescribing the "purposes or ends to which law is aimed," the classical tradition transcends particular judicial institutions and arrangements through "genuine concern for the common good at ever higher levels—individual, family, city, nation, and commonwealth of nations."[39] That common good is the "flourishing of the community" and the "well-ordered life in the *polis*," which includes but transcends all particular goods.[40] But the common good is also fragile. It is "dependent upon the flourishing of the political communities (including ruling authorities) within which humans are born, found, and embedded."[41] How quickly ostensible recovery becomes revolution. Constitutional order exists "to ensure that the ruler has both the authority and the duty to rule well," to "promote good rule, not to 'protect liberty' as an end in itself."[42] Liberty, then, is little more than the freedom to fall in line. Authority's legitimacy is not subject to the dialectical process of communal authorization. Instead, "the subjects' own perceptions of what is best for them may change over time . . . as the law teaches, habituates, and re-forms them."[43] The Lacanian trembles.

To call reaction an active intellectual project, a distinctively *modern* project, and to reject its own story about itself—that it is the "stupid" party, the steward of the past, the cautious counsel of continuity—is not lazy "both-sidesism." To call reactionaries revolutionaries is not to embarrass them by equating their motivations with those of their enemies. It is rather to name an asymmetry of political life. Ideologies of the glorious past and those of the glorious future have a structural advantage over any politics of everyday living. The strong gods are strong indeed. Whether history is a fall from grace or a march toward glory, revolutionary thinking cannot but view the present as an awkward age between the ages—either a decadence on the way to the restoration of the old regime or a decadence collapsing under contradiction, upon whose ruins the future will make its final, bloody entrance. What can a liberal offer the souls of the people that can compete with such apocalyptic splendor and world-historical consequence? Compared with the pathos of the king's return or the revolution's arrival, what is the ethos of rights? The logos of law? The demos of representation? Liberalism is not everything, but hopefully it is enough. Not enough to supply humanity with a destiny, but enough to ensure us all our chance to pursue one.

Jane Jacobs calls forgetfulness "the fifth horseman of the apocalypse."[44] Nostalgia is a sixth. "Hopes can be disappointed," writes Lilla, but "nostalgia is irrefutable."[45] Such irrefutability inspires devotion—to ideas, histories, and their consequences. "Post hoc, propter hoc," he says, "is the reactionary's profession of faith."[46] Faith built upon fallacy, though, is sinking sand. Liberalism is more than a set of procedures. It is a tradition. It is, in Adam Gopnik's telling, a moral adventure.[47] But it does not inspire the soul to its metaphysical excellencies. It is not supposed to. Even so tireless a champion of the liberal tradition as Francis Fukuyama concedes that liberalism "deliberately lowered the sights of politics, to aim not at a good life as defined by a particular religion, moral doctrine, or cultural tradition," and instead seeks "the preservation of life itself in conditions where populations could not agree on what the good life was."[48] Liberal orders, then, have a "spiritual vacuum" that is a feature, not a bug. They do not command us to renounce existing fellowships, forget our ancestors, or hide our light under a bushel. They ask us only to grant one another the liberty by which association, memory, and devotion are the prerogatives of free people, not the gilded chains of those born to time's captivity.

## CONCLUSION

This brief chapter is not a map. It has not defined a route. It has not even specified a destination. It has instead counseled against two destinations too many of today's intellectuals all too often pursue: forgetting and misremembering. The journey that follows and the destination it prescribes are not easy. But neither are they crooked. The watchwords will be memory and creativity. The mile markers are classical, but the destination is cosmopolis. To appraise any tradition requires an adequate memory of it.[49] It is, thus, the burden of the next chapter to show that a full realization of John XXIII's *aggiornamento* includes a *ressourcement* of speculative method. Such recovery involves a prior hermeneutical gamble. One must decide how one wishes to remember, and so how one will understand and evaluate the horizons of concern that animate and organize the intentions of a prior age. One must elect whether to remain forever a pupil of the school of suspicion, or instead to bear its lessons along in tutelage to the school of recovery, with the hope that ultimately "extreme iconoclasm belongs to the restoration of meaning."[50] And while the reader is free to make this choice, so too is the author. What follows, then, is an attempt to go beyond (not around) suspicions of the speculative toward its critical recovery. It offers no *apologia* for the entire tradition, and it grants the legitimacy of many features of the modern forms of resistance. But it moves through them toward the restoration of meaning by "remembering" the exemplarity of that tradition and letting that memory be the basis of recovery.

The project of recovering speculative theology could be attempted using multiple strategies on multiple fronts for multiple ends. Some of these efforts may be allied and complementary.[51] Others may be simply at odds.[52] But, individually, all are limited in scope. I will present two fragments of speculative recovery derived from the work of Bernard Lonergan. The first concerns intelligence and time. It examines Lonergan's theory of speculative form and its developmental order in the history of theology as the unfolding of understanding in history. The second element treats of theological understanding itself, of speculative theology as the specification of human inquiry and understanding to the questions of God and the doctrinal judgments that answer them. But because the recovery of the past is for the sake of renewal in the present, the next chapter concludes with a provisional glance at the transformations in thought emblematic of the modern situation that indicate the ways a recovered speculative method must be transformed if it is to be at the level of our time.

## NOTES

1. Lewis Ayres notes that "the distinction between 'positive' and 'Scholastic' or 'speculative' theology arose in the early sixteenth century, probably in the work of John Mair (1467–1550), and remained one of the main divisions in Catholic theology through the early 1970s." See Lewis Ayres, "The Memory of Tradition: Postconciliar Renewal and One Recent Thomism," *The Thomist* 79 (2015): 538. Ayres directs readers to several classic and recent historical studies that trace this developmental process, including, Ulrich G. Leinsle, "Sources, Methods and Forms of Early Modern Theology," in Ulrich Lehner, Richard Muller, and A. E. Roeber, eds., *Oxford Handbook of Early Modern Theology* (Oxford: Oxford University Press, 2016), 25–42; Yves Congar, *A History of Theology*, trans. and ed. Hunter Guthrie (Garden City, NY: Doubleday, 1968), 170–75; Riccardo Quinto, *Scholastica: Storia di un concetto* (Padua: II Poligrafo, 2001), 238–55; Hubert Filser, *Dogma, Dogmen, Dogmatik: Eine Untersuchung zur Begründung und zur Entstehungsgeschichte einer theologischen Disziplin van der Reformation bis zur Spätaufklärung* (Munster: LIT Verlag, 2001). Jean-Louis Quantin, *Le catholicisme classique et les pères de l'église: Un retour au sources (1669–1713)* (Paris: Ètudes augustiniennes, 1999), 103–11. A much older study, cited multiple times by Bernard Lonergan, highlights Peter Lombard's role in assembling dogmatic data in his *Sentences*, while leaving to others the task of finding systematic coherence in that data. See Franz Pelster, "Die Bedeutung der Sentenzenvorlesung für die theologische Spekulation des Mittelalters. Ein Zeugnis aus der ältesten Oxforder Dominikanerschule," *Scholastik* (1927) 250–55.

2. See Jürgen Mettepenningen, *Nouvelle Théologie: Inheritor to Modernism, Precursor to Vatican II* (London: T&T Clark, 2010), 11. For Mettepenningen, a concern for the renewal of positive theology is among four characteristics shared by the diverse strands of thinkers that comprise the four phases of the *nouvelle théologie*. The other characteristics include: (1) French language and culture; (2) the role of history in faith and understanding; (3) a critical attitude toward neoscholasticism.

3. Mettepenningen, *Nouvelle Théologie*, 11.

4. See Hans Urs von Balthasar, *Presence and Thought: An Essay on the Religious Philosophy of Gregory of Nyssa*, trans. Mark Sebanc (San Francisco: Communio and Ignatius Press, 1995); idem, *Cosmic Liturgy: The Universe according to Maximus the Confessor*, trans. Brian Daley (San Francisco: Communio and Ignatius Press,

2003). In this introduction, Daley suggests that *Cosmic Liturgy* should be considered a classic "because of its crucial importance in the development of modern scholarship's estimate of Maximus" (11). Elsewhere, Daley notes that though subsequent scholarship has often been critical of Balthasar's analysis of both Gregory and Maximus, Balthasar's efforts have been pivotal in raising awareness and interest in these figures in western scholarship. See Brian Daley, "Balthasar's Reading of the Church Fathers," in *The Cambridge Companion to Hans Urs von Balthasar*, Edward T. Oakes and David Moss, eds. (Cambridge: Cambridge University Press, 2004), 202: "His studies of Gregory of Nyssa and Maximus were catalysts for a new appreciation of the originality and significance of these figures, an interest which remains strong sixty years later."

5. See Massimo Faggioli, *True Reform: Liturgy and Ecclesiology in* Sancrosanctum Concilium (Collegeville, MN: Liturgical Press, 2012), 19–58.

6. See Leo XIII, *Providentissimus Deus* §17; *Dei verbum* §12. *Dei verbum*'s approach was anticipated in Pius XII's 1943 encyclical, *Divino afflante Spiritu*, commemorating the fiftieth anniversary of *Povidentissimus Deus*.

7. See Marie-Dominique Chenu, *Introduction a l'étude de Saint Thomas d'Aquin* (Montreal: Institut d'études médiévales, 1950); idem., *St. Thomas d'Aquin et la théologie* (Paris: Les Editions du Seuil, 1959); Henri Bouillard, *Conversion et grâce chez s. Thomas d'Aquin* (Paris: Aubier, 1944); Bernard Lonergan, *Grace and Freedom: Operative Grace in the Thought of St. Thomas Aquinas*, Frederick E. Crowe and Robert M. Doran, eds., CWL 1 (Toronto: University of Toronto Press, 2000). To these figures, one must add Thomistic philosopher-historians like Étienne Gilson.

8. There were Catholic theologians in the twentieth century writing within a speculative register, including Hans Urs von Balthasar, Karl Rahner, Edward Schillebeeckx, and Bernard Lonergan. The theologies of Lonergan and Balthasar figure heavily in later chapters. At least one notable effort at a modern Catholic systematic theology is the collaborative text, *Systematic Theology: Roman Catholic Perspectives*, 2nd ed., Francis Schussler Fiorenza and John P. Galvin, eds. (Minneapolis: Fortress Press, 2011). While this work is systematic in its scope, its method remains more historical than speculative.

9. Sarah Coakley, *God, Sexuality, and the Self: An Essay "On the Trinity"* (New York: Cambridge University, 2013), 42.

10. This critique is perhaps most famously associated with Jean-Luc Marion and his *God without Being: Hors Texte*, 2nd ed., trans. Thomas A. Carlson (Chicago and London: University of Chicago Press, 2012).

11. Katherine Sonderegger, *Systematic Theology, vol. 1: The Doctrine of God* (Minneapolis: Fortress Press, 2015), xi–xii.

12. Sonderegger, *Systematic Theology, vol. 1*, xii.

13. Sonderegger, *Systematic Theology, vol. 1*, xvii.

14. Coakley, *God, Sexuality, and the Self*, 42.

15. Coakley, *God, Sexuality, and the Self*, 42.

16. This is especially true of the philosophical form of resistance. Even Marion was eventually compelled to retract his earlier charge, in *God without Being*, that Thomas Aquinas was an ontotheologian. See Marion, "Thomas Aquinas and Onto-theology,"

in *Mystics: Presence and Aporia*, Michael Kessler and Christian Sheppard, eds. (London and Chicago: University of Chicago Press, 2003), 38–74. William Desmond has charted a new path toward an affirmation of so-called "classical theism" from within the continental philosophical tradition that stands up to the ontotheological critique. See his *God and the Between* (Malden, MA, and Oxford: Blackwell, 2008), 281–340, for his retrieval of the classical divine attributes. Desmond sees his work sharing many of Marion's own aims, but finds Marion's account of being to be overdetermined by Heidegger, and so containing an antagonism between being and *agape*. While Marion opts for *agape* beyond being, Desmond advances an "agapeic being." See Desmond, *God and the Between*, 242n3.

17. Lionel Trilling, *The Moral Obligation to Be Intelligent: Selected Essays*, Leon Wieseltier, ed. (New York: Farrar, Strauss and Giroux, 2000), 543.

18. Richard Hofstadter, *Hofstadter: Anti-Intellectualism in American Life, The Paranoid Style in American Politics, Uncollected Essays 1956–1965*, Library of America (New York: Library of America, 2020), 503.

19. Garry Wills, *Nixon Agonistes: The Crisis of the Self-Made Man* (New York: Signet, 1971), 545–46.

20. Mark Lilla, *The Shipwrecked Mind: On Political Reaction*, rev. ed. (New York: New York Review Books, 2016), xv.

21. Corey Robin, *The Reactionary Mind: Conservatism from Edmund Burke to Donald Trump*, second edition (New York: Oxford University Press, 2018), 18.

22. Alasdair MacIntyre, *Three Rival Versions of Moral Enquiry: Encyclopedia, Genealogy, and Tradition* (Notre Dame: University of Notre Dame Press, 1990), 39–40.

23. Lilla, *The Shipwrecked Mind*, 84.

24. Lilla, *The Shipwrecked Mind*, 84–85.

25. Alasdair MacIntyre, *After Virtue: A Study in Moral Theory*, third edition (Notre Dame: University of Notre Dame Press, 2007), 72.

26. Robin, *The Reactionary Mind*, 34.

27. Sam Tanenhaus, *The End of Conservatism: A Movement and Its Consequences* (New York: Random House, 2010), 94.

28. Lilla, *The Shipwrecked Mind*, 85.

29. Mark Lilla, *The Reckless Mind: Intellectuals in Politics* (New York: New York Review Books, 2016), xi.

30. Rémi Brague, *Curing Mad Truths: Medieval Wisdom for the Modern Age* (Notre Dame: University of Notre Dame Press, 2019), 6.

31. R. R. Reno, *Return of the Strong Gods: Nationalism, Populism, and the Future of the West* (Washington, DC: Regnery Gateway, 2019), xxiv.

32. Reno, *Return of the Strong Gods*, 152–53.

33. Reno, *Return of the Strong Gods*, 153.

34. Reno, *Return of the Strong Gods*, 159.

35. Sohrab Ahmari, *The Unbroken Thread: Discovering the Wisdom of Tradition in an Age of Chaos* (New York: Convergent, 2021), 9.

36. Ahmari, *The Unbroken Thread*, 21.

37. Adrian Vermeule, *Common Good Constitutionalism: Recovering the Classical Legal Tradition* (Cambridge and Medford, MA: Polity Press, 2022), 24.
38. Vermeule, *Common Good Constitutionalism*, 19.
39. Vermeule, *Common Good Constitutionalism*, 19, 23.
40. Vermeule, *Common Good Constitutionalism*, 28.
41. Vermeule, *Common Good Constitutionalism*, 29.
42. Vermeule, *Common Good Constitutionalism*, 37.
43. Vermeule, *Common Good Constitutionalism*, 38.
44. Jane Jacobs, *Dark Age Ahead* (New York: Random House, 2004), 8.
45. Lilla, *The Shipwrecked Mind*, xiv.
46. Lilla, *The Shipwrecked Mind*, xii.
47. Adam Gopnik, *A Thousand Small Sanities: The Moral Adventure of Liberalism* (New York: Basic Books, 2019).
48. Francis Fukuyama, *Liberalism and Its Discontents* (New York: Farrar, Strauss and Giroux, 2022), 115–116.
49. On the distinction between misremembering and forgetting, see Cyril O'Regan, *The Anatomy of Misremembering: Von Balthasar's Response to Philosophical Modernity, vol. 1: Hegel* (New York: Herder & Herder, 2014), 1–27.
50. Paul Ricoeur, *Freud & Philosophy: An Essay on Interpretation*, trans. Denis Savage (New Haven and London: Yale University Press, 1970), 27, 32.
51. What is attempted in this project has a clear dependence on Robert M. Doran's *What Is Systematic Theology?* (Toronto: University of Toronto Press, 2005). Doran's retrieval of Lonergan's pre-*Method in Theology* account of systematic/speculative theology focuses on the various forms of the first chapter of his systematic text on the doctrine of the Trinity. On the way to writing *What Is Systematic Theology?* Doran wrote extensive commentaries on these texts, which are vital to recovering Lonergan's evolution. See Robert M. Doran, "The First Chapter of *De Deo Trino*: The Issues," *Method: Journal of Lonergan Studies* 18.1 (2000): 27–48; idem, "*Intelligentia Fidei* in *De Deo Trino, Pars Systematica*: A Commentary on the First Three Sections of Chapter One," *Method: Journal of Lonergan Studies* 19.1 (2001): 35–84; idem, "The Truth of Theological Understanding in *Divinarum Personarum* and *De Deo Trino, Pars Systematica*," *Method: Journal of Lonergan Studies* 20.1 (2002): 33–76. Rather than rehearsing Doran's arguments, this chapter complements them by showing how his conclusions can be reached from other texts in Lonergan's corpus not central to Doran's project.
52. There is a generic resemblance between this project and the *ressourcement* Thomism advocated by Reinhard Hütter, Thomas Joseph White, Romanus Cessario, and others. But such resemblance is superficial. While this project is broadly "Thomist" in conviction, the sources of its Thomism and the implications drawn out from them differ, at times starkly, from those of *ressourcement* Thomism.

## Chapter 2

# Form and Action

"Speculation," writes John Henry Newman, "is one of those words which, in the vernacular, have so different a sense from what they bear in philosophy. It is commonly taken to mean a conjecture, or a venture on chances; but its proper meaning is mental sight, or the contemplation of mental operations and their results."[1] Quite apart from the term's common connotation, speculation's theoretical or philosophical denotation, and especially its theological gloss, developed over many centuries through a complex exchange between different religious, cultural, and philosophical traditions. According to Lewis Ayres, the emergence of *theologia speculativa* in the medieval writings of Alexander of Hales, Siger of Brabant, and Thomas Aquinas transformed the ancient Christian contemplative tradition (*theoria*) through the introduction of doctrines adapted from the Aristotelian corpus, particularly those of the *Posterior Analytics* and the *Metaphysics*, which had only recently completed their geographical and linguistic migration into medieval Europe.[2] And while this transformation did not leave unaltered the prior contemplative tradition, the ancient and medieval forms of *theoria* share three neuralgic features.

First, Ayres argues, Christian speculation is dialectical. It adapts and repurposes the classical tradition to articulate the distinctions and definitions relevant to advancing Christian self-understanding.[3] Second, Christian speculation is "*synthetic* and *extensive*."[4] It grasps an interior unity from among the diverse sources of Christian doctrinal literature and teaching, while experimenting with manners of extending this unity into the varied horizons of non-Christian thought. It assimilates what is discovered within those horizons into its synthetic structure, as it did first with certain strands of the Middle and Neoplatonist traditions and later with a reconstituted Aristotelian tradition. Lastly, Ayres notes that Christian speculative thought has a "reconstructive impulse."[5] It makes use of literary, philological, historical, but also metaphysical forms of analysis to re-create the contextual constellations within which texts, teachings, and questions emerge. For Ayres, these constitutive aspects of speculative theology indicate a "tensional" relationship between the poles of intellectual exploration and dogmatic submission, between "the darkness of faith" and the light of revelation. This tension consigns the speculative theologian to "an appropriate anxiety . . . inseparable from prayer for grace."[6]

However much maligned the speculative tradition is in the dominant discourses of modern thought, Ayres's identification of the characteristics broadly shared across that tradition suggests that a "chastening" of intellectual desire always accompanies faith's "enkindling" of that desire.[7] One need not assume that speculative theology is ontotheological, hegemonic, or idolatrous from the root. But, while Ayres highlights the thematic linkages common to various epochal expressions of speculative theology, this chapter takes an allied, but distinct approach, one that examines speculation's analytic and developmental structure. It is this latter way that Bernard Lonergan explores in his early study of Thomas Aquinas, *Gratia operans*.[8]

## RECOVERING SPECULATION AS FORM

### Intelligence, Time, and Order

In *Gratia operans*, Lonergan attempts an intervention into the debates concerning the theology of operative grace that had vexed both the interpretation of Thomas Aquinas and the interpretation of the Council of Trent. As the leading lights of the sixteenth-century Protestant Reformation criticized human freedom in order to safeguard divine providence, the Tridentine Fathers responded by reaffirming the doctrinal veracity of both human free will and the gratuity of divine grace, but they declined to offer any speculative reconciliation between these doctrines. This silence was not out of some undue conciliar timidity. Rather, it recognized that the fault lines of the Reformation were doctrinal, not speculative. They had to do with the truth or falsity of magisterial teaching, and not with the distinct, sometimes contradictory manners in which that teaching was understood.

Jaroslav Pelikan describes the situation of Catholic theology between Trent and the end of the seventeenth century as comprised of two tasks. It had to consolidate "the doctrinal achievements of the council as a reaffirmation, against the teachings of the Protestant Reformers, of the authentic tradition of the church," while also "clarifying, within the household of faith, some of the theological inconsistencies that had been inherited from the doctrinal pluralism of previous centuries but had been left unresolved by the council."[9] While Trent limited itself to the first task, its silence on the second left Catholic theology vulnerable to various, even violent controversies within its own ranks.

The *de auxiliis* dispute between Molinist Jesuits and Bannezian Dominicans grew out of the Catholic Counter-Reformation's need to work out the speculative theory of grace and freedom demanded (but not provided) by the Tridentine formulations.[10] And while Molinists and Bannezians each labored toward such a theory, their respective routes eventually collided with one another, resulting in a bitter controversy that eventually required papal intervention, and led not to a resolution of the speculative question of grace and freedom, but only to a sanction against further debate.[11] Yet, the basic understandings of grace and freedom that Molina and Báñez articulated informed centuries of subsequent scholastic interpretation of Thomas Aquinas among both Jesuits and Dominicans.[12] Jesuits read Thomas and found confirmation that he was a Molinist, while Dominicans conducted the same exercise but discovered that he was, rather, a Bannezian.[13] But upon taking up his study of Thomas, Lonergan found "an attitude and direction of thought distinct from the one resulting in the impasse of the controversy *de auxiliis.*"[14]

Convinced that neither sixteenth-century thinkers nor their partisan interpreters had grasped Thomas's thirteenth-century achievement, Lonergan directed his attention to the history of speculative development on the doctrines of grace and freedom in the centuries prior to Thomas's synthesis, and to the developments within Thomas's own understanding, as his thinking evolved through the gradual accumulation of insights over the course of his career. Lonergan sought "a method that of itself tends to greater objectivity than those hitherto employed," one that would grasp scientifically the form of intelligence unfolding through the history of speculative development.[15] For to amass the relevant historical materials is not yet to understand them. And even careful curation does not provide a theory that would grasp within the multiplicity of materials and sources an intelligible developmental order. Such a theory would be a "form of development," a scientific explanation of "the unity and coherence of a vast body of historical data," "a matrix or system of thought that at once is as pertinent and as indifferent to historical events as is the science of mathematics to quantitative phenomena."[16]

*Gratia operans* provides this theoretical structure and deploys it to interpret the multiphase advance from doctrinal clarification in Augustine's distinction between divine operation and cooperation to nascent speculative understanding in Anselm's theory of grace as the cause of rectitude. And from Peter Lombard's presentation of the four states of human freedom to Philip the Chancellor's theorem of the supernatural and Albert the Great's distinction between the form of grace as operative and the form of merit as cooperative, culminating in Thomas Aquinas's mature formulation of habitual and actual grace as both operative and cooperative.[17] Furthermore, as Lonergan shows, Aquinas's achievement itself is the fruit of his own personal development of speculative understanding from the *Scriptum* to the *De veritate* and from the *Summa contra Gentiles* toward his final, mature synthesis in the *Summa theologiae*.[18]

There is both a negative and a positive rationale for adopting a scientific, theoretical mentality in inductive research. Negatively, theory "eliminates a host of impertinent questions which otherwise would spontaneously be introduced into the inquiry to give it a false bias and encourage a search—too often successful—to find in an author what the author never dreamt of."[19] But in addition to guarding against such anachronism, theoretical control has the positive effect of allowing "one who lives in a later age to understand those whose thought belongs to almost a different world, and it does so, not by the slow and incommunicable apprehension that comes to the specialist after years of study, but logically through ideas that are defined, arguments that can be tested, and conclusions that need only be verified."[20]

Lonergan's theory has four points. First, he defines speculative theology and its content. Second, he enumerates the constitutive elements of speculative elaboration. Third, he indicates the distinct manners in which those elements combine in the outworking of the progressive stages of speculative thought. And fourth, he makes application to the specific speculative phases in western theological reflection on the doctrines of grace and human freedom. Given the aims of the present study, attention to the first three points will suffice for understanding Lonergan's theory of speculative form.

## The Content

Central to Lonergan's notion of theory is what he calls "pure form." Speculative theology is not the cause of the objects within its intellectual field. Of itself, it neither makes discoveries nor produces knowledge. Without prior knowledge, there can be no speculation. Theory grasps the relation between terms but establishes neither the terms nor their relations. Theological theory, therefore, intends only the "unity and cohesion" of the knowledge affirmed and communicated in Church doctrines. For Lonergan, this means there can be no speculative theology sanitized from the historicity of revelation and doctrinal formulation. Theory in theology can never have the clinical precision of mathematics. Its work of relating, understanding, elaborating, defining, and clarifying applies to data, not of the imagination but rather of history.

Revelation, for the Christian tradition, occurs not through private, mystical enlightenment but rather through public histories. Speculative theology introduces into revelation nothing other than an intellectual mentality. The speculative is the aspect of theology that "penetrates the whole structure," which "has brought to light and formulated this organicity in revealed truth."[21] It is an enrichment and an enlargement of the human grasp of the truth. The biological imagery of a living, growing "whole" discernible in the concrete developmental order is consonant with the conclusions of earlier Catholic thinkers like John Henry Newman, Johann Sebastian Drey, Johann Adam Möhler, and Maurice Blondel.[22] Lonergan, though, in a way distinct from his forebears, emphasizes that this organic whole is the fruit of intending intelligence grasping an intelligible form. It is not "there" in a spatialized field of biological perception; it is not some "thing" one "sees." It is the content of the theologian's act of understanding. And while earlier theologians sought the nature of Catholic tradition and of the historically unfolding character of Catholic doctrine, Lonergan's concern is the systematic understanding and expression of that unfolding.

This means that speculative understanding is not the object or product of an act, but rather the quality of an act. "It is not something by itself," Lonergan writes, "but the intelligible arrangement of something else."[23] In theology, speculation "enters everywhere," but "it is also true that everywhere its role is very subordinate. It provides the technical terms with their definitions; it does not provide the objects that are defined."[24] For Lonergan, speculative theology can be provisionally defined as the arrangement of doctrinal affirmations that promotes a theoretical grasp of the coherence of those affirmations and their conjunctions. Nowhere is this clearer than in Lonergan's statement that speculative theology "is not systematic theology but the system in systematic theology."[25]

## The Elements

While the content of speculative theology is the pure form of intelligence grasping explanatory coherence, the distinct features of this form comprise speculative theology's basic elements. Lonergan identifies four classes of elements in speculative thought: theorems, terms, dialectical positions, and techniques. The psychoanalytic and feminist critic may object that systematic thought's phallocentric drive to clarify, control, and master has yet again surfaced. The procedures of natural science and mathematics seem to be the overriding criterion for valid knowledge, such that there is an unreflective disciplinary transgression occurring when a theologian imagines that they can generate from within theological discourse notions like "theorems" and "techniques," notions that may have their place in mathematics but have no truck with the human sciences. And while such suspicion is perhaps not unfounded, its anxiety in this case turns out to be only an allergy to certain words.

The language of theorems and technique is not symptomatic of a symbolic attempt to control or domesticate revelation by imposing the canons of scientific method. It is not self-aggrandizement or the pretension of angelic knowledge. As features of speculative form, theorems and techniques are accommodations of intelligence to its own spatiotemporality, its historicity, its contingency—its incarnate nature. Absent the constraints of bodily knowledge, historical mediation, and the disproportion of the natural to the supernatural, no speculative thought would be required, for all would see face-to-face and know even as they are fully known. The elements of speculative theology—the emergence of theorems, the articulation of terms, dialectical positions, and specialized techniques—are how a limited, finite, historical, incarnate theologian advances their incarnate understanding toward the incomprehensible mystery of God, and even then, never fully outside the mist of analogical dissimilarity.

By "theorem," Lonergan means, "the scientific elaboration of a common notion."[26] Theorems, like speculation itself, are not generative; they do not discover. They enrich and expand the already generated and discovered. Their elaborations provide generalizations that can transpose a common notion from one world to another, from the world of common sense to the world of theory. Lonergan illustrates the dynamic between commonsensical notions and their theoretical elaborations with the example of the relationship between the differential equation for acceleration and the experience of "going faster." He writes,

> The common notion of "going faster" and the scientific concept of "acceleration" partly coincide and partly differ. They coincide inasmuch as both apprehend one and the same objective fact. They differ inasmuch as the common notion apprehends no more than the fact, while the scientific concept elaborates it by understanding it. First, "acceleration" generalizes "going faster" to include "going more slowly." Second, it submits it to the subtle analysis of the calculus and enriches it with the endless implications of $d^2s/d^2t$. Third, it gives it a significant, indeed a fundamental, place in the general theory of natural phenomena.[27]

The differential equation $d^2s/d^2t$ is not the experience of "going faster" in this instance or in that. It is the scientific expression of experience made possible by grasping the theoretical meaning immanent to the experience. It is what speculative explanation adds to descriptive notion. But this elaboration is not simply a translation from the common to the recondite for complexity's sake. It is instead what allows intellect to abstract from this or that experience to the generalized context of the intelligible. In this sense, speculation liberates thinking from the parochialism of experience, to the wider—in fact, universal—context of understanding. But this liberation does not leave experience behind. Without experience, there could be no understanding, but without understanding, there could be no symbolization or expression of the intelligible contents of experience. To live in a world of the merely experienced is to live in a world not yet fully or adequately human. Theorems are the fruit of the intervention of one's intellect on one's experiences. They are the result of intellect grasping the inner unity and coherence of those experiences and so the generalizable and universal meanings they contain.

"Universality," in this instance, does not imply a God's-eye view, enabling one to observe from some remote vantage point the whole seen only as a changeable fragment from the world below. It refers instead to what Jean Piaget calls "mobility."[28] The theorem is a structure, but because it is an intellectual structure, it is not static or unidirectional. It is reversible and mobile. It can be applied to this set of questions or ambiguities in one instance and that set in another with no diminution of its explanatory power. A theorem's universality or generality is demonstrated precisely through this mobility of explanation. The differential equation for acceleration is universal because it has the mobility to coordinate the explanation of any given instance of "going faster." Beyond that, though, a theorem's universality also makes possible the elimination of misapprehension and illusion that can easily affect experiential conjugates. "Going faster," as experienced, can be mimicked or simulated in the absence of actual acceleration. But the theorem cuts through the ambiguity of the experiential conjugate and lays bare the elaborated intelligibility of the pure conjugate.[29]

But when one pivots from theorems generally conceived in mathematics or physics to the theorems of a speculative theology, the analogical character of the application comes into relief. In the example of acceleration, the theorem elaborates scientifically the intelligibility immanent to the experience of "going faster" under the formality of questions like "What is happening?" or "What is the relationship between distance, motion, and time in this happening?" In a speculative theology, however, theorems do not elaborate the intelligibility of experience; they articulate the meaning and coherence of antecedent truths. The quiddity intended by the speculative deployment of theorems is the answer to the question "What does this revealed truth or teaching mean?" or "How do these truths relate to one another?" Answers will be hypothetical, revisable, and imperfect.

In *Gratia operans*, Lonergan identifies two theorems that led to Thomas's mature articulation of the speculative coherence of human freedom and divine grace: the theorem of the states of man and the theorem of the supernatural. The first theorem emerged in the thought of Peter Lombard, and the second in that of Philip the Chancellor, who adapted and analogically applied Aristotle's theory of habit and disengaged through it the entitative disproportion between the human soul and the created communication of the divine nature that is God's grace. The theorematic elaboration of this disproportion enabled Thomas Aquinas to conceive of grace as both *sanans*, healing the soul's wounds, and *elevans*, enriching the soul toward participation in the divine life, which is its proper end. Such disproportion is not given in the data of sense or experience. It is the term of a theory, and so a doctrine of speculative intelligence.

Forgetfulness of the abstractness of such distinctions, argues David Burrell, leads to a forgetfulness of the contingency and gratuity of the natural order.[30] Such forgetting can result in a lapse back into the pagan cosmology of the eternality of the world or even the two-tiered universe of decadent scholasticism and its doctrine of pure nature. It is this latter result that, according to Henri de Lubac, has proved the most harmful. Insofar as theologians after Aquinas treated of the distinction between the natural and the supernatural as a cartography of the concrete universe, they imagined that universe as divided into two. One tier was the realm of "pure nature," separable, sufficient, and secular, supplying to human nature its own natural desire, authority, and end, each fully realizable by natural powers. A second, supernatural tier was the realm of grace, the domain of the sacred, which furnished a supernatural end to the human soul and supplied the supernatural means for the soul's attainment of that end. A concrete universe so divided made possible, argues de Lubac, the genetic emergence of atheist humanism, its elevation of the givenness of autonomous nature, and its rejection of transcendent meaning.[31] Whether one concurs with de Lubac's genealogy, the episode dramatically demonstrates the social and religious consequences of the forgetfulness of theorematic function. And so, while the postmodern suspicion of theory as scientism is not unwarranted, rejecting theory in favor of a ready-made practicality has long-term deleterious effects for theology and even for faith.

Speculative acts have effects, products, *facta*. Lonergan calls these "terms."[32] It is important to note from the outset that, as products of speculative intelligence, the terms are not *a priori* to understanding but *a posterori* to the understood. They are not features of a Kantian synthetic manifold of concepts always already backgrounded in consciousness, nor are speculation's productions merely the linguistic expressions of prior concepts and present applications. Terms, rather, are the culminations of movements in thought. "The analytic processes of speculative thought," Lonergan writes, "necessarily result in a complex transition from the latent to the evident, from the vague to the definite, from the implicit to the explicit, from the naked fact to its scientific elaboration."[33]

Terms are the effects of this dynamic migration of intelligence toward explication. In some instances, existing rhetorics or symbolizations are repurposed, transformed, adapted, and made to be adequate carriers of meaning for the terms resulting from speculation (as is the case for the term "sacrament" in the history of theology), but in other cases, no existing symbolizations are available, and so new terms are introduced (for example, "actual grace" as a term formalizing what is not yet explicit in Thomas's *auxilium divinum*).[34] But unlike the differential equation for acceleration, which symbolizes a scientific elaboration of any instance of "going faster," the terms of speculative theology will require the theologian to distinguish carefully theoretical from dogmatic grammars, because the notions elaborated by the theorem both belong to the common sense of another age and are regarded as features of a divinely originated deposit of revealed truth. The gap that opens between the scientific term and the historically revealed reality indicates the need for a third element in the speculative form, what Lonergan calls "the dialectical position."

Dialectical positionality deals with the encounter of the known, the known unknown, and the formally unknown in an analytical investigation. It is related analogically to the natural scientist's methodical position, which enables the affirmation of multiple explanatory frameworks that, at least at the present stage of understanding, are contradictory. For example, experimental data indicate light's duality as, in the general case, a wave, and, in a special case, a particle. Yet, the physicist operates with the belief that the law of noncontradiction has not been violated, and that the present appearance of contradiction already suggests the basic shape of a future explanation that would account for both sets of experimental conclusions in a single theory. Investigation can proceed because the unknown of the present is a known unknown, and so contains the anticipatory promise that "in the future, as far removed as you please, [the scientist] will possess the complete explanation of all phenomena."[35] Such methodical control can make progress toward a full solution to a present problem without getting bogged down in anxiety over the incompleteness of current understanding—even if that incompleteness is indistinguishable from contradiction at the present stage of discovery.

When one moves from the methodical position of the natural sciences to the dialectical position of speculative theology, however, one discovers that the situation is "at once more radical and more coherent."[36] For speculative theology, a dialectical position confronts difficulties on multiple fronts. The contradictions it seeks to explain are not the experiential data of experimental procedure but rather the apparent antinomies between the doctrines of faith and the conclusions of human reason. As theology, speculation affirms that "truth is one, and God is truth."[37] Thus, the "negative coherence of non-contradiction" must be advanced. But because the God revealed in the doctrines of faith is transcendent mystery, no speculative articulation of a doctrine can attain—even methodologically—the "positive coherence of complete explanation." Speculative thought "may construct the terms and theorems apt to correlate and unify dogmatic data; but the unification it attains cannot be explanatory in its entirety; the mind attains a symmetry, but its apex, the ultimate moment and the basis of its intelligibility, stands beyond the human intellect."[38]

Speculation's method is thus dialectical in its "yes" to noncontradiction and its "no" to complete explanation. The former "yes" mobilizes speculative theology toward the unification and correlation of the *nexus mysteriorum*, but the latter "no" chastens the theological mentality against the delusion of a finite instance of the infinite act of understanding. This "no" is not a false humility or an overeager apophaticism but a recognition of the disproportion between the finite means deployed in acts of human knowing and the infinite term those acts intend. At the same time, there exists a temptation to invoke the final dialectical position of this disproportion and its "no" anytime speculative difficulties arise. Some difficulties are merely philosophical; they crop up due to an inadequate set of philosophical tools and are overcome not through apophatic silence but through philosophic differentiation.

To advance the dialectical position, a speculative theology requires a technique to generate the distinctions, terms, and methods that, when transposed to the speculative context of theology, can tip the scales of probability in favor of resolving apparent contradictions. For Lonergan, any such technique must be able to grasp and survey the entire field of data on the problem; it must analyze accurately the natural element in the problem; and it must deal with questions pertaining to the problem in the correct order.[39] *Philosophia ancilla theologiae* is the traditional name designating the technique for speculative theology that ably responds to this threefold necessity.

There exists what Lonergan calls an "influence by analogy" between philosophy and theology owing to the theophanic quality of both the natural and the supernatural orders. If nature is a domain of divine appearing, then philosophical analysis—"the natural" in rationality—is analogous to theology in a manner corresponding to the relation between these orders of theophany, the natural order truly but dimly, and the supernatural order in a disproportionate mode and with a brighter brilliance. As an element in speculative theology, the philosophical technique provides methods, distinctions, and terms that can be augmented, adapted, transformed, and transposed into a theology, specifically into the theological theorems that seek the unity and coherence of dogmatic affirmation.

Absent the distinctions articulated in the natural order, the negative coherence of the dialectical position is unable to be advanced, because the theologian is unlikely to "make his first discovery of them in the supernatural."[40] Important speculative questions in theology are thus left unasked, and so the insights that would answer the unasked questions also fail to emerge. Without philosophical technique, "speculation is defective," making the theologian guilty not of the error of doctrinal negation but rather guilty of "ignorance or even of nescience."[41]

## The Phases

These four elements of the speculative—theorems, terms, the dialectical position, and technique—have various forms of interrelation, resulting in discrete phases of speculative development in theological intelligence. These combinations occur within a logical order of emergence, with some being "naturally prior" to others, resulting in a phased succession of progressive interrelation. For Lonergan, a "phase" is not a temporal designation, and so the succession of phases is not a diachronic series. Rather, a phase indicates a complex function of elements, especially the primary variables of theorems and technique.[42] Because the sequencing of phases is ordered by the natural functions of various elemental combinations, the phases are not *a priori* to development. Developmental order is not a logical formalism imposed upon historical unfolding. For Lonergan, rather, the phases of development are the "sets of abstract categories that have a special reference to historical process."[43]

Lonergan identifies a preliminary phase of speculative development in which theologians collect and classify the dogmatic data points relevant to their speculative problems. "Since speculative theology is the systematic element in the presentation of dogmatic truths," he writes, "its preliminary phase will consist in the first movements toward an explanatory unification of the data to be found in the dogmatic sources."[44] Concretely, these movements include those of prespeculative genres of doctrinal reflection (e.g., patristic commentaries on the Bible, Thomas's *Catena aurea*, and the *Glossa ordinaria*) to proto-speculative works (e.g., patristic polemical treatises and medieval books of sentences).[45] The emergence of organizational schemes for presenting dogmatic materials makes possible the subsequent phases of speculation properly so-called because "one cannot speculate without having something to speculate about."[46]

The intermediate stages of development arise from two sources: (1) the external circumstances of philosophic advancements, clarifications, and analogies that drive the ongoing growth of speculative technique; and (2) the attainment of internal coherence through developing theorems. Of the four elements of speculative form, technique increases (owing to external philosophic developments), theorems and their terms change (leading to and flowing from internal coherence), but, Lonergan argues, the dialectical position remains stable throughout the developmental progression. It is "the constant element," that which "constitutes the identity of any particular development in speculative theology."[47]

Lonergan demonstrates how the constancy of the dialectical position entails a migration from initial apprehension to final articulation. What is grasped first is the coexistence of two apparently opposed truths that, because each is affirmed in the dogmatic context, must be the case. The opposition has both philosophical and theological valences, and so technique is employed and theorems are utilized to resolve or remove all but the essence of the mystery intended in the doctrines. This essence, as divine mystery, is beyond technique; it is beyond the encompassing capacity of human understanding, and so the final "no" of the dialectical position receives its utterance. Speculation must resist invoking the final dialectical position as a cloak for ignorance that appeals to the superrationality of divine mystery to avoid the complexities of merely philosophical challenges. The dialectical "no" is a response to the disproportion between human reason and divine life, not a "no" to reason itself.

While the formal principle of the dialectical position remains constant throughout its process of elaboration, the phased development of speculative technique drives the migration. In both the classical tradition and in its appropriation in different forms of Christian thought, there is a simultaneous affirmation of both philosophic development and of *philosophia perennis*, of "man's apprehension of the eternal and immutable."[48] This apprehension, as Aristotle argued, has the love of wisdom as its potency, and this potency comes into act through "the triumph of reason systematically revealing the light of the eternal in the light of common day."[49] And despite the seeming divergences between philosophers or philosophies, the developmental trajectory of the *philosophia perennis* is a straight line from potentiality to achievement, *dynamis* to *energeia*, potency to act.[50] The "rectilinear" shape of this movement "can embrace differences as wide as those that exist between the pagan from Stagira and the Christian saint of Aquino; yet, however great such differences may appear outwardly, it remains that they emerge only to make more systematically certain and secure a position that is unique because it is central."[51]

Lonergan's analysis of *philosophia perennis* considers philosophy not as the achievement of any single philosopher or age but as the formality of philosophical activity, as the *systematic* disclosure of the eternal term of wonder in and through the mutability of creatureliness and its history. Divergences from this formality are not only the dead ends of a philosophy but betrayals of the eternal that accrue as the philosopher redirects his or her gaze to the problems of the age and crises of a cultural moment. This rerouting of reason can yield "the flux of philosophies," but this flux only confirms the formality of *philosophia perennis*.[52] But if one looks ahead to Lonergan's later thought, perhaps his greatest revision of this early analysis of speculative form is the legitimacy he accords *philosophia perennis*. As his sensibility increasingly turns to the operational, the empirical, and the historical, he comes to regard even the formality of *philosophia perennis* with increasing suspicion, viewing it as a residue of a world that no longer exists. And so, attention to the unique transformations in technique that these philosophic revolutions occasion will prove vital to transitioning from a speculative retrieval that mediates from the past to a speculative renewal that is mediated in the future. For the Lonergan of *Grace and Freedom*, the linear development of technique that drives the migration of the dialectic from initial apprehension to final position has an "essential moment" for speculative theology, in which emerges "a systematic distinction between faith and reason."[53] When the general distinction emerges, it can be specified to discrete speculative questions (such as the relationship between grace and freedom), acting to isolate incomprehension before the divine mysteries grasped loosely in faith from difficulties belonging to the operation of reason.

These elements and phases of speculative form are, for Lonergan, the *a priori* of theory to specific histories of dogmatic definitions, the relations between them, and the drive to understand those definitions coherently, synthetically, and theoretically. Speculative form as a developmental order in history interrelates the historical mediation of divine revelation, the magisterial proclamation of the church, and the diachronic series of efforts to disengage the synchronic meaningfulness of belief. But in addition to the historical unfolding of the speculative, there is the operation of speculation itself. And so beyond thematizing the structure of development, Lonergan outlines the conscious operations of intelligence by which the coherence and unity of dogmatic truth is attained.

## RECOVERING SPECULATION AS ACTIVITY

Theology always suffers the disproportion between its operator and its object. Theologians are human beings. They are bounded by a world, a history, a horizon, the natural limitations of their creatureliness. But their words intend God, who is unbounded, eternal, and unconditioned. Medieval theologians not only dared to utter words about God but even organized their utterances with the notion of *scientia*. They strived not merely to speak of God but to do so systematically. As a *scientia*, theology is a specification of human inquiry to the data of divine disclosure. It is a structured nexus of operations performed by the theologian effecting the emergence of theological understanding. But even the most robust account of theology still faces the basic disproportion between the natural and the supernatural, which leads to several questions. What is human inquiry in general? What is scientific inquiry? And how and to what degree do these notions apply to theological inquiry? Answers to these questions are many and often contradictory. And so, a brief account of the tradition of these disputed answers will serve as a pivot between speculative form as a developmental order in history and speculative operation as a specialized mode of human inquiry.

## Faith, Knowledge, and Understanding: A Disputed Tradition

The elusive relation between faith, understanding, and scientific elaboration has been a disputed one throughout the development of speculative theology. In *Gratia operans*, Lonergan articulates the form of speculative thought. He shows how various combinations of its constitutive elements comprise a phased developmental order of cumulative and progressive understanding. Implicit in his analysis of formal order is the operational order of human knowing. There is a tacit distinction in that early text between an act of judgment that gives its "yes" to doctrine, and an act of understanding that elaborates that judgment scientifically, theoretically, and speculatively to promote an intellectual grasp of the truth affirmed. And while this cognitional distinction operates implicitly in the background of *Gratia operans*, it is the dominant focus of Lonergan's subsequent efforts. His *Verbum* articles of the 1940s and his Latin theological works of the 1950s and '60s such as *The Ontological and Psychological Constitution of Christ*, and *The Triune God: Systematics*, as well as various essays over the same period, analyze the structure of cognitional operations within the consciousness of the theologian engaged in speculative theology.

Of singular importance is the role understanding *(intelligere, intellectus)* plays in interrogating dogmatic data, an importance only fully grasped against the backdrop of Lonergan's entire career.[54] But bound up in this emphasis is a dispute about the meaning and implications of Vatican I's Dogmatic Constitution on the Catholic Faith, *Dei filius*, and its articulation of the relationship between faith, science, and understanding. In his 1954 essay, "Theology and Understanding," Lonergan reaches into the debate through engaging the work of the Jesuit theologian, Johannes Beumer, noted for his critique of neoscholasticism's *"Konklusionstheologie."*[55]

According to Beumer, *Dei filius*'s account of the *intelligentia mysteriorum* is the culmination of a centuries-long tradition of conceiving of theology as the understanding of faith (*Glaubensverständnis*). The genesis of this tradition is the Christian transformation of *gnosis* in second- and third-century Alexandria with Clement and Origen.[56] The Augustinian and Anselmian *crede ut intelligas* builds off that earlier phase and leads to the subsequent medieval development of the *intellectus fidei* in William of Auxerre and Henry of Ghent.[57] Between the *intellectus fidei* of the Middle Ages and the *intelligentia mysteriorum* of Vatican I stands Josephus a Spiritu Sancto and the noetic connection between theology and contemplation.[58]

Conspicuously absent from Beumer's genealogy, or at least Lonergan's summary of it, is Thomas Aquinas. For while Beumer does treat of Thomas, his account is not flattering. The patristic, scholastic, and mystical theologians he surveys affirm theology as *Glaubensverständnis* and represent distinct phases of development toward Vatican I's synthesis, but Thomas's position, for Beumer, is ambiguous, even potentially deleterious. Beumer is suspicious that Thomas's *Theologie als Glaubenswissenschaft* is a regrettable departure from the Augustinian *Theologie als Glaubensverständnis* that had been the western approach since the patristic period.[59] The latter is theology's goal, while the former is the method by which that goal is attained.[60] And while a steady balance between *scientia* and *intellectus* is necessary, individual theologians may make disproportionate contributions to the development of one area over another. Thomas's methodological advances in speculative theology, for instance, occasioned through the application of Aristotelian theory, are major achievements in the history of theology. Yet, for Beumer, Thomas (especially the Thomas of the *Summa theologiae*) overemphasizes theology as *scientia* to the neglect of theology as *intellectus*.[61] Beumer concludes that whatever merit accrues to Thomas for his method, he represents a regrettable loss of the clear expression of the mysteries of faith that were so ably expounded in Augustine and in earlier scholasticism.[62]

Lonergan finds in this analysis much with which to sympathize. Like Beumer, Lonergan critiques theology's inattention to the act of understanding, its "oversight of insight." Beumer's reconstruction lionizes Matthias Scheeben as the proper exponent of Vatican I's teaching, arguing that if more theologians would have followed Scheeben's approach, mid-century Catholic theology would be less fragmentary and far closer to a methodical speculative theology.[63] Lonergan too sought the controls of meaning that would make a modern methodical theology possible, and insisted that such a theology would be a mediation rather than a fragmentation. But while Beumer finds his exemplar in Scheeben, Lonergan finds his in Thomas. And so, it is with Beumer's interpretation of Thomas that Lonergan takes issue.[64]

Retrieving Thomas's theory of understanding was the principal task that Lonergan gave himself in the early phase of his career, resulting in *Verbum: Word and Idea in Aquinas*, in which he painstakingly reconstructs Aquinas's cognitional theory, its Aristotelian origins, and its Trinitarian applications. But in "Theology and Understanding," Lonergan's account of Aquinas is streamlined. He presents Thomas's position in only six points. And he does so with the conviction that an accurate account of Thomas's notion of theology and understanding will significantly bolster Beumer's larger thesis concerning *Theologie als Glaubensverständnis*.

First, Thomas conceives of theology neither as a *scientia* nor an *intellectus* in any univocal sense, neither as axiomatic propositions nor indubitable truths. Theology's subject is the reality of God, and so its methods and modes of understanding resemble those of other sciences (those with proportionate objects) only analogically—that is, truly, but with ever greater dissimilarity. Lonergan's principal line of refutation runs through Aquinas's own account of the act of understanding itself.

Second, while Beumer treats of Aquinas's use of Aristotelian syllogism as grist for the mill of his thesis that Thomas privileges method over understanding, Lonergan shows that the syllogism does more than identify the grounds for judgments; it is an instrument of mind deployed to develop understanding.[65] It "is a vehicle for expressing an insight."[66] Logic is thus subordinated to intelligence.[67] The syllogism organizes the dynamism of intelligence as it moves "from principles to conclusions in order to grasp both principles and conclusions in a single view."[68] And that single view is the act of organizing intelligence—understanding.

Third, science is understanding in process. And so, parallel to the possibility of an understanding of God is the possibility of a science of God. For Aquinas, though, understanding is *quo est omnia fieri*, and so its term is the total and unrestricted context of being.[69] The unrestrictedness of the natural desire to know being manifests itself in the unrestrictedness of questions that provoke understanding. The desire to understand being unrestrictedly can only be fulfilled by an unrestricted act of understanding. For understanding to be fully in act, therefore, it must understand everything about everything in a single view. But an unrestricted act of understanding is beyond the capacity of human intellectual craft. It is God's knowledge of himself and all things through himself. So there arises what Lonergan calls the "apparent antimony" that created intelligence naturally desires to know God by his essence but cannot attain to such knowledge by its natural powers.[70]

Fourth, because *in via* there can be no natural attainment of the natural desire, any understanding of divine quiddity is negative understanding. It can refute objections and it can grasp the absence of inner contradiction, but it cannot know what God is.[71] But this incapacity to understand God's essence positively does not preclude a revelatory disclosure that mediates through itself a positive understanding. Human intelligence can, in this life and through faith, understand that disclosure but not the reality it mediates.[72]

Fifth, as positive knowledge of revelation is the expression of a reality not itself understood, there are three distinct manners by which that understanding can be effectuated. One can conceive of understanding as a gift flowing from sanctifying grace.[73] One can make the nontechnical, conciliar assertion that though positive understanding will inevitably be imperfect, it will also be fruitful. And one can specify that theology is a *scientia subalternata*, a science that is subalternated to the reality of God. As such, theology's subject is a reality, not a set of propositions (as Thomas already showed in *ST* I. q. 1. a. 7). As *scientia*, theology is understanding in process. As *subalternata*, theological understanding is not of God himself but of God as God reveals himself. But because the God who reveals is not understood, even the understanding of God as revealed will be imperfect.[74]

Sixth, though Thomas claims that theological science deduces from the conclusions of the articles of faith, Lonergan argues that such a claim has to be interpreted "in light of both Aristotle's theory of science and of Thomas's own theological practice."[75] Aristotelian syllogism has both explanatory and factual forms. But, Aristotle makes finer distinctions within the explanatory syllogistic structure. He distinguishes between those middle terms that fix the cause of existence (*causa essendi*) of any particular thing and those that fix the cause of one's knowledge (*causa cognoscendi*) of that thing's way of existing.[76] The cause of being "is some being that is a source of existence for another being, either extrinsically as final cause or efficient cause, or intrinsically as a constitutive principle of that which is caused."[77] The cause of knowing, meanwhile, "is not a being but a truth that is the reason grounding another truth."[78]

The phases of the moon (as middle term between "moon" and "sphere"), for example, are the cause of our knowing that the moon is a sphere, but the moon's sphericity (as middle term between "moon" and "phases") causes its phases to exist in the way that they do.[79] Our knowledge of the phases is the principle of our knowledge of the sphericity, but the existence of the phases depends upon the existence of the sphericity. The cause of knowledge considers what is "first for us" (*priora quoad nos*) in our analytic investigation (*via inventionis*). But once knowledge of the moon's sphericity is discovered, knowledge of that discovery can be passed on synthetically. A student can begin with knowledge of the moon's sphericity rather than having to make that discovery all over again. The priority shifts to the *causa essendi*, to what is first in itself (*priora quoad se*) and to what comes first in the *via doctrinae*.[80]

Thomas's task was to transpose these distinctions into theology in order to speak of theology as a science. For a theological investigator, the conclusions of the articles of faith are the *causa cognoscendi* of theological truth. These truths are *priora quoad nos*, and they are first in the *via inventionis*. Thus, the analytic terms of Aristotelian science can be imported into theology without significant augmentation. But since the reality of God is the subject of theology, the synthetic terms (*causa essendi*, *priora quoad se*, and *via doctrinae*) present a much more difficult transpositional challenge. Theology considers God as the universal *causa essendi*, that upon which all things depend but which depends upon nothing. God himself has no *causa essendi*, and so theological science cannot understand God through understanding God's causes. Thus, theological science properly speaking considers only the causes of human knowledge of God.[81]

Neither can theological science determine God's constitutive relations according to the *priora quoad se*, "for in the Blessed Trinity there is *nihil prius aut posterius*."[82] This does not mean, however, that the *priora quoad se* has no utility for theology but only that its application is limited to the causes of human knowledge of the divine relations. As Lonergan writes,

> There are in theology some causes of knowing that are more evident with respect to us, namely those from which we begin when faith is enlightening reason by way of theological discovery, and there are other causes of knowledge that are more evident with respect to themselves, namely, those from which we begin when reason enlightened by faith acquires some understanding of the mysteries of faith by way of theological teaching.[83]

But if theological science has no *causa essendi*, and only has a *priora quoad se* as applied to the *causa cognoscendi*, can there be a synthetic *via doctrinae* or *via disciplinae* for theology?

The *Summa theologiae*, Thomas tells us in the *prooemium* to the work, was written for the benefit of beginners, those not yet entrenched in the polemics, disputes, and arguments of the schools, those who "have been considerably hampered by what various authors have written."[84] The problem lies not with the students but with the texts and teachers meant to instruct them. These failures, Thomas insists, owe to a defective pedagogy, one that subordinates the intellectual *ordo* of teaching and learning to the expository and polemical demands of so many books and disputations. In the *Summa*, Thomas charts a different path. Proper theological pedagogy, he argues, should proceed not according to expositional or polemical *ordines* but according to the *ordo disciplinae*.[85] In the *ordo doctrinae/disciplinae*, the dogmatic discoveries that conclude the *ordo inventionis* are the starting points for systematic understanding. No longer needing to establish those dogmatic truths, this alternative *ordo* sets itself instead "to a systematic presentation of the truths that have been revealed."[86]

For Lonergan, Thomas walks the *via doctrinae* most clearly in his presentation of the doctrine of the Trinity in questions 27–43 of the *Summa*'s *Prima pars*. In the *prooemium* to question 27, Thomas states that the *ordo doctrinae* treats first of the processions, then of the relations, and concludes to the divine persons. This approach cannot prove that God is one nature existing eternally in three divine persons, and it cannot establish that the church's understanding of the revelation of the divine persons is correct. It assumes the revelation, and it assumes the doctrinal formulation of what has been revealed. But that is all it assumes. And from these givens, Thomas labors "to the synthetic or constitutive procedure in which human intelligence forms and develops concepts."[87]

Thus, the notion of God elaborated in QQ. 2–26 do not demand of students a detailed understanding of Trinity; they do not ask Trinitarian questions at all. In question 27, Thomas asks, considering the notion of God previously outlined, whether in such a God there is procession. Having imperfectly but fruitfully understood the meaning of procession in an eternal, simple God through an analogy of intelligible emanation, Thomas considers the two processions in God as four mutually opposed relations of origin (Q.28). Further reflection on the four real relations yields the understanding that three of the relations are intellectual and subsistent and so can be understood as persons (Q.29). Thus, what in a dogmatic *via inventionis* treatise on the Trinity is first (the divine persons) is, in the systematic *ordo doctrinae* of the *Summa*, last. But since there is no *priora quoad se* in the Trinity, the Trinitarian questions evince "the order of the genesis in our minds of our imperfect *intelligentia mysteriorum*; and by identity it is the order of Aquinas's *scientia subalternata* presented in the *ordo doctrinae*."[88]

For Lonergan, Thomas's theological method corroborates rather than contradicts Beumer's basic contention that *Glaubensverständnis* is the fundamental task of speculative theology. And beyond mere corroboration, a Thomistic *Glaubensverständnis* has distinct advantages over the patristic frame Beumer champions. But if the goal of speculative theology is an "imperfect, analogical, obscure, gradually developing, synthetic, and fruitful theological understanding" of the *nexus mysteriorum*, then mere recovery of Thomas is not sufficient. Having established that the understanding of faith is the central activity and goal of speculation, Lonergan provides an incisive examination of understanding itself, as well as understanding's specification to theology.

## Explanatory Understanding and Theological Speculation

Through his engagements with Aristotle, Aquinas, and the history of their contested interpretation, Lonergan demonstrates how the classical idea of science, so rigorously expressed in the *Posterior Analytics* has, at best, an analogical application to the unique context of theology. Theological science is a limit case to the universality of Aristotle's definition. For Lonergan, the central purpose of Aristotelian science, and even Aquinas's adaptation of it, is obscured by an oversight of insight, an inattention to understanding as both the purpose of syllogistic structure and the goal of theological exploration. And, further, the inexactness of the analogy of science itself is a source of that inattention. Beyond his dialectical efforts at interpreting Aristotle and Aquinas, Lonergan articulates a philosophical account of understanding and understanding's relation to judgment that, though compatible with the classical tradition, aims to make explicit the structured activities of empirical, intellectual, and rational consciousness operative but only implicit in that tradition's leading lights.

Insofar as they are brought out of the context of logical procedure and placed into that of conscious intentionality, the basic terms of Aristotle's science are transformed. Intellectual consciousness not only embraces what is included in Aristotelian *theoria* but expands its range to embrace all intelligible domains of terms and relations. The *priora quoad nos* becomes descriptive understanding (a grasp of the intelligible relations between the term of inquiry and the inquirer), while the *priora quoad se* becomes explanatory understanding (a grasp of the nexus of intelligible relations obtaining among the terms of inquiry themselves). Science defined as certain knowledge of things through their causes is redefined as a revisable, methodically controlled inquiry aiming at complete explanation, where explanation means the grasp of the relational nexus in a given domain of inquiry, and complete explanation means the grasp of all relational nexuses in all intellectual domains. But even in the transformed context, the application of science to theology is analogous, and so a generalized form of the operational structure needs clarification before its specialized, theological meaning can be expressed.

In his 1959 lecture, "Method in Catholic Theology," Lonergan summarizes the basic position regarding the generalized form of understanding and understanding's theological specification under five imperatives: (1) understand; (2) understand systematically; (3) reverse counter-positions; (4) advance positions; and (5) accept the responsibility of judgment.[89] In the pivot from the generalized form of these imperatives to their theological application, the specific analogical valence of science to theology comes into relief.

No single issue dominates Lonergan's thinking more than the recovery of the act of understanding in philosophical and theological discourses.[90] "[J]ust as man does not live on bread alone," Lonergan writes, "so knowledge does not live on certitude alone."[91] Between the experience that elicits philosophical wonder and the certitude that follows upon true judgments of fact is the act of understanding, the operation of organizing intelligence that grasps from within data an intelligible form, a quiddity, an essence. And as there exists a real distinction between essence and existence, so too is there a real distinction between the noetic operations that intend them. There is an act of direct understanding that grasps essences, and the act of reflective understanding and judgment that affirms or denies whether those essences exist.[92]

The essences or intelligibilities grasped in understanding are "no more than ideas, definitions, hypotheses, theories. They may prove to be correct; far more commonly they prove to be incorrect; but in themselves they are neither true nor false."[93] The intelligent grasp of the intelligible in sense or in consciousness is not merely certitude by another name; it is a distinct activity with a distinct criterion: coherence. It does not answer the question of whether some state of affairs exists or is the case, but only what that state of affairs is, what it means, and why its meaning is what it is. The product of understanding, in the Aristotelian language, is an intelligible species. It falls to the higher court of reflective understanding and judgment to determine whether the conditions of existence of any intelligible species have, in fact, been fulfilled such that an essence can rightly be said to exist.

Significantly, because the act of understanding is a grasp of the intelligible in the data of sense or of consciousness, it is a grasp of concrete intelligibility. Against a nominalism in which understanding is the grasp or intuition of abstract universals and the classification of concrete particulars under the banner of those universals, Lonergan writes, "When we are able to abstract, it is because we understand."[94] Abstraction relates "to the sensible only as the universal to the particular," but " it is in the sensible, in the concrete, that understanding grasps intelligibility."[95] And although similars are similarly understood, and so understanding can be said to grasp universals, "it remains that understanding may or may not exploit its capacity for generalization."[96]

To pursue the generalizations of abstractness is to move from understanding in a generic sense to systematic understanding in a specific one. Such pursuits intend intelligibilities beyond those grasped in descriptive understanding. Beyond the utility of common sense, human intelligence "heads for complete explanation of all phenomena; it would understand the universe."[97] This systematic pursuit of complete intelligibility, intelligibility that includes relational nexuses between terms, is what Lonergan means by explanatory understanding or science. "It distinguishes endlessly," he writes, "but it does so only to relate intelligibly; and ideally the network of relations is to embrace everything. It is this complete network of relations, making intelligible every aspect of the concrete universe, that is to be thought of when I say that understanding is to be systematic."[98] And against the suggestion that explanatory understanding is the proprietary ground of the hard sciences, he insists that "it is relevant not only to the natural sciences but also to the human sciences, to philosophy, and to theology. I base this relevance on the fact that such a technique merely makes explicit what already is implicit in all intelligent and reasonable knowing."[99]

As the distinction between understanding and understanding systematically implicitly suggests, intellectual consciousness is polymorphic. There exists a plurality of patterns to human experience, evincing a plurality of intelligibilities and demanding different nuances of intellectual operation proportionate to those intelligibilities. In *Insight*, Lonergan distinguishes between the biological, aesthetic, intellectual, and dramatic patterns of experience.[100] Some experiential flows pertain to survival (biological), others to symbolic liberation (aesthetic), some to theoretical mastery (intellectual), and still others to human social living (dramatic). In a concrete subject, however, the patterns are often not well-ordered. They "alternate; they blend or mix; they can interfere, conflict, lose their way, break down."[101] As they do, counter-positional thinking interferes with explanatory understanding. Biological, aesthetic, and dramatic constraints threaten to undermine the difficult work of system or theory. Often they do so under the guise of philosophical or scientific opinion, and, in the history of ideas, these interferences sometimes yield entire traditions of philosophy. They may be erudite, accomplished, and widely successful in gathering adherents and advocates, but they have within them a rotten core, an interference of insights proper to biological, aesthetic, or dramatic patterns of experience misapplied to philosophical inquiries. These counter-positions are opportunities for transformations, but transformations that occur not only in the doctrine of a philosophical school but in the basic intellectual horizon of the philosopher. As Lonergan writes,

> The root of the problem, I believe, its really baffling element, lies within the subject, within each one of us. For the problem is not solved merely by assenting to the propositions that are true and by rejecting the propositions that are false. It is a matter of intellectual conversion, of appropriating one's own rational self-consciousness, of finding one's way behind the *natura naturata*, the *pensée pensée*, of words and books, of propositions and proofs, of concepts and judgments, to their origin and their source, to the *natura naturans*, the *pensée pensante*, that is oneself as intelligent and as reasonable.[102]

The enactment of this intellectual transformation results in both the reversal of counter-positions and the advancing of positions.

If the recovery of understanding is the central element in Lonergan's philosophy, his doctrine of judgment is perhaps his greatest positive philosophical contribution. The grasp of essences, Lonergan demonstrates, is not a matter of seeing, intuiting, or imagining. It is an act of understanding, of intelligence. Similarly, knowledge of existence is not passive perception, but active rationality, or judgment. As Lonergan writes, "Minds reach knowledge only through judgment. And there is no recipe for producing men of good judgment."[103] In judgment, one has already understood some essence, grasped what the conditions of its existence are, reasoned that those conditions have been fulfilled, and so said "yes" to the question of an essence's existence. As Lonergan puts it, "Judgment demands more than adequately developed understanding. It supposes a transformation of consciousness, and ascent from the eros of intellectual curiosity to the reflective and critical rationality that is the distinguishing mark of man."[104]

It is this distinguishing mark that Augustine referred to as the contemplation of eternal reasons, and Aquinas named a created participation in uncreated light. For Lonergan, this distinguishing mark is termed rational consciousness.[105] In rational consciousness, "there emerges the proper content of what we mean by truth, reality, knowledge, objectivity; and by the movement we ourselves in our reasonableness are involved, for every judgment is at once a personal commitment, an endeavor to determine what is true, and a component in one's apprehension of reality."[106]

In the ordinary course of the development of a science, these imperatives succeed one another in an upward moving dynamism, from the first rudiments of intellectual comprehension to theoretical grasp, to dialectical transformation of horizons, to rational adjudication between the formality of intellectual coherence and the actuality of rational existence. But like the application to theology of the Aristotelian *priora quoad se*, *causa essendi*, and *via doctrinae*, the theological application of Lonergan's scheme has an analogical valence. Yet, the manner of its analogical difference illuminates the relation between theological speculation and doctrinal affirmation with greater clarity and explanatory force than that of the Aristotelian framework.

As Lonergan demonstrates in his engagements with Beumer, the notion of *intellectus* is central to the Catholic theological tradition, and the development of that tradition is in many respects the development of its *intellectus* from implicit to explicit, from common sense to theory, from the negotiation of doctrinal appositions and aporias to the breakthrough to the distinction between faith and reason. Like other sciences, theology's historical development is one of migration toward elaborated systematic understanding. And like other scientists, the development of an individual theologian is the maturation of intellectual habits and powers in response to the systematic exigence. For Lonergan, it was the thirteenth-century theoretical distinction between the natural and supernatural orders that made possible the systematic breakthrough to a formally theological domain of systematic understanding, to a "total viewpoint" that distinguished in order to relate theology, philosophy, and other disciplines of inquiry. As Lonergan writes, "Things are ordered when they are intelligibly related, and so there is order inasmuch as there is a domain of intelligible relations. The discovery of a supernatural order was the discovery of a domain of intelligible relations proper to theology."[107] And in discovering its proper domain of intelligible relations, theology discovered its essential relation to all other departments of knowledge.[108]

But if, for Beumer, the loss of theological *intellectus* begins in Aquinas, for Lonergan, this disappearance is the scandal of the late Middle Ages. The condemnations of Aristotle in the generation after Aquinas was "an acceptance of Aristotelian logic but a rejection of the ancient pagan's views on science and philosophy. Theology was to be pure. In the hands of Duns Scotus and of William of Ockham it quickly became very purely logical, and while logic is a valid systematic ideal, its atmosphere is too thin to support life."[109]

Theology as logic evinces the counter-position that speculation intends certainty, and it disguises its flight from understanding behind deductive rigorism. But as Lonergan argues, the process of coming to understand, especially the unique, analogical form of understanding that is speculative theology is haphazard and full of uncertainties.[110]

It has become commonplace in contemporary theology to critique late medieval Franciscan theology, assigning to it blame for the negative effects of the Reformation, modernity, capitalism, secularism, nihilism, and even liturgical decline. Lonergan's claim, though, is different. And his prescription for reversing this counter-position also runs contrary to the impulses of many critiques of the late Middle Ages. Rather than trying to get back behind the Scotist conception of theology to a more viable high medieval frame, Lonergan argues, "The achievement of the thirteenth century is not a goal but a starting point."[111] Lonergan's own theological and philosophical project was not simply to excavate and recapitulate the Thomistic synthesis as a panacea for modern philosophical and theological impasses, but to incarnate Thomas's achievement by doing in the present age what Thomas did in his. The position Aquinas advanced required the breakthrough to the notion of the supernatural order and the consequent line of reference termed nature, making possible the theoretical distinction between nature and grace, and between reason and faith, but "it lacked what we call the historical sense, namely, an awareness that concepts are functions of time, that they change and develop with every advance of understanding, that they become platitudinous and insignificant by passing through minds that do not understand, and that such changes take place in a determinate manner that can be the object of a science."[112]

By taking cognizance of the ways concepts are temporally (and, implicitly, geographically) textured, of how intelligence develops within histories, Lonergan indicates not only a path back to the unity of positive and speculative theology but also a path forward to a more critical reconciliation of systematic and historical knowledge. The precepts of theological method, "serve to unite historical and speculative theology as past process and present term. Historical or positive theology is concerned with the becoming of the speculative; and speculative theology is the term of historical process."[113] The reciprocity and inner unity between the positive and the speculative secures the legitimacy of both theological tasks. And to forget that unity is also to undermine them. Without an integral relation to the speculative task, positive theology "becomes lost in the wilderness of universal history; it ceases to be a distinct discipline with a proper field and competence of its own; for it is only from speculative theology that history can learn just what its precise field is and what are the inner laws of that field in their enduring manifestations."[114] But the dependence of the positive on the speculative is mutual. Without positive theology, speculative theology withers away; for its proper task is, not just understanding, but understanding the faith; its positive basis is historical, and without that basis it may retire into an ivory tower to feed itself with subtle memories, it may merge with the general stream of philosophic thought, or it may attempt to take over, modestly or despotically, the teaching office of the church, but the one thing necessary it cannot do: continue today the process begun so long ago of adding to living faith the dimension of systematic understanding.[115]

Speculative recovery, therefore, involves the recovery of the inner unity between the history of divine self-disclosure in time and the explanatory understanding of the nexus between the terms of that disclosure. And as the emergence of modern historical consciousness complicates the notion of history in positive theology, so too it demands a renewed formulation of the inner unity between the positive and the speculative, between history and system. To deliver upon this demand is, for Lonergan, to advance the position achieved in Thomas by integrally expanding the tradition he represents to encompass what it as yet does not.

The last of Lonergan's methodological precepts strains the analogical influence between science, philosophy, and theology. Judgment, evaluation, the rational "yes" or "no" to an understanding is "the supreme rule in any and every science."[116] Scientific inquiry interrogates some circumscribed range of data, seeking to understand what is to be understood, postulating possible answers, testing them through controlled procedures, before discovering at the conclusion of those procedures whether what is understood is, in fact, the case. Judgment, therefore, stands to truth as understanding to coherence. And so, to refuse the responsibility of judgment is to reject the possibility of truth, a prospect that Lonergan calls "sub-human."[117] But while in all mundane sciences intelligence interrogates data, theological science interrogates truths; it seeks to understand faith. Speculative theology "begins from revealed truth: it does not move towards them through an understanding of data. The truth is had right from the beginning."[118] These truths are secured in the mystery of God, revealed in history, known in faith, expressed in doctrine, and understood through the explanatory nexus between the terms. And yet, the speculative theologian cannot avoid making their own judgments. "Theology is not exercise in repetition," Lonergan writes, "it is an understanding that grows with the passage of time."[119]

For an understanding to grow, one must evaluate it, either ratifying its veracity, or deeming it defective, leading to a new quest for understanding. The theological responsibility of judgment is the theologian's willingness to reflect critically upon the hypothetical postulations of his or her speculations. Such critical reflection is not simply a repetition of the act of understanding. It is something different. It is a new operation in the consciousness of the theologian and "the only way by which a fuller understanding can for the first time pass into the realm of truth."[120] The success of this transition from intelligence to reason, from understanding to judgment happens "in accordance with a certain wisdom."[121] And while wisdom makes adequate all true judgments, only the wisdom of God can fully judge the adequacy of the understanding of faith. But although lacking divine wisdom, the theologian must nevertheless judge. A speculative theologian must "make a judgment according to their own considered opinion," and if the wisdom underwriting the judgment is discovered to be defective, they "readily submit their judgment to that of the church, because they know that the church's teaching authority is guided by the Holy Spirit."[122] The responsibility of judgment subordinates the theologian both to the wisdom of God and to the teaching authority of the church. Such subordination means that "theologians will refrain from rendering a definitive value judgment upon their understanding, but will humbly state their opinion and accept the judgments of the church."[123]

## CONCLUSION

The previous chapter began with the recognition that a once commonplace division of labor in theology—between the positive and the speculative—has fallen out of fashion and that this fall has resulted from multiple causes. The rise and maturation of the human sciences, especially the study of history, demanded an ecclesial transformation of positive theology. This transformation commanded much of the intellectual energy of continental theologians during the first half of the twentieth century and contributed to the various reforms of the Second Vatican Council. An unhappy result of this overwhelmingly fortunate development was the relative neglect that speculative theology suffered over the same period.

The twentieth century saw not only the ecclesial transformations leading to and following Vatican II but also major transformations in philosophy, especially on the continent. The rise of deconstruction, psychoanalysis, and various forms of Marxist political theory leveled critiques against the speculative systems of not just theologians but of philosophers, political economists, and scientists too. All systems, precisely as systems, occlude a will to power, an unjust set of social relations, and a psychosexual symbolic perversity. And as such, they deserve to be razed.

These two sources of speculative decline could not differ from one another more starkly. Yet, they have both contributed to the loss of the speculative tradition in much of modern theology. This chapter argued that the first step toward an honest reevaluation of the speculative tradition is to recover a memory of its form and operations in their exemplarity. Theologians cannot ignore the moral and intellectual urgency of postmodern suspicion toward speculative thought, but they need not let the legitimacy of suspicious questions prevent them from seeking answers.

Through a detailed examination of several early texts of Bernard Lonergan, this chapter has tried to make clear what exactly speculative theology is, how it develops, and the nature of the conscious operations by which its work is accomplished. In so doing, the argument does not seek direct confrontation with the modern forms of resistance to the speculative tradition. Rather, it has tried to let that tradition, at least insofar as it is reflected in Lonergan's early work, speak for itself. Yet, while this foregrounding reveals the superficiality of several features of the critics' case, it leaves unaddressed their more central claims. To pass through the modern forms of resistance, recovery is only the first phase. A subsequent renewal of the speculative tradition is required, one that does more than rehearse the broad lines of the past, but that invites the development of the tradition in light of the transformations in the cultural and intellectual situation that distinguish the present stage of theological reflection from that of the bulk of the speculative tradition's main currents.

Hints of these transformations are scattered throughout this chapter's analyses, and indeed throughout much of Lonergan's early writings. Lonergan identified three revolutions in western consciousness that together establish the new context of theology and with which any theological *aggiornamento* must contend. First, based especially on his reading of Herbert Butterfield, Lonergan calls attention to the revolution in science that overturned the Aristotelian worldview. The transition from a conception of science as the sure knowledge of things through their causes to science as the heuristic procedures aiming toward complete explanation of all phenomena demands, he argues, a reexamination of the *scientific* nature of theology.

Second, following Hans Georg Gadamer, Christopher Dawson, and Carl Becker, Lonergan highlights the challenge that the rise of historical consciousness and the empirical notion of culture represent for a global religion, and a theology that elaborates the faith of that religion. The notion of culture as the social objectification of human nature, an immutable and universal achievement crumbles with the discovery of the multiplicity of cultures. The theological task must broaden to be able to effectuate a mediation of revealed meaning within this multiplicity.

Finally, Lonergan's own work aims toward a revolution in philosophy, one in which cognitional theory overturns metaphysics as first philosophy, as the critical ground for epistemology, metaphysics, ethics, and the philosophy of God. Such reorganization results in a new emphasis on method, and a greatly reduced, decentered role for logic. Philosophy grounded in cognitional theory and method yields a new notion of theology as the mediation of religious meanings to a cultural matrix. The next chapter integrates these revolutions into a synthetic account of the structure of a renewed speculative theology. It highlights especially the revolutions in history and philosophy in the development of such a theology. And it presents an experimental account of that in which a renewed speculative theology consists.

## NOTES

1. John Henry Newman, *An Essay in Aid of a Grammar of Ascent* (Notre Dame: University of Notre Dame Press, 1979), 75.

2. Ayres, "The Memory of Tradition," 535. As *loci classici*, Ayres identifies Alexander of Hales, *Summa* pars 1, inq. 1, tr. 4, q. 2, cap. 4. 4; Siger of Brabant, *Quaest. in Metaph.* 6. *Comm.* 1; Thomas Aquinas, I *Sent.*, prol., q. 1, a. 3. In the *sed contra* to *Summa theologiae* I. 1. 4., Aquinas argues, against the objector's application of *Metaphysics* Ia, I, that because *sacra doctrina* is primarily concerned with God, not humanity, "it is not a practical but a speculative science." And in the *respondeo* he insists that because *sacra doctrina* is one and extends to a consideration of the objects of all sciences under the aspect of the knowledge granted by divine light, *sacra doctrina* includes both speculative and practical *scientiae*, but "it is more speculative than practical, because it is more concerned with divine things than with human acts." Of course, the extent to which *sacra doctrina* can be considered synonymous with theology is a matter of dispute. See Brian Davies, "Is *Sacra Doctrina* Theology?" *New Blackfriars* 71 (1990): 141–147.

3. Ayres, "The Memory of Tradition," 535.

4. Ayres, "The Memory of Tradition," 536 (emphasis original).

5. Ayres, "The Memory of Tradition," 536.

6. Ayres, "The Memory of Tradition," 538.

7. On the dynamic of pneumatological enkindling and chastening of desire, see Coakley, *God, Sexuality, and the Self*, 13–15, 266–300.

8. Lonergan, *Grace and Freedom*, CWL 1. This volume contains both Lonergan's doctoral dissertation, *Gratia Operans*, which he completed in 1940 (though he was not granted the degree until the end of 1946 due to the political and social situation in Europe) and his revision of the dissertation published in *Theological Studies* as four articles from 1941 to 1942. In the process of adapting his work for *TS*, Lonergan elected to cut the first chapter of the dissertation, which is devoted to the developmental form of speculative theology. Accordingly, this chapter's reflections on speculative method in conversation with *Grace and Freedom* depends completely on the dissertation, not the *TS* articles. Because the chapter was unpublished, it did not invite extended treatment in the early reception of Lonergan's work. It was first published as Bernard Lonergan, "The *Gratia Operans* Dissertation: Preface and Introduction," *Method: Journal of Lonergan Studies* 3.2 (1985): 9–46.

9. Jaroslav Pelikan, *Reformation of Church and Dogma (1300–1700)*, The Christian Tradition: A History of the Development of Doctrine 4 (Chicago and London: University of Chicago Press, 1984), 374.

10. See Pelikan, *Reformation of Church and Dogma*, 374–385.

11. For an account of this history, see Friedrich Stegmüller, *Geschichte des Molinismus* (Münster: Aschendorff, 1935); Gerald Smith, *Freedom in Molina* (Chicago: University of Chicago Press, 1966).

12. For a thematic outline of the various positions associated with these schools, see J. Michael Stebbins, *The Divine Initiative: Grace, World-Order, and Human Freedom in the Early Writings of Bernard Lonergan* (Toronto: University of Toronto Press, 1995), 183–211.

13. Lonergan, *Grace and Freedom*, CWL 1, 155.

14. Lonergan, *Grace and Freedom*, CWL 1, 155. Kathryn Tanner argues along the same lines as Lonergan that both sides of the debate violate the "rules" for coherently speaking of God and the world, and so deform modern theological discourse. See Tanner, *God and Creation in Christian Theology: Tyranny or Empowerment?* (Minneapolis: Fortress Press, 2005), 141–152. For an appreciative, but critical response to Lonergan's reading of Thomas and his solution to the *de auxiliis* problematic, see J. R. Matava, *Divine Causality and Human Free Choice: Domingo Báñez, Physical Premotion and the Controversy de Auxiliis Revisited*, Brill Studies in Intellectual History, vol. 252 (Leiden: Brill, 2016), 213–241.

15. Lonergan, *Grace and Freedom*, CWL 1, 155.

16. Lonergan, *Grace and Freedom*, CWL 1, 162. For an allied account of the first chapter of *Gratia operans* and a theory about its relation to the account of doctrines and systematics in *Method in Theology*, see Mark T. Mealey, "Lonergan's Notion of Speculative Theology in His Dissertation on *Gratia operans*, in Comparison with the Notions of Method in *Method in Theology*," *Method: Journal of Lonergan Studies* 19.1 (2001): 113–141. See also Frederick E. Crowe, *The Lonergan Enterprise* (Cambridge, MA: Cowley Publications, 1980), 14–18.

17. See Augustine, *De Gratia et Libero Arbitrio* c. 14, §27 (PL 44, 897), cc. 14–17, §§27–33 (PL 897–901); Anselm, *Tractatus de concordia*, c. 14, 524–25 (Schmitt 2: 267–68); Peter Lombard, *Libri IV Sententiarum* 2, d. 25, cc. 5–6; Albert the Great, *Commentarium in II Sententiarum* d. 26, a. 6; Thomas Aquinas, *Summa Theologiae* I-II, 109–114.

18. Lonergan cites numerous passages in his account of this history, but highlights *Super II Sententiarum* d. 28, q. 1, a. 2; *De veritate* 24, 14; *Summa contra Gentiles* 3, cc. 52, 147–163; and *ST* I-II, 109.2. It is worth noting that studying Aquinas's texts with a sensitivity for internal development was, even at the time Lonergan wrote *Gratia operans*, a relatively recent development in post-Leonine Thomism. As Alasdair MacIntyre notes, in addition to the systematic, often deductive reduction of Aquinas to Suarezian scholasticism, "*Aeterni Patris* also produced generated a quite different set of intellectual enterprises, in which retrieving stage by scholarly stage the historical understanding of what Aquinas himself said, wrote, and did, recovered for us an understanding of what is distinctive about the mode of enquiry elaborated in its classical and most distinctive form by Aquinas." See MacIntryre, *Three Rival Versions of Moral Enquiry* (Notre Dame: University of Notre Dame Press, 1990), 77.

19. Lonergan, *Grace and Freedom*, CWL 1, 162.

20. Lonergan, *Grace and Freedom*, CWL 1, 162–163.

48                               Chapter 2

21. Lonergan, *Grace and Freedom*, CWL 1, 163.

22. See John Henry Newman, *An Essay on the Development of Christian Doctrine*, 6th ed. (Notre Dame, IN: University of Notre Dame Press, 1989); Johann Sebastian Drey, *Brief Introduction to the Study of Theology with Reference to the Scientific Standpoint and the Catholic System*, trans. Michael J. Himes (Notre Dame, IN: University of Notre Dame Press, 1994); Johann Adam Möhler, *Unity in the Church, or the Principle of Catholicism: Presented in the Spirit of the Church Fathers of the First Three Centuries*, trans. Peter C. Erb (Washington, DC: Catholic University of America Press, 2016); Maurice Blondel, *The Letter on Apologetics & History and Dogma*, trans. Alexander Dru and Illtyd Trethowan (Grand Rapids: Eerdmans Publishing Company, 1994).

23. Lonergan, *Grace and Freedom*, CWL 1, 163.

24. Lonergan, *Grace and Freedom*, CWL 1, 163.

25. Lonergan, *Grace and Freedom*, CWL 1, 163.

26. Lonergan, *Grace and Freedom*, CWL 1, 164.

27. Lonergan, *Grace and Freedom*, CWL 1, 164.

28. See Jean Piaget, *The Psychology of Intelligence*, trans. Malcolm Piercy and D. E. Berlyne (London: Routledge, 1950), 10: "To define intelligence in terms of the progressive reversibility of the mobile structures which it forms is therefore to repeat, in different words, that intelligence constitutes the state of equilibrium towards which tend all the successive adaptations of a sensori-motor and cognitive nature, as well as all assimilatory and accommodatory interactions between the organism and the environment."

29. On experiential and pure conjugates, see Bernard Lonergan, *Insight: A Study of Human Understanding*, ed. Frederick E. Crowe and Robert M. Doran, CWL 3 (Toronto: University of Toronto Press, 1992), 102–103.

30. David Burrell, "Incarnation and Creation: The Hidden Dimension," in *Faith and Freedom: An Interfaith Perspective* (Oxford and Malden, MA: Blackwell, 2004), 235: "An unintended connotation of that distinction, which identified grace with the supernatural order, was to imply that the natural order was not a grace, not a gift. And what is not a gift is a given. But taking the world as a *given* is precisely the pagan outlook which the revelation to Moses explicitly countered in the ancient world."

31. Henri de Lubac, *The Drama of Atheist Humanism*, trans. Edith M. Riley, Anne Englund Nash, and Mark Sebanc (San Francisco: Ignatius Press, 1995).

32. Lonergan, *Grace and Freedom*, CWL 1, 165: "Terms are the obvious product of speculation."

33. Lonergan, *Grace and Freedom*, CWL 1, 165.

34. Lonergan, *Grace and Freedom*, CWL 1, 165.

35. Lonergan, *Grace and Freedom*, CWL 1, 166.

36. Lonergan, *Grace and Freedom*, CWL 1, 166.

37. Lonergan, *Grace and Freedom*, CWL 1, 166.

38. Lonergan, *Grace and Freedom*, CWL 1, 166.

39. Lonergan, *Grace and Freedom*, CWL 1, 166.

40. Lonergan, *Grace and Freedom*, CWL 1, 168.

41. Lonergan, *Grace and Freedom*, CWL 1, 168. In a footnote to this assertion, Lonergan explicitly invokes this distinction as Thomas Aquinas articulates it in *De malo* q.3 a.7. There Thomas defines ignorance as a privation of knowledge; it is a state in which one finds oneself lacking knowledge proportionate to one's nature. As a state, not an act, not knowing is not a sin. Like concupiscence, it is a material element in sin, but not a sin itself. Nescience, on the other hand, involves an act. It is to make judgments about that which one is ignorant. It brings into act the material element of ignorance, and so bears with it the nature of sin.

42. Lonergan, *Grace and Freedom*, CWL 1, 168.

43. Lonergan, *Grace and Freedom*, CWL 1, 168.

44. Lonergan, *Grace and Freedom*, CWL 1, 169.

45. Peter Candler uses the metaphor of "manuduction" to analyze the *Glossa* and its thematic connections to the *Summa theologiae* in *Theology, Rhetoric, Manuduction, or Reading Scripture Together on the Path to God* (Grand Rapids: Eerdmans Publishing Company, 2006), 70–107. In addition to his constructive thought, Candler provides an overview of contemporary historical scholarship on the *Glossa*.

46. Lonergan, *Grace and Freedom*, CWL 1, 170.

47. Lonergan, *Grace and Freedom*, CWL 1, 171.

48. Lonergan, *Grace and Freedom*, CWL 1, 172.

49. Lonergan, *Grace and Freedom*, CWL 1, 172.

50. Lonergan, *Grace and Freedom*, CWL 1, 172.

51. Lonergan, *Grace and Freedom*, CWL 1, 172–173.

52. Lonergan, *Grace and Freedom*, CWL 1, 173.

53. Lonergan, *Grace and Freedom*, CWL 1, 173.

54. Lonergan believed that the major problem in late medieval and modern philosophy was its inattention to the act of understanding, the "oversight of insight." His *Verbum: Word and Idea in Aquinas* (ed. Frederick Crowe and Robert Doran, CWL 2 [Toronto: University of Toronto Press, 1997]), *Insight: A Study of Human Understanding*, and *Method in Theology* (ed. Robert M. Doran and John D. Dadosky, CWL 14 [Toronto: University of Toronto Press, 2017]) all investigate the nature of understanding and its various methodic specifications in the sciences, philosophy, and theology.

55. Johannes Beumer, *Theologie als Glaubensverständnis* (Würzburg: Echter-Verlag, 1953), 90–91. For his earlier analysis of post-Vatican I "conclusions theology," see Beumer, "Konklusionstheologie?" *Zeitschrift für katholische Theologie* 63 (1939): 360–365. Lonergan also rejected conclusions theology. See Lonergan, *The Triune God: Systematics*, ed. Robert M. Doran and H. Daniel Monsour, trans Michael Shields, CWL 12 (Toronto: University of Toronto Press, 2007), 53: "The view that is usually called 'conclusions theology' should be abandoned."

56. Beumer, *Glaubensverständnis*, 32–47.

57. Beumer, *Glaubensverständnis*, 71–80, 105–110.

58. Beumer, *Glaubensverständnis*, 116–120. He also presents the positions of Bernard of Clairvaux and Denis the Carthusian in sections immediately prior.

59. Beumer, *Glaubensverständnis*, 80–81: "Nur in *einem* Punkte müsste wohl die Untersuchung weitergeführt oder von neuem aufgenomen werden, ob Thomas von

Aquin durch seine Auffassung von Theologie als Glaubenwissenschaft wirklich nicht die augustinische Richtung mit ihrer Betonung des Glaubensverständnissses verändert hat."

60. Lonergan, "Theology and Understanding," in *Collection*, Frederick Crowe and Robert M. Doran, eds., CWL 4 (Toronto: University of Toronto Press, 1988), 115–116.

61. Lonergan, "Theology and Understanding," CWL 4, 117.

62. Beumer, *Glaubensverständnis*, 93: "Bedeutet also Thomas von Aquin einen Fortschritt oder einen Rückschritt in der Erkenntnis des Wesens der Theologie? Die Antwort auf diese Frage muss unterscheiden. Ein Fortschritt war besonders für die damalige Zeit zu verzeichnen, indem Thomas den Anschluss an die Geistesströmungen für die Theologie gefunden hat, ein Fortschritt auch absolut, indem er eine genauere Methode angeben konnte. Einen Rückschritt, allerdings begreiflich aus der Neuheit des Wagnisses, bedeutete es, dass er die positive Wendung zu den übernaturlichen Glaubensgaheimnissen nicht mehr so klar zum Ausdruck brachte wie Augustin und die ältere Scholastik."

63. Lonergan, "Theology and Understanding," CWL 4, 115.

64. Lonergan, "Theology and Understanding," CWL 4, 115: "Considerable misgivings will be felt over his views of St Thomas and on the relations between Thomist thought and *Glaubensverständnis*."

65. Lonergan, "Theology and Understanding," CWL 4, 118. During the early phases of Lonergan's development and career, he frequently reflected on the role of the syllogism in rational reflection and inference. His reading of John Henry Newman's *Essay in Aid of a Grammar of Ascent* was foundational for this interest. Lonergan's later work on Aquinas's notion of *verbum* ratified what he had already learned from Newman, and would be the basis of his analysis of the reflective grasp of the virtually unconditioned and the procession of judgement in chapters 9–11 of *Insight*. See Lonergan, "The Form of Mathematical Inference," in *Shorter Papers*, Robert C. Croken, Robert M. Doran, and H. Daniel Monsour, eds., CWL 20 (Toronto: University of Toronto Press, 2007), 3–12; idem, "The Syllogism," *Shorter Papers*, 13–33; idem, "True Judgment and Science," *Shorter Papers*, 34–44; idem, "The Form of Inference," *Collection*, Frederick E. Crowe and Robert M. Doran, eds., CWL 4 (Toronto: University of Toronto Press, 1988), 3–16; idem, *Insight*, CWL 3, 296–371. On Lonergan's early development, see Richard Liddy, *Transforming Light: Intellectual Conversion in the Early Lonergan* (Collegeville, MN: Liturgical Press, 1993), 16–40; William A. Matthews, *Lonergan's Quest: A Study of Desire in the Authoring of* Insight (Toronto: University of Toronto Press, 2005), 32–48.

66. Lonergan, *Understanding and Being: The Halifax Lectures on "Insight,"* Elizabeth Morelli and Mark Morelli, eds., 2nd ed., rev. Frederick Crowe et al., CWL 5 (Toronto: University of Toronto Press, 1990), 49.

67. Lonergan, "Theology and Understanding," CWL 4, 118.

68. Lonergan, "Theology and Understanding," CWL 4, 118. According to Lonergan's interpretation, "Plainly, Aristotle and Aquinas formulated with technical precision the very relations between understanding and science that Fr Beumer advocates"

("Theology and Understanding," CWL 4, 118). See *ST* I. q. 14. a. 7; I. q. 79. q. 8; II-II. q. 8. a. 1.

69. Lonergan, "Theology and Understanding," CWL 4, 118; *ST* I. q. 79. a. 7.

70. Lonergan, "Theology and Understanding," CWL 4, 118; *ST* I. q. 12. a. 4. See Lonergan, "Natural Desire to See God" CWL 4, 81–91. Lonergan shows that this difficulty stems from an inadequate consideration of material and formal objects. Materially, desire and fulfillment have the same object. But formally, desire's object is specified by the already known (in this case, the already known is the existence of God—a "yes" to the question "an sit Deus?"), but fulfillment's object is nothing other than what is presently not known (in the case, the answer to the question, "quid sit Deus?"). "Thus the object of the natural desire is transcendental; but the object of the fulfilling vision is supernatural" ("Natural Desire to See God," CWL 4, 87). Lonergan presents a philosophical form of this basic argument in chapter 19 of *Insight*.

71. Lonergan, "Theology and Understanding," CWL 4, 119; *ST* II-II. q. 8. a. 2.

72. Lonergan, "Theology and Understanding," CWL 4, 119; *ST* II-II. q. 8. a. 6.

73. Lonergan, "Theology and Understanding," CWL 4, 119; *ST* II-II. q. 8. a. 5.

74. Lonergan, "Theology and Understanding," CWL 4, 119.

75. Lonergan, "Theology and Understanding," CWL 4, 119.

76. Lonergan, "Theology and Understanding," CWL 4, 119; Aristotle, *Posterior Analytics* II.1–2.

77. Lonergan, *The Ontological and Psychological Constitution of Christ*, trans. Michael Shields, CWL 7 (Toronto: University of Toronto Press, 2002), 89.

78. Lonergan, *The Ontological and Psychological Constitution of Christ*, CWL 7, 89.

79. Lonergan, "Theology and Understanding," CWL 4, 120; idem, *The Ontological and Psychological Constitution of Christ*, CWL 7, 89.

80. Lonergan, "Theology and Understanding," CWL 4, 120; idem, *The Ontological and Psychological Constitution of Christ*, CWL 7, 89; idem, *Understanding and Being*, CWL 5, 48.

81. Lonergan, *The Ontological and Psychological Constitution of Christ*, CWL 7, 89.

82. Lonergan, "Theology and Understanding," CWL 4, 120.

83. Lonergan, *The Ontological and Psychological Constitution of Christ*, CWL 7, 91.

84. Thomas Aquinas, *Summa Theologiae*, Prologue.

85. Thomas Aquinas, *Summa Theologiae*, Prologue.

86. Lonergan, "Theology and Understanding," CWL 4, 121.

87. Lonergan, "Theology and Understanding," CWL 4, 122.

88. Lonergan, "Theology and Understanding," CWL 4, 122.

89. Lonergan, "Method in Catholic Theology," in *Philosophical and Theological Papers, 1958–1964*, Robert C. Croken, Frederick Crowe, and Robert M. Doran, CWL 6 (Toronto: University of Toronto Press, 1996), 30. This text is one of Lonergan's early efforts to elaborate the basic issues involved in theological method. While still years before many of his key breakthroughs that led to his mature analysis in *Method in Theology*, this early essay is an illuminating transitional text that connects the

speculative concerns of his dogmatic writing to his emerging account of consciousness and its attendant focus on method. The five precepts he enumerates are adapted from his course, "*De Intellectu et Methodo*," which he taught at the Gregorianum in the spring of 1959. A critical reconstruction and English translation of the original Latin manuscript are included in Bernard Lonergan, *Early Works on Theological Method 2*, ed. Robert M. Doran and H. Daniel Monsour, trans. Michael G. Shields, CWL 23 (Toronto: University of Toronto Press, 2013), 3–229.

90. This claim is more than justified by even a cursory read of *Verbum: Word and Idea in Aquinas* and *Insight: A Study of Human Understanding*. *Verbum* demonstrates that the act of understanding was central to Aristotle and Aquinas, though only implicitly articulated. *Insight* demonstrates how the traditional account, so obfuscated in late medieval and modern philosophy, can be recovered and enriched in the context of modern science and modern cognitional theory.

91. Lonergan, *The Triune God: Systematics*, CWL 12, 117.

92. On the medieval origins of the real distinction between essence and existence, see Etienne Gilson, *Being and Some Philosophers*, 2nd ed. (Toronto: Pontifical Institute of Medieval Studies, 1949 and 1952), 74–107.

93. Lonergan, "Method in Catholic Theology," CWL 6, 32.

94. Lonergan, "Method in Catholic Theology," CWL 6, 34.

95. Lonergan, "Method in Catholic Theology," CWL 6, 34.

96. Lonergan, "Method in Catholic Theology," CWL 6, 34.

97. Lonergan, "Method in Catholic Theology," CWL 6, 35.

98. Lonergan, "Method in Catholic Theology," CWL 6, 35.

99. Lonergan, "Method in Catholic Theology," CWL 6, 36.

100. Lonergan, *Insight*, CWL 3, 204–212.

101. Lonergan, *Insight*, CWL 3, 410.

102. Lonergan, "Method in Catholic Theology," CWL 6, 38.

103. Lonergan, "Method in Catholic Theology," CWL 6, 39.

104. Lonergan, "Method in Catholic Theology," CWL 6, 40.

105. Lonergan, "Method in Catholic Theology," CWL 6, 40.

106. Lonergan, "Method in Catholic Theology," CWL 6, 40–41.

107. Lonergan, "Method in Catholic Theology," CWL 6, 45.

108. Lonergan, "Method in Catholic Theology," CWL 6, 45.

109. Lonergan, "Method in Catholic Theology," CWL 6, 46.

110. Lonergan, "Method in Catholic Theology," CWL 6, 46.

111. Lonergan, "Method in Catholic Theology," CWL 6, 46.

112. Lonergan, "Method in Catholic Theology," CWL 6, 46.

113. Lonergan, "Method in Catholic Theology," CWL 6, 50.

114. Lonergan, "Method in Catholic Theology," CWL 6, 51.

115. Lonergan, "Method in Catholic Theology," CWL 6, 51.

116. Lonergan, "Understanding and Method," in *Early Works on Theological Method 2*, Robert M. Doran and H. Daniel Monsour, eds., Michael Shields, trans., CWL 23 (Toronto: University of Toronto Press, 2013), 207.

117. Lonergan, "Understanding and Method," CWL 23, 207.

118. Lonergan, "Understanding and Method," CWL 23, 211.

119. Lonergan, "Understanding and Method," CWL 23, 213.
120. Lonergan, "Understanding and Method," CWL 23, 215.
121. Lonergan, "Understanding and Method," CWL 23, 215.
122. Lonergan, "Understanding and Method," CWL 23, 215.
123. Lonergan, "Understanding and Method," CWL 23, 215.

*Chapter 3*

# Why Speculative Theology Failed

Speculative theology was never a ready-made achievement. Its emergence in scholastic craft was not inevitable. Its successes were never guaranteed. Speculative theology arose as the term of a series of distinct but interrelated developments in western, Christian consciousness. The story of speculative theology was a chapter in the story of that consciousness—of its birth, its growth, and its maturation. The early conciliar struggles against heresy led theologians to safeguard the deposit of faith through the introduction of metaphysical terms—substance, nature, person, union—to communicate an understanding of the revelation of God in Jesus Christ that maintained the coherence of Christian practice, worship, and devotion.[1] But the exegetical, homiletical, and polemical achievements of the patristic and conciliar age did more than rebuff heresy. They also contributed to a growing, diverse, sometimes contradictory tradition of self-understanding handed on to and expanded by later generations of Christians.

So diverse were these contributions that it fell to the early medieval schoolmen to bring systematic order and intellectual reconciliation to a steadily expanding doctrinal pluralism. Peter Abelard identified and collected from the tradition's many sources and texts the affirming *sic* and the negating *non* for numerous theological theses. But such dialectical collision only codified the ambiguities embedded in the theological patrimony. It could not resolve them. The subsequent development of the scholastic *quaestio* proved to be the subtler stratagem, and with it "Abelard's *non* became *videtur quod non* and his *sic* became *sed contra est*."[2] Peter Lombard's *Sentences* further amassed the vast and varied opinions, expositions, and postulations of the Christian textual heritage, and the *Sentences*'s commentary tradition applied the *quaestio* to communicate the unity and coherence contained within the manifold of that heritage. But it was not until scholastic thinkers, most famously Thomas Aquinas, encountered, adapted, and integrated elements of Aristotelian theory into their quest for coherence that speculative theology possessed a philosophical technique adequate to move beyond collection, collation, and nascent *intellectum* to a comprehensive synthesis, a systematic understanding of the doctrinal nexus, and an intellectual resolution to long-standing theological debates.[3]

This integration was not simply an elegant eclecticism, "a term that should only be applied to syntheses that have been insufficiently thought through."[4] Instead, as Hans Urs von Balthasar notes, "It is humanity, thinking symphonically, polyphonically. And it is characteristic of its greatest thinkers that the intuitions at the heart of their systems always assimilate scattered elements they find to hand."[5] By Balthasar's lights, Thomas Aquinas is "perhaps the most extreme" example of polyphonic thinking, a theologian whose "originality lies, not exclusively but substantially, in his lucid arrangement of the vast and confused volume of thought that had preceded him."[6] The lucidity of Thomas's synthesis and its explanatory range represent major intellectual achievements in the history of the West. And yet, for all his considerable talents, Thomas's accomplishments rested upon more than the force of his genius and the dint of his labor. They required an entire apparatus of material, social, intellectual, and cultural conditions without which their emergence would have been improbable.

The Thomistic speculative resolution of the twelfth century's "tortured" pluralism required the gradual deployment of Aristotelian logical method to organize varied doctrinal sources.[7] It demanded the material and linguistic transmission of Aristotle's nonlogical works to furnish an adequate philosophical technique. It necessitated the practical intellectual infrastructure of the medieval university to house and support the intellectual vocation. It involved the westward migration of Byzantine learning after the Fourth Crusade to make available vital philosophical and theological sources. It entailed the philosophical labors of Islamic and Jewish interpreters of Aristotle to bring philosophy into an Abrahamic horizon. And it needed the trailblazing thought of Albert the Great to provide a model for the integration of these various elements.[8] There was, in other words, a sequence of related but independent historical developments that resulted in a unified intellectual and practical cultural matrix, a matrix that formed a foundation for the medieval synthesis that resolved the doctrinal pluralism of earlier theologies. And while the intellectual residues of that synthesis have imperfectly but truly endured from the thirteenth century to the twenty-first, the unified cultural matrix that formed its foundation has been razed.

The church and its institutions are no longer central actors in the western sociopolitical order. Theology's philosophical handmaid has resigned her theological commission and has redirected her critical powers away from metaphysical theory and toward the interrogation of her own *via inventionis*. Natural philosophy has gained autonomy from metaphysics, rebranded itself as "natural science," and has lifted creation's explanatory veil through the emergence, application, and refinement of the canons of empirical method. Furthermore, the very notions of society and culture have undergone a radical change. Culture is no longer viewed in classicist terms, as the immutable social manifestation of the human soul—the *physis* beyond *nomoi*. It is rather the historical, specific, contingent, and concrete set of meanings and values by which people organize their common life. And as there are many discrete sets of such meanings, so are there many distinct cultures.

These scientific, philosophical, and cultural revolutions have led to what Lonergan calls "the passing of Thomism," and thereby to a pluralism of a sort quite distinct from that of the twelfth century.[9] The older doctrinal pluralism was the consequence of diverging, competing, and often inadequate philosophical strategies for expressing or even securing church doctrines. The new pluralism has its origins in distinct patterns and traditions of cultural making and ecclesial inculturation; in the varied and imperfect personal attainments of intellectual, moral, and religious authenticity; and in the conflicts that result from the complexities of the polymorphism of consciousness and the methods of analysis determined by distinct abstractive viewpoints.[10] And so it is right to ask, absent the intellectual and cultural unity of the high Middle Ages, is speculative theology still possible?

Both conservative and revisionist answers have denied its possibility. But the implications of that denial pull in opposite directions. Conservative opinion has tried to secure speculative theology by rebuilding the cultural and social unity of the world that gave it birth.[11] This tendency is evinced in many conciliar, curial, and papal statements from the mid-nineteenth century through the mid-twentieth.[12] And while the conservative response to the decline of speculative theology in modernity has often been a rigorous antimodernism and a robust effort of classicist cultural repristination, the revisionist responses, such as those Sarah Coakley identifies as the "modern forms of resistance" to speculative or systematic thinking, so closely associate speculation with hegemonic cultural classicism that they rule it out as a legitimate feature of religious expression. Instead of speculation, revisionist theologies prize contextual, practical, and critical projects. They seek grassroots theologies that make use of modern methods of analysis and that comport with their specific, concrete cultural and moral situations.[13]

But while both conservative and revisionist theologies have denied the possibility of speculative theology under current intellectual and cultural conditions, this chapter argues that there can and should be a postclassicist speculative theology. While the previous chapter drew from Lonergan's early theology to recover a particular vision of the speculative, a memory of its development and unfolding in the history of theology that could pass through postmodernism's critical gaze with its integrity intact, this chapter draws from later work on meaning, culture, and the methods of human inquiry to propose a heuristic account of the elements of a renewed speculative theology, a renewal provisionally termed "speculative pluralism." It is speculative insofar as it identifies that form of theological inquiry which intends an imperfect but highly fruitful understanding of the mysteries of faith in a way that is hypothetical, analogical, and revisable. It is a pluralism insofar as it anticipates a dynamic multiplicity of such speculative understandings correlated with a dynamic multiplicity of concrete cultural, intellectual, and moral exigencies. And it presents a basic heuristic structure to coordinate the material, formal, and dialectical elements of these multiplicities. The result, rather than new theological contents, is a contribution to what Robert Doran calls "a systematic theology of theologies," one that moves from the mere fact of theological pluralism to the methodical grounds of speculative collaboration.[14] Doran's account of the theology of theologies envisions a genetic sequence of advancing intelligence through shifts in historical stages of meaning and so considers systematic theological pluralism in diachronic terms. This chapter seeks to complement Doran's analysis by drawing out the correlated synchronic pluralism suggested by the empirical notion of culture.

## THE CLASSICIST WORLDVIEW AND ITS BREAKDOWN

To say that the sun has set on the cultural world of Aquinas is not simply to recognize the collapse of one scheme of civilizational circumstances and the emergence of another. It is not a matter of adding new metallurgical layers to the statue of Nebuchadnezzar's imperial dream.[15] It is rather to claim something far more radical, that what has ended is not only the practical order of Thomas's *milieu* but also the very notion of culture as he, his contemporaries, and his predecessors understood it. For them, culture was absolute, normative, and invariant. As classical philosophy abstracted from the material individuations of human living in order to posit its residues as the formal contents of human nature, so too the classical, normative notion of culture was the abstract social substance beneath and beyond all the concrete varieties of vital and political convention. Culture was the social embodiment of the human soul. And as the soul's formality does not suffer change from the empirical vicissitudes of time and place, neither does human culture.

This view, what Christopher Dawson calls "the old unitary conception" of culture, held that "men may be more cultured or less cultured, but in so far as they are cultured, they are walking along the same high road which leads to the same goal."[16] And because the goal was fixed, progress toward its realization could be measured by the standards "of Greek *paideia* and Roman *doctrinae studium atque humanitatis*," of education, cultivation, and

*Bildung*.[17] Becoming cultured was "a matter of acquiring and assimilating the tastes and skills, the ideals, virtues, and ideas that were pressed upon one in a good home and through a curriculum in the liberal arts," while culture itself was "a matter of models to be imitated, of ideal characters to be emulated, of eternal verities and universally valid laws."[18] Such were the aristocratic values that organized classicism's normative notion of the good life and the good society. So potent was the psychic momentum of the classicist worldview that it did not fall with the rest of the antique world. Its basic norms and ideals were taken up, modified, sometimes criticized, but largely maintained in the Christian West. As Lonergan describes Christian classicism, "Though there did exist the simple faithful, the people, the natives, the barbarians, still career was open to talent. One entered upon it by diligent study of the ancient Latin and Greek authors. One pursued it by learning Scholastic philosophy and theology and canon law. One exercised it by one's fluent teaching or conduct of affairs in the Latin tongue."[19] The accumulated wisdom of the ancient and medieval worlds was the normative course toward the cultivation of the self.

Classicism's great intellectual achievement is what Bruno Snell calls the discovery of mind.[20] By it, mentality and technique intervened upon the homogenous world of myth, magic, and practical intelligence. It objectified and distinguished between "feeling and doing, knowing and deciding," and it "clarified just what it is to know."[21] The discovery of mind was the discovery that when the intellect knows, it knows a meaning—a form, an intelligibility, a quiddity. And that clarification laid bare an additional discovery, that the range of meanings vulnerable to inquiry and knowledge includes two distinct classes. There are meanings whose terms have their intelligibility in their relation to the inquirer, and there are those whose intelligibility is the formality of the terms and the relations that obtain between and among them. The former are the meanings that populate the world of common sense, that are known through practical intellectual inquiry, that lead to language, economy, technology, politics, and—after a long time and with some epochal luck—the great civilizational orders of the ancient world.[22] But the latter are those meanings that belong to the distinct realm of theory, a realm discovered when inquirers ask questions whose answers lay outside the competence of common sense.

Such questions are those that Socrates posed and his interlocutors failed adequately to answer. They are questions that intend definitions of specific and universal applicability—*soli et omnia*. Theoretical inquiry asks not merely "Is this city just?" but also, "What is justice?" By clarifying that to know is to know a meaning, and that the world mediated by meaning includes both commonsensical and theoretical forms of mediation, the scientific, philosophical, and theological disciplines of the ancient and medieval worlds had their charter and their method. As such, notions like "justice" were taken out of the practical contexts that struggled to proffer stable definitions and set within a normative, universal moral psychology.

By distinguishing theory from homogeneous common sense, the discovery of mind clarified that the world human beings labor to know is mediated by meaning, explored through inquiry, and grasped by the intelligent apprehension of the intelligible. Knowing, in other words, is distinct from sensation, the intelligible from the sensible, and the known from the merely given. And while the mediation of meaning can take commonsensical or theoretical forms, it is only by making explicit the difference between them that one comes to thematize the world as mediated by meaning at all. For inasmuch as the discovery of mind is in part the discovery of the abstract realm of theory, it is also, by contrast, the discovery of the concrete realm of common sense as something distinct, circumscribed, and worthy of investigation because it has a discernible character all its own.

The classicist breakthrough to theory made possible by the discovery of mind allowed for the development of specialized, theoretical disciplines of inquiry: a perennial philosophy distinct from proverb, a universal science distinct from tacit understanding, and—in the Christian context—a speculative theology distinct from catechetical instruction. In the theoretical orientation, philosophy was, formally, a metaphysics. Its basic terms and relations were the general categories not just for philosophy but for natural and even (albeit imperfectly) theological science as well. In the theoretical realm, logic, especially the explanatory syllogism, was the primary control of meaning for every science. And because the conclusion of a syllogism is contained implicitly in the premises from which it proceeds, science could be conceived as the certain knowledge of things through their causes. Thus, theology, as the science of God and all things in relation to God, took its place atop the scientific hierarchy as *regina scientiarum*, for its object was the idea of being and its knowledge was effected with a certainty secured by divine revelation. Theory's universality, certainty, and logical control were fruits of the classicist worldview, a notion of order in which fixity, eternality, and generality were the ideals and norms of knowledge.

But as the medieval world gradually gave way to the modern, the notions and practices of science and philosophy underwent a sequence of dramatic revolutions that fractured the hierarchical unity of knowledge as it was imagined in the classicist scheme. That classical unity, argues Lonergan, "habituat[ed] the human mind to theoretical pursuits," but it "could be no more than a transitional phase."[23] The Aristotelian logical ideals that organized the "construction both of the nature of science and of the relations between sciences turned out to be a procrustean bed on which science cannot lie."[24] The transition from the medieval to the modern is marked by a series of revolutionary migrations in which theory moves from the generic to the specific, the abstract to the concrete, the certain to the probable, the normative to the historical, and from the objective context of truth to the subjective conditions of its constitutive judgments. The cumulative effects of these migrations contributed to the passing away of the classicist worldview, though word of its passing has only slowly spread and only reluctantly been received.

The specialized disciplines of philosophy, science, and theology that developed through the differentiation of sensibility from intellect and common sense from theory turned, one after another, from the verities and certitudes of universal definitions and axioms to the empirical contexts of inquiry and thought. The first migration of theory occurred in the development of modern science and its break with the Aristotelian method. Late medieval and early modern science had embarked on a gradual, cumulative process "to develop its own proper basic concepts and thereby achieve its autonomy."[25] The result is a notion of science quite at odds with that of the *Posterior Analytics*. "The content of modern scientific doctrine" Lonergan writes, "is not an intelligibility that is necessary but an intelligibility that is (1) possible and (2) probably verified."[26] Modern science advances from the empirical analysis of phenomena toward its ideal of complete explanation through a refined methodical process by which the scientist selects a field of sensible data within which he or she observes, experiments, and makes applications in order to understand the immanent intelligibility of that sensible field in accord with classical and statistical laws.[27] The laws themselves are true not because they are necessary, but only insofar as they are verified. And the understanding resulting from empirical analysis is not a certainty secured in logical control, but is rather the best of current opinion anchored to successful, recurrent methodical performance, and open to potentially radical future revision.[28]

The modern notion of science promoted, as a consequence, the emergence of a modern philosophy. Where the metaphysical formulations of classical thought furnished the universal definitions, categories, and relations basic to various subordinated inquiries, modern science's methodical independence from metaphysical doctrines and its usurpation of the theoretical mantle led to a second migration. Having ceded the responsibility for theory to the natural scientists, philosophers nevertheless followed their lead. They turned increasingly to the actual contexts of philosophy and philosophical data, to the manifold ways in which inquiry is embedded in existence, history, and community. "[P]hilosophy," writes Lonergan, "has invaded the concrete, the particular, and the contingent, of the existential subject's decisions and of the history of peoples, societies, and cultures."[29] Philosophy's criterion of validity moved from the rigorous deduction of conclusions from basic axioms to the critique of the philosopher's method. As a result, no philosophic doctrine or product can be affirmed without demonstrating the validity of the concrete process of discovery by which the doctrine came about. The antinomies between knowledge and opinion, the theoretical and the practical, wisdom and prudence, the ideal and real, the *res cogitans* and the *res extensa* thus yielded to Kant's Copernican revolution.[30] In its wake, "Hegel turned from substance to the subject. Historians and philologists worked out their autonomous methods for human studies. Will and decision, actions and results, came up for emphasis in Kierkegaard, Schopenhauer, Nietzsche, Blondel, the pragmatists. Brentano inspired Husserl, and intentionality analysis routed faculty psychology.[31]"

As the empirical turn in natural science rules out the possibility of realizing the ideal of certain knowledge, so the existential turn from substance to subject so radically multiplies the field of data relevant to philosophical inquiry that the classicist expectation of an objective, universal, and formal doctrine of human being invulnerable to the ambiguities of human living proves impossible. "The study of the subject," writes Lonergan, "is the study of oneself inasmuch as one is conscious. It prescinds from the soul, its essence, its potencies, its habits, for none of these is given in consciousness. It attends to operations and their center and source, which is the self."[32] If philosophy's object of study is the subject in his or her operative, active performance in the world mediated by meaning, then there are no mere opinions to be discarded, no accidents to be bracketed, and no contexts from which to flee through abstraction without intellectual cost. The subject is a subject in conscious operation, in existence, history, and community. The subject is incarnate. And the data on the subject are empirical.

But the philosophical migration of theory from the abstract to the concrete does more than expand the horizonal range of the world mediated by meaning. It also clarifies that the meaningfulness of the world of human phenomena is distinct from that of the world that natural science selects for its investigations. The human world has a history—a past, a present, and a future—and that history unfolds in accord not with the verified laws of physical-chemical emergence, but rather with the admixture of the authenticity and inauthenticity of human freedom, human decision, and human responsibility. The human world "does not come into being or survive without deliberation, evaluation, decision, action, without the exercise of freedom and responsibility. It is a world of existential subjects, and it objectifies the values that they originate in their creativity and their freedom."[33] Not only is the human world mediated by the cognitive contents of common sense and theory, it is also constituted by those meanings and the conscious acts by which they come about.

The human world is a human production, an effect of acts of meaning. Absent those acts, there is no human world. Such world-making, moreover, "is not restricted to the transformation of nature, for there is also the transformation of man himself."[34] That transformation, be it individual, cultural, or social, artistic, linguistic, or historical, "is in its essence a change in meaning:

a change of idea or concept, a change of judgment or evaluation, a change in the order of request."[35] Human worlds, and, by extension, the data of philosophy, are not only intelligible but are also intelligent.

Critically, the assertion of meaning's constitutive function in world-making is not to deny the reality of what is made, but merely to specify its provenance. Cultural constructivism, in other words, need not come at the cost of critical realism. Because such realism insists that the real is known intelligently, rationally, and deliberately, the meanings made through acts of understanding, judging, and deciding also have their reality in and through those acts. "[H]uman reality," Lonergan writes, "the very stuff of human living, is not merely meant but in a large measure constituted through acts of meaning."[36] The dwellings in which humans live, the clothes they wear, the social institutions to which they belong, the ideals and values to which they aspire, and even the explanatory constructions of theory have their origins not in some realm of pure nature or a higher world of forms but in the intentions, executions, and effects of intellectual, rational, and existential consciousness.

One could be forgiven for expecting that this pattern of migration, in which science and philosophy moved to the concrete and discovered their own methodical practices of investigation, would also have led to an empirical turn in theology. Given the historical relationship between theology, philosophy, and science, it is not unreasonable to expect that so dramatic a change in the methods of two fields of this triad would occasion a corresponding change in the third. And yet, as Lonergan notes, "When modern science began, when the Enlightenment began, then the theologians began to reassure one another about their certainties."[37] As the other domains of inquiry took aim at the contingent and verifiable, the daring speculative theologies of the Middle Ages were abandoned in favor of dogmatic theology, a method conceived "in opposition to Scholasticism," which "demoted the quest of faith for understanding to a desirable but secondary and, indeed, optional goal."[38] Instead of theology as *fides quarens intellectum* and the open-ended perspective of the *quaestio*, the dogmatic approach prized the certainty of the thesis and worked to unfold the consequences that derive from that certainty. Lonergan notes that this form of theological practice was normative in Catholic contexts even into the twentieth century, but that for seventy years before Vatican II and in the decades since, theology has been slowly coming to terms with the postdeductive, empirical, and historical contexts of the modern world and of the transformations of its own methods demanded by those contexts.[39] As Lonergan writes, "Just as theology in the thirteenth century followed its age by assimilating Aristotle, just as theology in the seventeenth century resisted its age by retiring into a dogmatic corner, so theology today is locked in an encounter with its age. Whether it will grow and triumph, or whether it will wither to insignificance, depends in no small measure on the clarity and the acc ~y of its grasp of the external cultural factors that undermine its past achie~ents and challenge it to new endeavors."[40]

These external cultural factors include the migrations of scientific and philosophical theory from the abstract to the concrete, migrations that represent decisive breaks with the dominant mentality of the classicist worldview. Where classicism sought cultural universality and scientific certainty and deployed its theoretical instruments in pursuit of that universality, the concrete contexts of modern science and philosophy have rejected those deployments. Without leaving theory behind, they have become empirical disciplines; they seek to explain the data of sense and the data of consciousness as they are given in the specific worlds of nature and human culture. And as the methodical selection of the phenomena of the natural world led to the development of a new science of nature independent from borrowed metaphysical doctrines, so a practiced attention to the varied phenomena of distinct human worlds invites the development of a new science of culture distinct from that of classicist expectation.[41] But, as we will see, that development has been uneven. Classicism promotes blind spots in even very earnest investigators. And those blind spots often obscure the data relevant for insights into the concrete situations of human culture and can yield a reflexive turn back to the unexamined pretension of classicist universality. Thus, before treating of the empirical context of a modern speculative theology, we must first address the development of the science of human meaning, the emergence of a new notion of culture, and the implications for speculative theory that follow upon them.

## THE NEW SCIENCE OF CULTURE BETWEEN PHILOSOPHY AND THEOLOGY

### The Empirical Notion of Culture

In his 1948 work, *Notes towards the Definition of Culture*, T. S. Eliot writes, "Just as a doctrine only needs to be defined after the appearance of some heresy, so a word does not need to receive this attention until it has come to be misused."[42] The misuse of the term culture, which provokes Eliot's protracted effort to elaborate a precise definition, is a consequence of its long, complex history, a history that Raymond Williams famously calls "one of the two or three most complicated in the English language."[43] For Eliot, such complexity, as a practical consequence, incentivizes the employment of the term in speech and writing, but not the careful examination of its meaning.[44] In a more metaphorical voice, F. R. Cowell notes that "culture has something of the elusive, attractive quality of the rainbow. When it appears it is generally welcomed and admired, and all the more so by those who find its composition, nature and essence, like its beginning and end, something of a mystery."[45] The classicist notion of culture, precisely because of its undifferentiated and normative perspective, has the advantage of clarity and simplicity. But, as H. L. Mencken remarked, "there is always a well-known solution to every human problem—neat, plausible, and wrong."[46] A new notion of culture has emerged. One that rejects classicism's neatness and plausibility and that hopefully overcomes its error.

As natural philosophy and metaphysical psychology could not resist the migration to the concrete, neither can the classical notion of culture abstract indefinitely from the material peculiarities, the conventions, the social biographies and artifacts of distinct expressions of human living. Those particulars, once set aside as mere *nomoi*, have become the data for a new science, a science which inquires into the immanent intelligibility of distinct patterns of convention. The result is what Lonergan calls the empirical notion of culture in which culture is defined as "a set of meanings and values informing a common way of life," and which entails the further recognition that there are as many cultures as there are distinct sets of such meanings and values.[47]

In an empirical frame, as Christopher Dawson notes, culture is not "the cultivation of the individual mind, which was the usual sense of the word in the past, but of a common social way of life—a way of life with a tradition behind it, which has embodied itself in institutions and which involves moral standards and principles."[48] Yet, if the empirical notion of culture clarifies the fields of data on human living relevant to a postclassicist theory of culture, a mentality coordinated and habituated to the empirical view has only unevenly come into being. As Dawson recognizes, "The idea that there are a number of different roads leading, perhaps, in opposite directions, still remains a difficult idea to assimilate."[49] And as Christian classicism was the heir of Greek and Roman classicism, so Modernity's displacement of Christian culture entailed its own classicist view. "Humanism, the Enlightenment and the modern conceptions of 'the democratic way of life' and the 'one world,'" argues Dawson, "all suppose the same idea of a single universal ideal of civilization toward which all men and peoples must move."[50] But unlike ancient and medieval classicism, these ideologies of more recent invention are not insulated from the unsparing facts of culture's multiplicity and empirical variety. And so, despite the western soul's imperfect purgation of its classicist spirit, the reality of the concrete fields of data on human living have led to a protracted effort to disengage a method of inquiry proper to the contours of those fields capable of grasping the constitutive meanings within specific patterns of human life. And in the actual courses of that effort, there emerge different and sometimes competing answers to vital questions: Where do the relevant data on culture lie? What relationship obtains between culture and civilization? By what means should culture be interpreted?

As the new natural sciences discovered the universal classical laws that explain mass and its motion, so also did nascent inquiry into the empirical situation of culture search for a unified set of universal norms or laws of culture analogous to the universal physical laws of nature. The early practitioners of the new cultural sciences conceived of their disciplinary standpoint as neutral, rational, and value-free, thereby bringing to bear upon human societies the procedures of analysis canonized in the Baconian ideals of science. Like the Newtonian physicist, early anthropologists idealized universality of application. They sought something like an equation that would unite various local expressions into a universal theory of human culture. Such a theory would relax modern anxieties about cultural and historical relativism that accompany the recognition of seemingly endless human variety, each with its own animating vision of truth, goodness, and beauty.

These so-called *consensus gentium* theories tried to derive from their empirical studies a grand explanatory paradigm, a set of generalizations verifiable in all cultural situations and eras. But cultural meanings are not the same kind of data as physical motion. And to the extent that early anthropologists investigated cultural meanings within the methodical framework of natural science, they failed to let their objects of inquiry determine their methods of analysis. Despite a turn to the empirical, *consensus gentium* theories remained thoroughly classicist in outlook, still borrowing the basic terms and relations of another, higher science (albeit modern physics rather than classical metaphysics) instead of generating those terms and relations themselves. This classicism was evidenced by the fact that the specific cultures from which anthropologists themselves came were left unexamined. And this omission was not accidental. The cultural particularities of western, European modernity were not countenanced as particularities. They were tacitly or even explicitly assumed to be normative, or at least neutral, and certainly not demanding of investigative scrutiny. Accordingly, as Bruno Latour writes, "For traditional anthropologists, there is not—there cannot be, there should not be—an anthropology of the modern world. . . . It is even because they remain incapable of studying themselves in this way that ethnographers are so critical, and so distant, when they go off to the tropics to study others."[51]

One of the great exponents of *consensus gentium* theory, Clyde Kluckhohn, required at least eleven different definitions of culture to enlarge the concept sufficiently to encompass the immense diversity of the empirical features he observed among distinct cultures.[52] This Enlightenment strategy for solving the problem of plurality leads to anthropologist Clifford Geertz's question, "Can this halfway house between the eighteenth and twentieth centuries really stand?"[53] Geertz answers in the negative. "My point," he argues, "is that such generalizations are not to be discovered through a Baconian search for cultural universals, a kind of public-opinion polling of the world's peoples in search of a *consensus gentium* that does not in fact exist, and, further, that the attempt to do so leads to precisely the sort of relativism the whole approach was expressly designed to avoid."[54]

In contrast to an experimental model aimed at discovering universal cultural laws, Geertz proposes a semiotic or interpretive model of inquiry.[55] For Geertz, culture is "an historically transmitted pattern of meanings embodied in symbols, a system of inherited conceptions expressed in symbolic form by means of which men communicate, perpetuate, and develop their knowledge about and attitudes towards life."[56] Geertz conceives of culture metaphorically as ensembles of texts. These ensembles are webs of self-spun signification (as Charles Taylor might call them) that require the straining anthropologist or ethnographer "to read over the shoulders of those to whom they properly belong."[57] The task of the cultural scientist is not to interpret the meaning of cultures through the imposition of a universal hermeneutics, but is rather to patiently internalize, albeit secondarily and artificially, the patterns of interpretation embedded within cultures themselves. As Geertz writes, "Societies, like lives, contain their own interpretations. One has only to learn how to gain access to them."[58]

With a semiotic approach similar to Geertz, but articulated in a more philosophical key, Susanne Langer argues that "a culture is the symbolic expression of developed habitual ways of feeling," where feeling refers to "rhythms of attention," "the strain of thought," "attitudes of mind," the "activity of imagination," "confidence in the goodness of life," but also "annoyance, boredom, cynicism," and "the countless modes of humor."[59] For Langer, feeling means "*everything that can be felt.*"[60] Culture is not just feeling but also feeling's pattern of direction, its way, or "the degree to which feelings are apt to go, their persistence or transience, the quickness of various responses, and their directness to certain events rather than others."[61] And if culture is the expression of this concrete pattern of feeling, then distinctions among expressions reveal distinctions in ways of feeling and thereby distinctions among cultures.

Echoing Erich Rothacker's distinction between the social and the cultural, Langer contrasts culture as the symbolic directedness of feeling with civilization as the "pattern of the practical implementation of life" that organizes human networks of association through the mechanisms of monetized commerce, statute law, transportation and communication infrastructure, and networks for the flow and distribution of goods.[62] Civilization, Langer argues, arises from advanced cultures, but also floats free of them. It can be "transplanted and live apart from its cultural roots. It can be grafted onto other cultures and thrive on them."[63] But civilization, Langer claims, is also a threat to culture. It can reduce human association to raw economic exchange, to productivity, to "nothing but usefulness."[64]

The distinction between the social and the cultural, while common to many approaches, is not definitive among modern theories of culture. The psychoanalytic theory of culture, flowing from the thought of Sigmund Freud, explicitly rejects any distinction of culture and civilization. According to Paul Ricoeur, there are three models of cultural interpretation in Freud's thought. There is an "economic model," which considers culture "from the viewpoint of a balance sheet of libidinal cathexes and anti-cathexes."[65] There is a "genetic model," which looks for the origins of these economic functions "in childhood and phylogenesis."[66] And there is a "topographic" model, which considers culture in terms of the dynamic interactions of the id, ego, and superego.[67] From a psychoanalytic viewpoint, "There is almost no distinction between the utilitarian enterprise of dominating the forces of nature (civilization) and the disinterested, idealist task of realizing values (culture)."[68] These models each locate the meaning and interpretation of culture in the psychic contexts of originating violence, be it the foundational murder of the father by his son or the internal war between and among competing appetites and principles of psychic order.

But while Freud conceived of the psychoanalytic interpretation of culture as definitive of a modern mentality, Paul Ricoeur's interpretation of Freud stresses that the importance of the psychoanalytic interpretation lies not in the accuracy of its explanatory diagnoses, but rather as a sign of a shift in cultural self-constitution toward explicit cultural interpretation. He writes, "Psychoanalysis takes part in the contemporary cultural movement by acting as a hermeneutics of culture. In other words, psychoanalysis marks a change *of* culture because its interpretation of man bears in a central and direct way *on* culture as a whole. It makes interpretation into a moment of culture: it changes culture by interpreting it."[69]

The anthropological, semiotic, and psychoanalytic responses to the challenge of the empirical, modern notion of culture bear witness to the immense challenge of adequately attending to the data of human living and of understanding those data in a comprehensive, systematic way. As such, the shift to a modern, empirical, historical, and pluralist notion of culture remains a precarious and incomplete achievement. The differentiations, skills, and orientations necessary to sustain and develop both the human subject and human culture are present, to invoke Thomas Aquinas, only in a few, only after much work, and accompanied by many errors. As Lonergan writes,

> Classical culture has given way to a modern culture, and, I would submit, the crisis of our age is in no small measure the fact that modern culture has not yet reached its maturity. The classical mediation of meaning has broken down;

the breakdown has been effected by a whole array of new and more effective techniques; but their very multiplicity and complexity leave us bewildered, disoriented, confused, preyed upon by anxiety, dreading lest we fall victims to the up-to-date myth of ideology and the hypnotic, highly effective magic of thought control.[70]

Even this brief survey of various modern attempts to understand culture in its concreteness and variety indicates the residual classicism that often attaches itself to any would-be modern science of culture. And while a truly postclassicist cultural science is *per se* possible in terms of the metaphysical symmetry between the known unknown of cultural intelligibility and the intellectual powers of human understanding *qua* human, it remains that the emergence of such a science is *de facto* improbable, at least in a form purified from the egoist and classicist biases that undermine understanding and mobilize misunderstanding. A truly postclassicist, historically-minded cultural mentality may be a proportionate effect of natural reason, but, in the concrete, the natural intellectual means to achieve that proportionate effect prove rare, precarious, and diluted with various biases, errors, and oversights.

It is not unreasonable to hypothesize, then, that historical-mindedness or the empirical notion of culture is a natural knowledge, a formal effect of human intelligence, but that, in the concrete order and on a civilizational scale, a supernatural effective means will be required to secure it.[71] According to such a hypothesis, stabilized historical-mindedness has its origins in world-transcendent value and in that value's self-communication to the world of human meaning. As such, historical-mindedness is a theological category. And if historical-mindedness is, at root and in the concrete, theological, then any would-be postclassicist speculative theology has a responsibility to organize itself around that mentality.

## The Empirical Notion of Culture as Theological

The foregoing analysis is controlled by what Maurice Blondel calls a method of immanence.[72] It treats of the objectification of the historical constitution of the human world as a "from below" phenomenon characteristic of a diverse array of disciplinary procedures and viewpoints that have proliferated since the nineteenth century. Whether one speaks with Dilthey and Gadamer of historical consciousness (*historischem Bewusstsein*), with Carl Becker, Alan Richardson, and Lonergan of historical-mindedness, or with Dawson, Langer, and Geertz of culture as anthropological, semiotic, or empirical, one is searching for and selecting a rhetoric adequate to denote the multidisciplinary convergence of scholarly inquiry upon the nexus of human meaning, history, and plurality. The discovery at the heart of this convergence, according to Gadamer, "is very likely the most important revolution among those we have undergone since the beginning of the modern epoch. . . . The historical consciousness which characterizes contemporary man is a privilege, perhaps even a burden, the likes of which has never been imposed on any previous generation."[73] For Gadamer, to be historically conscious is to possess the "full awareness of the historicity of everything and the relativity of all opinions"[74] and to recognize "the possibility of a multiplicity of relative viewpoints."[75] But, as Gadamer himself recognizes, jealous traditions tend to reassert their own normativity. And so even these new methods of cultural analysis can slouch toward classicism and its *de jure* singularity.

The "from below" methodologies of the sciences of empirical culture, while proportionate to their objects and thereby capable in principle of understanding them in a historically-minded way, are vulnerable to the restrictedness of individual and group biases. What is more, they suffer from the immaturities of youth. The human sciences are newcomers on the scene, and so their practices are bound to be unrefined and incomplete. But a "from below" approach to historical-mindedness is not the only possibility for cultivating a postclassicist cultural mentality.

In his massive work, *Theology and the Dialectics of History* (1990), Robert Doran dialogues with Eric Voegelin and his account of classical philosophy's discovery of the anthropological principle and its erotic, classicist, and aristocratic vision of the world-transcendent Good. For Voegelin, Philosophy exercises its resistance to social disorder and the processes of decline by "evoking a more integral order of existence" and by "constituting that order as the substantive center of a new community emergent by force of the resistant movement of the philosophizing spirit in the midst of the pressures of corruption."[76] The anthropological principle, according to Voegelin, governs this resistance such that "the integrity of the psyche measures the integrity of society, and God measures the integrity of the psyche."[77] There is a circularity of conditioning between psyche and society, within which the growth or decay of one order leads to the growth or decay of the other and back again. But "the circle is broken with the recognition of the inclinations in the psyche toward attunement with the world-transcendent measure of its integrity."[78] In Voegelin's account of the Platonic tradition, attunement to world-transcendent *Agathon*, evidenced by the philosopher's erotic anticipations, is the principle of transformation in both the psychic and public orders. The authentic psyche is attuned to and measured by world-transcendent *Agathon*, and, in turn, the authentic psyche resists the disordered orientations of the public order and offers itself as the measure for social integrity. The philosophical psyche, in other words, mediates transcendent value to the public sphere.

In Doran's analysis, this Platonic anthropological principle is true as far as it goes, but it suffers from a series of horizontal circumscriptions that must be transcended if it is to be transposed into a modern, global, pluralistic context. For the Platonic tradition, the notion of the world-transcendent *Agathon* that measures the integrity of the psyche is erotic in orientation, classicist in outlook, and aristocratic in values. For Doran, these circumscriptions are a consequence of the "from below" directionality of psychic dynamism toward transcendence. The responsibility for achieving psychic integrity lies solely with the philosophizing spirit. The philosopher must both resist public disorder and transcend his or her own limitations in the erotic striving for the world-transcendent measure. As a result, only the philosopher can realize the good and thereby achieve psychic integrity. Erotic elitism births aristocratic values and cultural classicism.

But if cultural normativity and aristocratic reductions of value are entailments of philosophical erotic striving, then a different order of desire and attainment is required, one in which the directionality of transcendence and psychic dynamism are reversed, one in which the world-transcendent measure not only is the term of erotic anticipation but is itself communicated to the psyche through its own initiative. An analysis of that shift in directionality requires a corresponding shift in abstractive viewpoint, a shift from philosophy and its erotic orientations to theology and its agapic testimony. As Doran writes, "The Christian soteriological differentiation of consciousness renders possible the transformation of a classicist, aristocratic, and psychic-erotic notion of the human good into one that is historical, universalist, and agapic."[79]

As eros is transformed into agape, it becomes the source of a consequent transformation of attitudes toward culture and value embedded in the philosophical anthropological principle. This transformation is not merely a dilation of the philosopher's native horizon, but is rather the radical and disproportionate reception of a new horizon, one beyond that of any natural love, any particular cultural achievement, or any parochial value. Whereas philosophy objectifies the dynamism of eros toward *Agathon*, theology objectifies "the gift of an antecedent and ultimately universal willingness as the ground of the integral resistance to social and personal disorder and decline."[80] This gift is what theologians call the grace of charity, "and it is offered by the divine ground to the eros of the psyche."[81] Through the divine initiative, the transcendent measure is given to the psyche and, through the psyche, to the community. The concrete form of agapic integrity, "the revelation of attunement with the divine ground," is "a visitation of humanity by soteriological truth."[82] In Christian theology, the truth of agapic attunement is revealed in the life, death, and resurrection of the Son of God incarnate in Jesus of Nazareth. The psychic integrity that measures the integrity of the community is, accordingly, the just and mysterious law of the cross, the love that returns good for evil, that transforms evil into good, that would lay its life down not only for one's friends but also for one's enemies.

Theology's testimony to soteriological revelation is also a "twofold agapic invitation," in which one is invited both "to receive the divine agape" and "to embody it in one's own existence."[83] In receiving divine agape, one receives that which eros can only desire. In embodying divine agape, one offers to the public order the fullness of its measure of authenticity and the means of resisting the forces of decline and for renewing those of progress. But because the psychic measure is the agapic law of the cross, soteriological revelation "pass(es) judgment on even the noblest achievements of thought, law, and religion. Thus the noetic truth disengaged by philosophy is no license to regard the cultural order that derives at least in part from this disengagement as either normative for genuine humanity or permanent."[84]

In this way, the reconfiguration of eros into agape "grounds the movement from classicism to historical mindedness and from aristocracy to universalism."[85] Because that reconfiguration is given freely by the divine ground, its realization in the psyche cannot be said to be an achievement of the human spirit. And since the realization of psychic integrity and its public mediation is not accomplished by the initiative of philosophy, then any claim to personal or cultural normativity is undermined at its root. A theological transformation of the anthropological principle holds that while the integrity of the psyche may be measured by God, it is God's gift of God's self to the psyche that both completes the psyche's native transcendental erotic orientation and elevates the psyche itself such that "integrity becomes cooperation with God, in any cultural order, as God effects the redemption of humanity from every consequence of sin by making the divine life the innermost constitutive element of human life."[86] Divine constitutive meaning rejects the normative claims of classicism and liberates the psyche from the narrowness of its vision to a historically-minded perspective, capable of bearing witness to the soteriological vector operative in the law of the cross at work in every culture and every age.

## SPECULATIVE THEOLOGY AFTER CLASSICISM

This chapter has, so far, attempted to indicate the major trend lines of the shift from the medieval context in which speculative theology arose to the modern context that has witnessed its decline. Speculative theology was a project built upon a unified, classicist cultural matrix. The material and intellectual fruits of classicism, most notably the discovery of mind, gifted to theology the materials and techniques for the adoption of a formally theoretical viewpoint, and thereby made possible a mediation between the doctrinal context of the received tradition and the intellectual horizon of the medieval world.

Classicism's genius was its disengagement of theory and its pursuit of the universal. But that genius also proved tragic. For theory's ideal of universal applicability has, in Robert Doran's terms, a "psychic-erotic" imaginary that underwrites its projects. Theory does not objectify and so does not know its own concreteness, its contingency, its location in the historical dialectic of progress and decline, and so it universalizes, normalizes, and makes abstract what is, in fact, local, empirical, and concrete. Classicism grasped the significance of theory as a realm of meaning in excess of common sense, but that achievement obscured the fact that theory is a product of acts of meaning and, as such, has its origins and exigencies in the concrete moral, cultural, intellectual, and historical contexts of the theorizer and his or her interrogative horizon. Theoretical meanings, like all meanings, are answers to questions. As such, the horizons and orientations of inquirers are essential constraints on possible terms of inquiry, even if those terms intend a universal scope.[87]

The breakdown of the classicist worldview brings with it the suspicion that all the achievements of classicism are so many fruits of a poisoned tree. But while that suspicion is perhaps well-earned, it need not be the last word on the matter. The argument of the remainder of this chapter is that speculative theology can be disentangled from the classicist context in which it arose, and situated within the postclassicist perspective that characterizes the modern mentality. Where classicism's discovery of mind brought with it the recognition that the human world is mediated by meaning, modern historical-mindedness recognizes that meaning not only mediates but also constitutes that human world, and so distinct situations of constitutive meanings reveal distinct human worlds. Thus, a theology that aspires to theoretical meaning in a postclassicist context must take cognizance of those distinct worlds. It must recognize its own situatedness within a particular world. And, it must systematically confront the challenge of the pluralism of human worlds, the unity of doctrines, and the intellectual mediation from one to the other.

As Lonergan argues in the opening paragraph of *Method in Theology*, a postclassicist theology mediates between a cultural matrix and the significance and role of a religion in that matrix. But because a postclassicist perspective recognizes a pluralism of cultural matrices, it must recognize, as a consequence, a pluralism of theological mediations. And if such mediations are the goal of the whole of theology, then speculative theology has the more exact task of mediating between the concrete religious, moral, and intellectual questions that occasion the speculative exigence's emergence in a particular pattern of culture and the transcultural permanence, validity, and personal enactments of religious doctrines.

The result will be a pluralism of speculative theologies, wherein the multiplicity of concrete cultural matrices and the various occasions of their speculative exigence demand a multiplicity of speculative mediations, within which the transcultural elements of the unified dogmatic-theological context and the normative human subject both are a bulwark against radical relativism and make possible an analogical and methodical cooperation among distinct speculative theologies. Such a speculative pluralism has four principal heuristic elements: a material element that pertains to the concrete pluralism that becomes explicit in the shift from classicism to historical-mindedness; a subjective formal element that is the pluralism of theologians engaged in the enterprise of mediation between religion and their respective cultural matrices; an objective formal element that is the pluralism of understandings effected through the subjective formal acts of theologians; and a dialectical element that attempts to diagnose the complementary, genetic, contrary, and contradictory relationships between theologies with the goal of coordinating constructive collaboration among them.

## The Material Element

Material pluralism is the human situation of the meaningfulness of social living as understood according to the empirical notion of culture. The concrete variety of distinct intellectual, moral, and historical contexts in various states of development or decay, flowering or decadence, progress or decline set the conditions for distinct trajectories of speculative thought. This pluralism has both synchronic and diachronic aspects that correlate with the spatial-geographic multiplicity of cultural matrices at a given time, and a temporal-historical multiplicity that results from the development or decline of the organizing meanings and values of particular matrices. And because development or decay both involve a change in the meanings and values (or indeed disvalues) that animate a culture's living, they also indicate a change in the moral and intellectual conditions to which a speculative theology mediates the meaningfulness of the doctrinal confessions of the Christian religion.

While many historical examples of speculative intervention pertain principally to problems in the order of understanding that vexed the medieval mind (e.g., the challenge of reconciling divine simplicity with eternal procession, or human freedom with the gratuity of divine grace), there are also speculative interventions that respond to problems in the order of understanding that result from moral disvalues in a culture and the dissonance they create for grasping the meaningfulness or value of religion. Moral disvalue can create the conditions for distinct forms of speculative exigence, which in turn commits the resulting speculative theology to mediate the meaning and value of the self-revealing God within the circumstances of moral decay that call the significance of such a God—and even more so the community that confesses him—into question. These situations in which the social surd of objective meaninglessness and the patterned experience of oppression, subju tion, alienation, and the collective suffering it promotes condition the ,ecula- tive exigence no less than those formal intellectual *ambigua* that weighed upon the religious imagination of medieval schoolmen. Thus, synchronic and diachronic variances in the conditions of speculative exigence anticipate synchronic and diachronic variations of speculative understanding.

For example, M. Shawn Copeland's *Enfleshing Freedom* argues that in an American culture partially constituted by the meanings and values of white supremacy and its long history, the embodied experience of poor Black women becomes the locus of the question of the theological understanding of human personhood as reflective of divine dignity, and of incarnation as the union of God with the really existing experience of being human.[88] Her speculative reconstruction of theological anthropology mediates the doctrinal affirmations of creation and incarnation into a cultural matrix organized around the dehumanization and abuse of poor Black women. While some may be tempted to classify Copeland's efforts as no more than an instance of so-called "contextual theology" at a praxiological remove from the labors of an Aquinas or a Lonergan, it is far truer to say that hers is a fully postclassicist speculative theology, which eschews the chasm between knowing and doing; responds to the unique ways in which the speculative exigence arises in a cultural matrix constituted by the dehumanization of poor Black women; utilizes the symbols, images, ideas, and organizing meanings of that matrix; and makes use of theoretical technique to render visible the meaning of Christian doctrines through the icon of the experience of poor Black women themselves.[89] And while Copeland's work exemplifies the speculative theological task of mediating the truth of Christian doctrines to the intellectual and moral horizon of a particular culture, it remains that there exists a plurality of cultures and, with it, an exigence for additional speculative mediations. And so, correlative with the material pluralism of cultural situations that follows upon the shift to historical-mindedness, there is a formal pluralism that responds to that shift, both a subjective formal element that is the various theologians in their speculative operations and an objective formal element that is the resulting plurality of speculative theologies.

## The Subjective Formal Element

The previous chapter presented Lonergan's early theory of speculative form and operation. It indicated the generic shape of speculative theology as a modality of theological practice distinct from positive and moral theology, with a unique charter and a specialized technique. By speculative form,

Lonergan means a generic orientation of intellectual mentality that is ordered to the pursuit of *intellectum* from within the horizon of *fides*. But such a gen ` orientation only becomes actualized within specific lines of speculative . iry that emerge from specific patterns of attention to specific problems in the order of understanding in specific constellations of meaning and value. As a consequence, the generic form of speculation will be specified differently in distinct lines of inquiry, as those inquiries interrogate distinct problems of understanding. And while those problems emerge spontaneously in the process of living, the coordination of activities and practices that meet those problems require what Sarah Coakley calls contemplation or "an attentive openness of the whole self (intellect, will, memory, imagination, feeling, bodiliness) to the reality of God and creation."[90] Specific speculative inquiries, then, even of the most assiduously theoretical nature, emerge from concrete circumstances and respond to those circumstances through the operation of theoretical understanding.

What Thomas Kuhn notes of scientific theory is no less true of speculative theology. He writes, "An apparently arbitrary element, compounded of personal and historical accident, is always a formative ingredient of the beliefs espoused by a given scientific community at a given time."[91] Theoretical understanding, even as it abstracts from the concreteness of common sense in the pursuit of the *soli et omni*, remains a human enterprise. And as a human enterprise, it remains tethered to the contexts of the minds engaged in the abstraction. Thus, the cultural, intellectual, moral, and religious orientations of theorizers play an essential role not only in the emergence of the speculative exigence but also in any speculative response. A theory's mobility across the borders of contexts lies in the correspondence between the meaning expressed in the theory and the specific questions of abstractive intelligence posed from within a different context. If a concrete situation of inquiry does not lead to the formulation of the question to which a given theory purports to be an answer, then the theory itself cannot become enacted in that context until the relevant question emerges.

Such orientations, the historical accidents of concrete circumstances, belong to the ordinary constitution of the human subject and the human world. And because there exists a material plurality of such worlds, there will also exist many distinct formal species of speculative theological inquiries that respond to those circumstances by deploying the specialized mentality of theory so as to mediate an understanding of faith back to those circumstances in a way that resolves the ambiguities embedded in them. Further, because all specific speculative inquiries and their answers bear an analogical relationship to the genus of speculative form, they also obtain an analogical relationship to one another. Thus, speculative understandings reached in one context may prove to possess adequate mobility to be resituated within another. As analogous classes of speculative questions are asked in different ways at different times and in different places, analogous speculative theories may prove cross-cultural, cross-temporal, and cross-spatial in their significance.

The theologian as subject, in terms borrowed from Michael Novak, "is both social gift and personal achievement: dove and mountain."[92] The cultural situation of the theologians is had in the givenness of their histories, but theologians as originating values also contribute to the maintenance and transformation of cultural situations themselves. A commerce obtains between the material context of a cultural matrix and the speculative insights that both arise from it and mediate new meanings and values back into it, transforming the common meanings of the cultural matrix through the process of mediation. The material element and the subjective formal element of speculative pluralism thus exercise a reciprocally conditioning influence on one another that unfolds dynamically in the process of theologizing.

## The Objective Formal Element

The commerce that obtains between the material element of speculative pluralism and its subjective formal element includes the formal effects of the subjective acts. These effects are the objective speculative theological mediations between the dogmatic context of a religion and the concrete circumstances of speculative exigence within a cultural matrix. Thus, coextensive with the subjective formal element of speculative pluralism that is the multiplicity of theological operators, there is the objective formal element that is the multiplicity of theological objects or understandings that result from the theological operations. As Elizabeth Johnson notes, "Words about God are cultural creatures, entwined with the mores and adventures of the faith community that uses them. As cultures shift, so too does the specificity of God-talk."[93] Such words are cultural, but they emerge from the intellectual practices of theologians within those cultures. For example, Johnson argues, "Feminist theology results when women's faith seeks understanding in the matrix of historical struggle for life in the face of oppressive and alienating forces."[94] As such, the formal functions at work in the emergence of a feminist speculative theology, then, are the same functions at work in, for example, the seven-century-long effort of western theologians to reconcile intellectually competing vectors of their Augustinian theological heritage with their own philosophical culture. In a speculative theology, one seeks "a complete vision of Christian doctrine," and such visions "have taken many forms—appropriate to the philosophical, cultural, and political ethos of their times, or sometimes in conscious reaction to the same."[95] This formal diversity, as has already been argued, includes both synchronic and diachronic forms, and as such, "one cannot therefore speak of systematic theology as a fixed or unchanging entity in Christian tradition."[96]

Furthermore, theological objects or productions that result from theological operations enter the nexus of common meanings and values that organize cultural existence. And when they do, they can lead to transformations and reorientations of cultural circumstances themselves. As Elizabeth Johnson argues regarding the emergence of feminist symbolic speculative discourse, "The symbol of God functions. Language about God in female images not only challenges the literal mindedness that has clung to male images in inherited God talk; it not only questions their dominance in discourse about holy mystery. But insofar as 'the symbol gives rise to thought,' such speech calls into question prevailing structures of patriarchy."[97] In other words, the accumulation of new and transformational meanings and values—even those of a rigorously theoretical nature—can lead to a transformation of culture, for culture itself is but a relatively stabilized nexus of meanings and values.

Taken together, the material, subjective formal, and objective formal elements comprise a situation in which, both at any given moment and across time and place, there will be not a single normative speculative theology mediating the Christian faith to a single normative culture, but rather a descriptive, empirical plurality of speculative theologians, speculative theologies, and cultural matrices. The analogical relationship between genus and species suggests a consequent analogical relationship between species themselves. Thus, one can expect a kind of "family resemblance" between distinct speculative theologians and their speculative theologies. But the character of that resemblance, because it is analogical and so has difference encoded within it, invites analyses of a more dialectical character. Differences between cultures, differences between theologians, and differences between theologies may be complementary, genetic, contrary, or contradictory. And so, an adequate heuristic structure for speculative pluralism must include a dialectical element beyond the material and formal elements.

## The Dialectical Element

In his 1974 essay, "Dialectic of Authority," Lonergan proposes a heuristic structure for understanding the dynamic relationship between authority, power, and legitimacy.[98] Without rehearsing his entire argument, one can say that 1) authority is legitimate power; 2) power is the result of past cooperation; 3) cooperation occurs both diachronically through time and synchronically in the here and now; 4) community carries power along through time; 5) community entrusts power to authorities; 6) the legitimacy of communal power is measured by the authenticity or inauthenticity of the meanings and values that the community holds in common; and 7) the authenticity of meanings and values is a matter of a cumulative process of communal attentiveness, intelligence, reasonableness, and responsibility. Analytically, the diagnosis of authenticity or inauthenticity is fraught and often inconclusive, but synthetically, one can judge the authenticity of authority by its fruits: collective progress indicates authenticity, while collective decline reveals inauthenticity. On its own, the dialectic of authority is a valuable tool for analyzing the state of a culture. But its invocation here is for a different purpose. The basic form of the dialectic of authority can be repurposed as a heuristic structure for understanding the dialectical element of speculative pluralism.

In the dialectic of authority, communal cooperation over time yields power, the community mediates that power as authority and entrusts it to particular authorities, and the dialectic of authenticity or inauthenticity measures the legitimacy of the meanings and values expressed in community, authorities, and those under authorities. In the case of speculative theology, communal cooperation both in and over time consists in what Lonergan calls a functionally specialized method that coordinates the efforts of theologians into a dynamic and intelligible whole of operations, relations, and effects. Embedded within and enabling that methodical collaboration is the anterior gift of God's love and human cooperation with that love in the pursuit of theological truth. Coordinated theological collaboration is the source of theological achievements, of an ongoing series of theological judgments that populate and expand into a tradition and, with it, a dogmatic-theological context. Particular cultures carry the meaning of the tradition forward into the realm of speculative understanding. The theologian is the agent of speculative understanding, who, through his or her acts, effects objects or theological meanings. Culture, agent, and object form a circle of mutually conditioning relationships in which culture contextualizes the agent in communal meaning, the agent effects objects, and the objects mediate new understanding or meaning back into the common context of a culture.

The dialectic of authenticity measures the legitimacy of this ongoing process. It looks to the progress or decline of the cultural situation as an indication of the authenticity or inauthenticity of the meanings and values that constitute it. It poses itself to the agent in terms of intellectual, moral, and religious conversion and the presence or absence of distinct differentiations of consciousness. And it addresses the objects or effects of speculative operations, the understandings or meanings grasped by the agent. But diagnosing the legitimacy of theological objects requires a distinct criteriological strategy. The speculative understandings that result from the speculative operation of the theologian as agent must be judged in terms of their adequacy to the horizon of meaning and value of the cultural matrix, to the interrogative determinations of theologian's questions, and to the dogmatic-theological judgments whose meaning they are to communicate. But while the dialectic of authenticity can work out the legitimacy of a set of meanings and values in accord with an analysis of progress or decline, and it can measure the completeness or incompleteness of the theologian's act of understanding through recourse to the transcultural unity of the normative human subject, reaching a judgment about the adequacy of the achieved understanding to the revealed mystery requires a confrontation with the transcultural unity of revealed truth itself. The hypothesis pursued here and in the next chapter is that this confrontation is best executed theorematically.

Analogous to the medieval function of theorems in which they serve to establish a framework of mental perspectives that allow relevant theological data to be distinguished from the irrelevant, investigated with rigor, and arranged in thought such that resolutions to received problems become possible, a postclassicist speculative theology invites a theorematic intervention into the dialectical multiplicity of perspectives and realized understandings. Such an intervention has two principal functions. First, it discloses the analogous congruities between complementary, genetic, and contrary theologies. Second, it aids in identifying contradictory viewpoints and exercises a criteriological operation whereby the positional element of the dialectic of contradictories is distinguished from the counter-positional element.[99] But if the perspective of speculative pluralism is truly postclassicist, and thereby rejects any source of normativity in the contents of a specific cultural matrix, where does the normativity operating in the theorems come from?

While the normativity of the formal element of speculative pluralism lies in the transcultural structure of the human subject as attentive, intelligent, reasonable, and responsible, the normativity of the dialectal theorems is secured in the dogmatic-theological context itself. Theological doctrines disclosed in the narrative universe of biblical revelation, refined through the intellectual and rhetorical process of creedal expression, can also be elaborated as theorems, that is, as systematic articulations that can organize whole networks of thinking, that can take on a mobility of application, and so both direct consequent theologizing and pass judgment on its results.

For any speculative theology, the *via analogica* will be the principal path in which theological insight travels. But speculative pluralism anticipates *viae analogicae*. Thus, a main function of the dialectical element regards discerning legitimate from illegitimate *analogiae*, coordinating the legitimate toward collaborative plurality, while unburdening that collaborative effort from the need to integrate the illegitimate. The structure of this dialectical heuristic is open-ended and, as such, invites the development of additional theorems in the ongoing process of discernment and collaboration. But it is the argument of the next chapter that the first dialectical theorem to be deployed in organizing that process is a repurposing of a traditional one: the theorem of the supernatural.

## CONCLUSION

This chapter began with an assertion. It argued that the speculative theological practice of the medieval synthesis, while not *per se* reducible to its sociocultural location, was *de facto* an achievement built upon the historical and intellectual scaffolding of the classicist conception of culture. Its deployment of theory, of universal definitions, of the hierarchical unity of inquiry and knowledge was secured by a vision of the social order, the cultural matrix, and the human soul that was fixed, normative, and invariant. And while the doctrines and directives of that synthesis have survived the emergence of the modern world, the classicist worldview that nurtured them has not.

The demise of classicism brings with it the question of speculative theology's continued possibility. This chapter has attempted to chart a course between and beyond two forms of that possibility's denial. It rejects the antimodernist impulse that would secure speculative theology's survival by rebuilding and imposing a classicist cultural order, and it resists the revisionist conclusion that the intimacy of the relationship between speculative theology and a rightly despised classicism disqualifies speculation's ongoing legitimacy.

In the course of pursing a *via media* between these two modern tendencies, I have traced the emergence and decline of the classicist worldview and the notions of science, philosophy, culture, and theology it furnished. Further I have explained the new science of culture as it has emerged in philosophy, semiotics, anthropology, and psychoanalysis. In the course of that explanation, I have shown that there exists a residual classicism that floats to the surface of many of the would-be modern sciences of culture, a tendency that, while adverting to culture's empirical context, smuggles in normativity under the guise of the scientist's imagined neutrality or the philosopher's heroic resistance. Following Robert Doran's theological reconfiguration of Voegelin's anthropological principle, I have argued that a fully universalist and historical science of culture has its more durable root in a theology. As the divine ground of world-transcendent meaning is communicated to the various matrices of human culture through the incarnate proclamation of the law of the cross, all forms of cultural pretention, universality, normativity, and permanence are invalidated and undone.

And since a fully theological account of the modern science of culture rules out any retreat to classicism, a renewed speculative theology must be consciously postclassicist. But a postclassicist speculative theology is not characterized primarily by its contents, but rather by its method. In a modern methodical frame, speculative practice—the intellectual mediation between *fides* and *intellectum*—pluralizes in accord with the varied contexts of cultural making and the unique emergences of speculative exigence within those contexts. A principal task, then, of a methodical, postclassicist speculative theology is to work out the means of negotiating that pluralism.

Toward that end, this chapter has put forward a basic heuristic structure for analyzing, interpreting, and evaluating speculative pluralism. It has identified the material, subjective formal, and objective formal elements of speculative pluralism that owe to the empirical plurality of cultures, theologians, and theologies. It has, furthermore, identified the evaluative structure of speculative pluralism's dialectical element and with it the means of coordinating collaboration among complementary, genetic, and contrary theologies and of rejecting contradictory theologies.

The dialectical element of speculative pluralism calls for—to borrow a term from Robert Doran—a "world-cultural network" of speculative theologies, a matrix of cooperation and collaboration in the pursuit of the intellectual mediation of Christian constitutive meanings to the varied and dynamic contexts of human living. And while any particular mediation within that collaborative matrix has a definite shelf life owing to the dynamism of human cultural making, the methodical structure of speculative pluralism and its collaborative potential remains, even when particular theologies either pass away or reach the limits of their mediating potential. The next chapter will present the initial theorematic criterion for both rejecting speculations that run afoul of the doctrinal context and coordinating the authentic pluralism that is grounded in the twin poles of church doctrine and the eros of the human spirit.

## NOTES

1. See Bernard Lonergan, "The Origins of Christian Realism (1972)," in *A Second Collection*, CWL 13, Robert M. Doran and John D. Dadosky, eds. (Toronto: University of Toronto Press, 2016), 202–220.

2. Bernard Lonergan, "Doctrinal Pluralism," in *Philosophical and Theological Papers, 1965–1980*, CWL 17, Robert C. Croken and Robert M. Doran, eds. (Toronto: University of Toronto Press, 2004), 84.

3. This brief narrative is adapted from Lonergan's own account in "Doctrinal Pluralism," CWL 17, 84. And while its form is generic, the developmental steps bear a striking resemblance to Lonergan's description of the phases of the speculative development of the reconciliation of grace and freedom discussed in the previous chapter. It is, therefore, reasonable to assume that even in 1971, Lonergan held to the basic lines of his theory of speculative development he had put forward in *Gratia operans*. And, furthermore, the narrative recurs again in 1972's *Method in Theology*, ed. Robert M. Doran and John D. Dadosky, CWL 14 (Toronto: University of Toronto Press, 2017), 277.

4. Hans Urs von Balthasar, *Truth Is Symphonic: Aspects of Christian Pluralism*, trans. Graham Harrison (San Francisco: Ignatius Press, 1987), 48.

5. Balthasar, *Truth Is Symphonic*, 48.

6. Balthasar, *Truth Is Symphonic*, 48.

7. See Lonergan, *Method in Theology*, CWL 14, 288.

8. These are among the key elements Margaret Deansley identifies in her classic work, *A History of the Medieval Church, 590–1500*, 9th ed. (London and New York: Routledge, 1969), 168–170.

9. See Bernard Lonergan, "The Scope of Renewal," in *Philosophical and Theological Papers, 1965–1980*, CWL 17, ed. Robert C. Croken and Robert M. Doran (Toronto: University of Toronto Press, 2004), 282–287; idem, "Revolution in Catholic Theology," in *A Second Collection*, CWL 13, ed. Robert M. Doran and John D. Dadosky (Toronto: University of Toronto Press, 2016), 195–201.

10. See Lonergan, "Doctrinal Pluralism," CWL 17, 77–81, 86–88.

11. Such conservative opinion can be expressed as what David Tracy terms "orthodox theology," the first of his five basic models of theological engagements with modernity. See David Tracy, *Blessed Rage for Order: The New Pluralism in Theology* (New York: The Seabury Press, 1978), 24–25.

12. Such statements include Pius IX's *Syllabus Errorum* (1864), Vatican I's *Dei filius* (1870), Leo XIII's *Aeterni patris* (1879), Pius X's *Sacrorum antistitum* (1910), the 24 Thomistic Theses (1914), and Pius XII's *Humani generis* (1950). While each of these texts evince this tendency, they do not do so with a single strategy. The Leonine project that has its origins in *Dei filius* and especially *Aeterni Patris* led to a creative and constructive recovery of Aquinas, encouraging and facilitating the study of his texts as well as his concrete historical and intellectual contexts. This approach can be distinguished from the more defensive posture of the anti-Modernist Oath and the Syllabus of Errors. For an account of this tradition, see Aidan Nichols, *The Conversation of Faith and Reason: Modern Catholic Thought from Hermes to Benedict XVI* (Chicago: Liturgy Training Publications, 2011).

13. These approaches can be broadly grouped within what Tracy calls "the revisionist model." See Tracy, *Blessed Rage for Order*, 32–34.

14. Doran, *What Is Systematic Theology?*, 80.

15. See Daniel 2:31–45.

16. Christopher Dawson, *The Historic Reality of Christian Culture: A Way to the Renewal of Human Life* (New York: Harper Torchbooks, 1960), 60.

17. Bernard Lonergan, "The Absence of God in Modern Culture," In *A Second Collection*, ed. Robert M. Doran and John D. Dadosky, CWL 13 (Toronto: University of Toronto Press, 2016), 86.

18. Lonergan, "The Absence of God in Modern Culture," CWL 13, 86.

19. Lonergan, "Doctrinal Pluralism," CWL 17, 98–99.

20. Bruno Snell, *The Discovery of Mind: The Greek Origins of European Thought*, trans. T. G. Rosenmeyer (New York: Harper Torchbooks, 1960). See also, Karl Jaspers, *The Origin and Goal of History*, trans. Michael Bullock (New York: Routledge, 2010); Eric Voegelin, *Order and History, Vol. 1: Israel and Revelation*, Maurice P. Hogan, ed., CWEV 14 (Columbia and London: University of Missouri Press, 2001).

21. Lonergan, *Method in Theology*, CWL 14, 87.

22. See Lonergan, *Method in Theology*, CWL 14, 82–87.

23. Lonergan, *Method in Theology*, CWL 14, 92–93.

24. Bernard Lonergan "Religious Knowledge," in Robert M. Doran and John D. Dadosky, eds., *A Third Collection*, CWL 16 (Toronto: University of Toronto Press, 2017), 135.

25. Lonergan, *Method in Theology*, CWL 14, 93.

26. Lonergan, "Revolution in Catholic Theology," *Second Collection*, CWL 13, 198. For Lonergan's philosophy of modern natural science, see chapters 2–5 of *Insight*, CWL 3, 57–195. For a history of the development of modern science from natural philosophy, see A. C. Crombie, *Augustine to Galileo: The History of Science, A.D. 400–1650* (Cambridge: Harvard University Press, 1953); idem, *Robert Grosseteste and the Origins of Experimental Science, 1100–1700* (Oxford: Clarendon Press, 1953); see also Hebert Butterfield, *The Origins of Modern Science*, rev. ed. (New York: Free Press, 1997).

27. On these canons of empirical method, see Lonergan, *Insight*, CWL 3, 93–125.

28. For a classic treatment of the social dynamics of these revisions, see Thomas Kuhn, *The Structure of Scientific Revolutions*, 3rd ed. (Chicago: University of Chicago Press, 1996).

29. Lonergan, "Dimensions of Meaning," in *Collection*, ed. Frederick E. Crowe and R. Doran, CWL 4 (Toronto: University of Toronto Press, 1988), 240.

30. Lonergan, "The Subject," in *A Second Collection*, ed. Robert M. Doran and John D. Dadosky, CWL 13 (Toronto: University of Toronto Press, 2016), 61n2.

31. Lonergan, *Method in Theology*, CWL 14, 93.

32. Lonergan, "The Subject," CWL 13, 63.

33. Lonergan, "The Subject," CWL 13, 73.

34. Lonergan, "Dimensions of Meaning," CWL 4, 234.

35. Lonergan, "Dimensions of Meaning," CWL 4, 234.

36. Lonergan, "Dimensions of Meaning," CWL 4, 232.

37. Lonergan, "Theology in Its New Context," in *A Second Collection*, ed. Robert M. Doran and John D. Dadosky, CWL 13 (Toronto: University of Toronto Press, 2016), 49.

38. Lonergan, "Theology in Its New Context," CWL 13, 49.

39. Lonergan, "Theology in Its New Context," CWL 13, 51.

40. Lonergan, "Theology in Its New Context," CWL 13, 51.

41. Lonergan, "Dimensions of Meaning," CWL 4, 240.

42. T. S. Eliot, *Notes towards the Definition of Culture* (London: Faber and Faber, 1948), 13.

43. Raymond Williams, *Keywords: A Vocabulary of Culture and Society*, new ed. (Oxford: Oxford University Press, 2015), 49. This line is frequently quoted in secondary literature, often without context. For Williams, the difficulty in defining culture stems from its distinct connotations and history of usage in multiple European languages, but also and especially because it is part of the specialized vocabulary of multiple intellectual discourses and given meanings in these discourses that are incompatible with each other.

44. See Eliot, *The Definition of Culture*, 14n1: "The use of the word culture, by those who have not, as it seems to me, pondered deeply on the meaning of the word before employing it, might be illustrated by countless examples."

45. F. R. Cowell, *Culture in Private and Public Life* (London: Thames and Hudson, 1959), 3.

46. H. L. Mencken, *Prejudices: Second Series* (London: J. Cape, 1921), 158.

47. Lonergan, *Method in Theology*, CWL 14, 3.

48. Dawson, *The Historic Reality of Christian Culture*, 13. As Dawson explains, every civilization, from the most basic to the most developed, has its own culture, and that culture is precarious. It can be lost through violence and changes in the basic structures of a society. Culture, for Dawson, is historically emergent and historically contingent. Lonergan claims to have first understood culture empirically when, in 1930, he read Dawson's text *The Age of the Gods: A Study in the Origins of Culture in Prehistoric Europe and the Ancient East* (Works of Christopher Dawson [Washington, DC: Catholic University of America Press, 2012]). See Lonergan, *"Insight Revisited,"* In *A Second Collection*, ed. Robert M. Doran and John D. Dadosky, CWL 13 (Toronto: University of Toronto Press, 2016), 222.

49. Dawson, *The Historic Reality of Christian Culture*, 60.

50. Dawson, *The Historic Reality of Christian Culture*, 60–61.

51. Bruno Latour, *We Have Never Been Modern*, trans. Catherine Porter (Cambridge, MA: Harvard University Press, 1993), 7.

52. Clifford Geertz, "Thick Description: Toward an Interpretive Theory of Culture," in *The Interpretation of Cultures: Selected Essays by Clifford Geertz* (New York: Basic Books, 1973), 4–5. Geertz cites the chapter on culture in Clyde Kluckhohn, *Mirror for Man: The Relation of Anthropology to Modern Life* (New York: McGraw-Hill, 1959).

53. Geertz, "The Impact of the Concept of Culture on the Concept of Man," in *The Interpretation of Cultures*, 39.

54. Geertz, "Concept of Culture," 40.

55. Geertz, "Thick Description," 5. For a thorough analysis of semiotic theories of culture and their theological application to the problem of cultural pluralism, see Cyril Orji, *A Semiotic Approach to the Theology of Inculturation* (Eugene, OR: Pickwick Publications, 2015), 102–165. Orji helpfully situates Geertz's semiotic theory within the legacy of C. S. Peirce and Susanne Langer, and argues that Geertz's notion of culture, despite the criticisms raised against it by Martin Palecek and Mark Risjord, James Clifford and George Marcus, Richard Shweder, and Talal Asad, is uniquely situated to address the challenges of a theology of inculturation. Orji writes, "He provides us with a way by which we can talk about different conceptions of the self as these conceptions are made manifest by different groups of people in various ways of life" (125).

56. Geertz, "Religion as a Cultural System," in *The Interpretation of Cultures*, 89.

57. Geertz, "On Deep Play: Notes on a Balinese Cockfight," in *The Interpretation of Cultures*, 452.

58. Geertz, "On Deep Play," 453.

59. Susanne K. Langer, *Philosophical Sketches: A Study of the Human Mind in Relation to Feeling, Explored through Art, Language, and Symbol* (Baltimore: Johns Hopkins University Press, 1962), 87.

60. Langer, *Philosophical Sketches*, 87 (emphasis original).

61. Langer, *Philosophical Sketches*, 87.

62. Langer, *Philosophical Sketches*, 89. See also, Erich Rothacker, *Logik und Systematik der Geisteswissenschaften*, 2nd ed. (Bonn: H. Bouvier u. Co. Verlag, 1947). While Langer does not directly cite Rothacker, Lonergan refers to him specifically as the source of the distinction between civilization and culture. See, for example, Lonergan, "The Absence of God in Modern Culture," CWL 13, 87n3.

63. Langer, *Philosophical Sketches*, 90.

64. Langer, *Philosophical Sketches*, 90.

65. Paul Ricoeur, "Psychoanalysis and the Movement of Contemporary Culture," trans. Willis Domingo, in *The Conflict of Interpretations: Essays in Hermeneutics*, ed. Don Ihde (Evanston, IL: Northwestern University Press, 1974), 124.

66. Ricoeur, "Psychoanalysis and Contemporary Culture," 137.

67. Ricoeur, "Psychoanalysis and Contemporary Culture," 137

68. Ricoeur, "Psychoanalysis and Contemporary Culture," 124.

69. Ricoeur, "Psychoanalysis and Contemporary Culture," 121 (emphasis original).

70. Lonergan, "Dimensions of Meaning," CWL 4, 238.

71. I am using "empirical notion of culture" and "historical-mindedness" as functional synonyms in this context. Lonergan himself uses them in this way, as radical alternatives to classicism. The term "historical-mindedness" is Carl Becker's, and it comes into Lonergan's lexicon through Alan Richardson. See Lonergan, "The Transition from a Classicist World-View to Historical Mindedness," in *A Second Collection*, ed. Robert M. Doran and John D. Dadosky, CWL 13 (Toronto: University of Toronto Press, 2016), 3–10; idem, "Natural Right and Historical-Mindedness," in *A Third Collection*, ed. Robert M. Doran and John D. Dadosky, CWL 16 (Toronto: University of Toronto Press, 2017), 163–176. See also Carl Becker, *The Heavenly City of the Eighteenth Century Philosophers* (New Haven: Yale University Press, 1932); Alan Richardson, *History Sacred and Profane* (London: SCM Press, 1964).

72. See Blondel, *The Letter on Apologetics & History and Dogma*, 178–179.

73. Hans Georg Gadamer, "The Problem of Historical Consciousness," in Paul Rabinow and William M. Sullivan, eds., *Interpretive Social Science: A Second Look* (Berkeley, Los Angeles, and London: University of California Press, 1987), 89.

74. Gadamer, "The Problem of Historical Consciousness," 89.

75. Gadamer, "The Problem of Historical Consciousness," 89.

76. Robert M. Doran, *Theology and the Dialectics of History* (Toronto: University of Toronto Press, 1990), 485.

77. Doran, *Theology and the Dialectics of History*, 485.

78. Doran, *Theology and the Dialectics of History*, 485.

79. Doran, *Theology and the Dialectics of History*, 486.

80. Doran, *Theology and the Dialectics of History*, 486.

81. Doran, *Theology and the Dialectics of History*, 486.

82. Doran, *Theology and the Dialectics of History*, 486–487.

83. Doran, *Theology and the Dialectics of History*, 488.
84. Doran, *Theology and the Dialectics of History*, 489.
85. Doran, *Theology and the Dialectics of History*, 488.
86. Doran, *Theology and the Dialectics of History*, 489.
87. I take this to be a basic, if underdeveloped, consequence of Lonergan's position in *Method in Theology* that a threefold process of conversion is a prior condition of systematic or speculative theology.
88. M. Shawn Copeland, *Enfleshing Freedom: Body, Race, and Being* (Minneapolis: Fortress Press, 2009). For an analysis of American white supremacy in terms of the empirical notion of culture, see Bryan Massingale, *Racial Justice and the Catholic Church* (Maryknoll, NY: Orbis, 2010), 13–33. Massingale's use of Lonergan, Geertz, and Copeland within his analysis of racism and Catholic social ethics illustrates well both the benefit speculative or theoretical apparatuses can provide and the contextual character of theoretical applications.
89. Copeland's project extends beyond the limited tasks of speculative theology and includes those of historical reconstruction and retrieval, interpretation, dialectical critique, ethical injunction, and communication. But one should not overlook the speculative/theoretical elements and the guiding role of theory in her work out of the assumption that "contextual" or "praxis" theologies are antispeculative.
90. Coakley, *God, Sexuality, and the Self*, 88.
91. Kuhn, *The Structure of Scientific Revolutions*, 4.
92. Michael Novak, *Ascent of the Mountain, Flight of the Dove: An Invitation to Religious Studies* (New York and London: Harper & Row, 1971), 88.
93. Elizabeth A. Johnson, *She Who Is: The Mystery of God in Feminist Theological Discourse* (New York: Crossroad, 1992), 6.
94. Johnson, *She Who Is*, 18.
95. Coakley, *God, Sexuality, and the Self*, 40.
96. Coakley, *God, Sexuality, and the Self*, 40–41.
97. Johnson, *She Who Is*, 5–6.
98. Lonergan, "Dialectic of Authority," In *A Third Collection*, ed. Robert M. Doran and John D. Dadosky, CWL 16 (Toronto: University of Toronto Press, 2017), 3–9.
99. Lonergan's basic triplet of possible relations includes the complementary, genetic, and the dialectical. For Lonergan, the dialectical is the contradictory relationship between basic terms, as, for example, good's relationship to evil or affirmation's relationship to negation. Robert Doran has argued, however, that there are two forms of dialectical relationship: a dialectic of contradictories as articulated by Lonergan, and a further dialectic of contraries, wherein the basic terms remain linked, but opposed principles of change can be held in creative tension with one another. Such a dialectic would include, for example, the relationship of limitation and transcendence. They are not contradictory opposites like good and evil, but they also are not straightforwardly complementary. Thus, an integral dialectic of contraries maintains the balanced tension between the two poles without giving sway to one pole or the other. See Doran, *Theology and the Dialectics of History*, 9–10.

*Chapter 4*

# Repurposing Royal Ruins

The previous chapter concluded with a conceptual ellipsis. It presented a heuristic structure for clarifying the theological pluralisms that become visible in the shift from classicism to historical consciousness. It anticipated the generation of the synthetic and dialectical perspectives required for understanding the interlocking relationships between different kinds of pluralisms, and for making judgments about the authenticity or inauthenticity of theological subjects, theological products, and cultural worlds. That structure has four basic elements—the material, the subjective formal, the objective formal, and the dialectical. The first three structural elements pertain to the bare givenness of theological speculative pluralism, that is, the empirical multiplicity of theologians, their theologies, and the varied and various cultural matrices out of which and for which theologians deploy theoretical and speculative techniques to promote *Glaubensverständnis*. But while the concreteness of history, culture, and subjectivity have the material and formal elements of speculative pluralism as their basic entailments, the dialectical element of the structure pertains to the explicit theological and methodological tasks of identifying the complementary, genetic, contrary, and contradictory relationships among synchronic and diachronic pluralities of theologies; of promoting and coordinating collaboration between complementary, genetic, and contrary theological products; and of developing the means of discriminating between contradictory speculative theologies by which to venture an affirmative judgement to one and not the other.

Lonerganian dialectic orders the plurality of cultures and of theologians in terms of progress and decline, conversion, the polymorphism of consciousness, and the transcendental imperatives—be attentive, be intelligent, be reasonable, be responsible.[1] But a dialectic of authenticity is not sufficient for the adjudication of speculative theological products. For, as Lonergan notes, "there is a real difference between the continuity of the history of dogma and the succession of theses and antitheses which characterize the human effort of *fides quarens intellectum*; and precisely because there is a real difference, speculative failure is not the same as heresy."[2] If speculative failure is not heresy, neither is it inauthenticity—indeed, it is an attempt to *be intelligent* with respect to a set of doctrinal judgments and the questions for understanding they elicit. Conversely, assiduous devotion to the transcendental precepts is no guarantee of speculative success. Canonical recognition of one's sanctity, surely, is at least a recognition of one's authenticity. Yet, the sainthood of an Augustine or an Anselm did not secure theories fully adequate to either theologian's speculative questions and basic doctrinal commitments.[3] The transcendental precepts order the moral *élan* of the human subject's conscious and intentional operations, but they do not of themselves vouchsafe the sufficiency of those operations' noematic effects.

Some other dialectical means, then, is required to discriminate among the results of distinct speculative labors. Such means, if they are to have ongoing viability, must be coordinated both with the dynamic succession of speculative contexts and viewpoints that unfold in the course of a speculative tradition, and with the analogical coexistence of speculative traditions within a single age.

The dialectical element of speculative pluralism will thus be an open-ended context of theorematic perspectives, that is, a series of theoretically elaborated articulations of the religious, moral, and intellectual conditions out of which speculative questions emerge and by which speculative answers are judged. The previous chapter outlined the dialectical element as a feature of speculative pluralism, but it did not articulate the theorematic content that the heuristic structure anticipates. It is the task of the present chapter to provide such an articulation, to move from the conceptual ellipsis of the heuristic to the *initial* methodical frame it anticipates.

Any open-ended frame must begin somewhere. Precedent and prudence suggest that one should look to the *vetera* for clues—and even capital—that might illuminate and fund the *nova* and be conscripted into their service. This chapter proposes a repurposing of what Bernard Lonergan calls the theorem of the supernatural, a synthetic insight that emerged in the thirteenth century that made possible an incisive breakthrough in the speculative theology of Thomas Aquinas. What began as a medieval theoretical means of clarifying properly theological domains of terms from "the line of reference termed nature"[4] can be repurposed in a modern context in which its basic function is to organize the plurality of speculative analogies and entitative orders of analogs such that the complementary, genetic, and contrary relationships between analogies are brought into focus and made the subject of methodical interrogation, while the negative pole of dialectically contradictory analogies may be set aside as a perhaps coherent but ultimately inapt hypothesis.

First, this chapter provides an overview of Lonergan's historical reconstruction of the theorem of the supernatural and explains the role of theorematic operation in speculative theology through the example of grace and freedom. Second, it argues that the theorem itself can be transposed from the specific medieval context and its many *disputata* surrounding the doctrine of grace and situated within a generalized context wherein that same synthetic insight can organize systematic thinking concerning every speculative question. But as the pathway from the medieval to the modern passes through classicism to historical consciousness, so the transposition of the theorem of the supernatural requires an analysis of the intellectual nexus between religion, culture, and philosophy. While the medieval form of the theorem pertains principally to the task of understanding the coherence of doctrines, the modern form enlarges the problematic to include the theological coherence of the plurality of such understandings. I will show that the theorem of the supernatural, or what, in a more generalized scheme, Robert Sokolowski calls "the distinction" between God and the world, emerges concretely through a complex commerce between the religious doctrines, orientations, and traditions of a culture, the questions engendered by that commerce, and the philosophical mentalities and insights that are forged in the course of navigating such questions.

Following the work of Sokolowski and David Burrell, I argue that, in cultures informed by Christianity, the doctrines of creation and incarnation constitute a basic religious context for understanding the relationship between God and the world. The theorem of the supernatural is a speculative correlate to these doctrines capable of expressing that relationship in systematic, philosophical terms. There is, thus, a generic form of the theorem which speculatively renders the relationship between God and the world as understood according to the doctrine of free creation in general, and there is a specific form of the theorem which expresses God's relationship to the world as disclosed in the special case of the doctrine of the incarnation.

Both creation and incarnation are supernatural with respect to human understanding, but are so in different ways. Creation is supernatural to a human nature with regard to the cause of that nature's first act. Human beings, like all beings whose *esse* is not also their *essentia*, are not proportionate to the cause of the act of existence itself. Their existence is a dependent existence and thereby one insufficient to establish, sustain, or explain itself apart from that upon which it depends. All natures which subsist as dependent relations are proportionate to human intelligence, for human intelligence intends and anticipates the complete intelligibility of proportionate being.

Incarnation, though, is not only supernatural with respect to the cause of created *esse*'s first act, it is also supernatural with respect to the contents of its communication. Christ's human nature participates existentially in the eternal and uncreated *esse* of the Son of God who eternally proceeds from the Father. Neither this communication nor this participation are proportionate to any human *esse*. Thus, as Eric Mabry argues, what is dogmatically called the hypostatic union, systematically called the grace of union, and existentially called the *esse secundarium* is absolutely supernatural to human understanding and is itself a communication of the divine nature to the created order.[5] If Christ's human existence is a communication of the divine nature, then one should anticipate that that existence itself should be a source of analogs for the divine life that, though in themselves not proportionate to human understanding, are in fact communicated to human understanding through the *mysterium salutis*.

Finally, the chapter proposes that this generalization of the theorem of the supernatural can serve as an initial dialectical theorem and a basic systematic term for speculative pluralism. The generic and specific forms of the theorem correspond to the double consequence of the synthetic insight the theorem expresses. The theorem of the supernatural clarifies both the uniquely theological elements of an inquiry (that which is beyond the proportion of a created intellect and thereby could not be known apart from a revelation that comes both *ex auditu* and *ex infusione*) and the validity of the line of reference termed nature (that which is proportionate to created intellect and thereby capable in principle of being known by it).

By distinguishing the supernatural from the natural, the theorem of the supernatural gives warrant for theology to make use of both the supernatural and the natural in its speculative endeavors. Thus, the generic theorem, which speculatively corresponds to the doctrine of creation, suggests that nature itself possesses analogs by which faith might seek understanding. And, furthermore, the specific theorem, which expresses the disproportion between God and the world supernaturally communicated in the doctrine of the incarnation, indicates that the supernatural order revealed through Christ can itself be a source of analogical terms of which a speculative theology might make use. Because, intellectually, both orders of analogs are controlled by the same theorematic relation, and, theologically, grace is not contrary to nature, there is potential for cooperation and collaboration between speculative theologies that deploy analogs from either order. As an initial dialectical theorem for speculative pluralism, the theorem of the supernatural has a further, regulative function, as well. By clarifying distinct entitative orders of analogs, the theorem can go beyond enkindling and coordinating speculative collaboration. It can also chasten, criticize, and exclude speculative theologies that either obscure entitative orders and relations, or explode them altogether. The chapter concludes by indicating how the methodical elements of the first three chapters of this study may be applied to specific nexuses of speculative pluralism, and takes the coincidence of both natural and supernatural analogs for the Trinitarian processions in contemporary Trinitarian theology as a testing ground for the dialectical repurposing of the theorem of the supernatural.

## LONERGAN'S RECONSTRUCTION OF THE MEDIEVAL BREAKTHROUGH

### Augustinian Origins

The term "theorem of the supernatural" has its origins in Bernard Lonergan's doctoral dissertation, *Gratia Operans*. With it, Lonergan names a synthetic insight and an intellectual orientation that emerged in the writings of the thirteenth-century theologian Philip the Chancellor. Philip's discovery enabled Thomas Aquinas to clarify the objectives of inquiry unique to theology and thereby to make of theology a *scientia*. What Philip posited was a way of understanding the data of faith and reason in terms of an entitative disproportion between the absolutely supernatural self-communication of the divine nature that is grace and the "nature" to which that communication addresses itself. But like all theoretical breakthroughs, the theorem of the supernatural was discovered as a solution to concrete and long-standing problems in a tradition of thought. Those problems accumulated in the intellectual climate birthed in the aftermath of Augustine's contestation with Pelagius and the exigence it established for clarifying the *doctrinal* positions on divine grace and human freedom.[6]

Against the Pelagian teaching, which maintained the sufficiency of human agency to the realization of the divine command (given that human will is free and that human intellect grasps that in which the divine command consists), Augustine argued that the noetic and volitional effects of sin were such that a marred human will could not fulfill the divine command absent the gratuitous, healing operation of divine grace. The Pelagian position, though organized around the self-sufficiency of the will, was variable. That variability meant that "if grace existed, then it was not necessary. If necessary, then it was the law, or knowledge of the law, or nature, or free will, or the remission of sins. If none of these would do, then it was given man according to his merits. If forced to admit that the merit of good deeds presupposes the gift of grace, there were those who would reply that the grace that causes good deeds is meted out according to the previous merit of good will."[7] To counter these Pelagian "evasions," Augustine set forth a distinction between *gratia operans* and *gratia cooperans*. Through operative grace, God works in us without us (*Deus sine nobis operatur*), changing a heart of stone into a heart of flesh, establishing a good will where once there had been a bad will. But the good will that operative grace effects remains "weak and imperfect" in its own mode of operation.⁸ Thus, to move from good desire to good action requires a further, *cooperative* grace in which God's action works alongside our own to bring our operation to perfection, which is to say, to fulfill the good will with its coordinated act.⁹

For Augustine, the distinction of *gratia operans et cooperans* is a distinctior within the totality of grace, while grace itself is simply "any gratuitous gift of God."¹⁰ The resulting view is one in which the utter gratuity of divine grace raises a question even the possibility—let alone the actuality—of human free will and free operation. While the Pelagians so stressed human freedom as to posit its self-sufficiency to good action and merit, the monks at Hadrumetum took the opposed position and "so extolled the grace of God as to deny human liberty."¹¹ So total was sin's corruption of the will, they argued, that human freedom itself was illusory.¹² Augustine responded to reports of this teaching by asserting, not as a philosophic opinion but as a dogmatic truth, that the testimony of Holy Scripture clearly affirmed the reality of human freedom. As Lonergan writes of Augustine's *Letter 214*, "It was addressed not to their understanding but to their faith; and if they failed to understand what they were to believe, they were not to dispute but to pray for light."¹³ The result of this two-front battle over basic elements of the doctrinal tradition is what Lonergan calls "the celebrated paradox," which asserts that "the will of man is always free but not always good: either it is free from justice, and then it is evil; or it is liberated from sin, and then it is good."¹⁴ This paradox effectively settled the doctrinal questions of grace's gratuity and the will's freedom with normalized dogmatic answers. But in successfully consolidating these doctrinal matters (at least in the Latin church), Augustine opened the door for new questions to be asked, questions not of the truths of grace's gratuity and the human will's freedom, but rather questions about the coherence of their mutual affirmation. Thus, the dogmatic solution to these fifth-century controversies inaugurated a centuries-long effort to discover the speculative means of resolving the ambiguities of Augustine's paradox.

## Anselmian Rectitude

In Lonergan's account of the development of speculative method in post-Augustinian theology, Anselm of Canterbury took the first major step beyond doctrine and toward system. Anselm, in a manner distinct from his beloved Augustine, did not write against those who denied either grace or freedom. For, as Michael Stebbins notes, "The affirmation that grace is a gratuitously bestowed divine gift instead of a reward measured out on the basis of any human work or merit runs like a guiding thread throughout the labyrinthine wanderings of early scholastic speculation on the doctrine of grace."¹⁵ Instead, Anselm sought to address "the deep problem of reconciliation."¹⁶

Anselm "was driven by the imperious impulse of *fides quarens intellectum* to try and construct a mode of conception that would lend coherence to the mystery."[17] That drive led Anselm to the notion of rectitude, which enabled him to integrally relate four contested terms: truth, justice, freedom, and grace. Truth, he argued, is rectitude perceived in the mind. Justice, further, is the will's maintenance of rectitude. Freedom is the capacity of the will for justice. And grace is the cause of the rectitude that the will justly maintains. Grace has a prevenient character regarding rectitude's emergence in the will and a consequent character as the "main cause" of rectitude's ongoing perseverance. Thus, within this scheme of relation, "grace and freedom are the causes of justice, and justice is the ground of salvation."[18]

By using rectitude as an organizing notion for relating grace, freedom, and their correlated terms, Anselm went beyond doctrinal clarification to speculative articulation. He did not seek to add new elements to dogmatic data, but attempted instead to arrange the received data according to a theoretical principle so as to resolve ambiguities entailed in their affirmation. As Lonergan recognizes, "Not only are the questions St Anselm treated the most difficult; they are also the most obviously problems, the most apt to excite wonder and impose the necessity of speculative thought in the medieval re-creation of culture and civilization."[19] And so, irrespective of the sufficiency of Anselm's solution to the speculative problem of grace and freedom, he affirmatively settled what is in fact the prior and more basic question, "Is speculation possible and is it worthwhile?"[20] If one affirms with him the possibility and desirability of speculation and proceeds toward its actuality, the "problem of its method" moves to the center of theological rationality. But if he succeeded in foregrounding the problem of speculative method, Lonergan insists that "St. Anselm in no way solved it."[21]

According to Lonergan, the imperative enjoining one to believe in order to understand (*crede ut intelligas*), which serves as the Augustinian basis for Anselm's speculative method, "fails to point out that there are two standards for understanding: natural truths can be reduced eventually to perfect coherence, but the truths of faith have the apex of their intelligibility hidden in the transcendence of God."[22] This twofold structure of understanding is what the first Vatican Council controversially termed the *duplex ordo cognitionis*, a teaching that asserts a distinction between possible terms of inquiry and their corresponding cognitional acts on the basis of the grounding distinction between divine mystery (knowable solely on the basis of revelation) and the proportionate created order (knowable by natural reason *per se*).

The *duplex ordo cognitionis*, despite the objections leveled against it in the twentieth century, serves a vital *methodical* function in speculative theology.[23] It regulates the activity of thinking so as to avoid two potential errors. First, absent a methodical distinction between natural truths and divine mystery, one risks reducing divine mystery to the status of merely natural truth. Such is the practice of the rationalist. But the second and opposite error is no less serious. One can encounter difficulties in understanding the natural elements of a matter and conclude that the terms of the inquiry must be mysteries hidden away in divine life. According to Lonergan, Anselm tended toward the latter error. In developing the speculative notion of rectitude to reconcile the existence of grace and freedom, Anselm elevates human liberty into the order of divine mystery. By conceiving of justice as a state of the will that grace effects, Anselm could not conceive of justification in terms other than the will's operation. Thus, because an infant does not exercise its will in the baptismal sacrament, it receives forgiveness of original sin but does not receive justification as a state of its will. Its salvation, therefore, is a secondary effect of the justice of Christ and the church.[24] This "strange, explicitly speculative position," Lonergan argues, is a consequence of "the unformulated problem of speculative method."[25] But it would be another century before an adequate method of speculative analysis was made possible. "As a result," Stebbins observes, "a number of crucial issues touching on the definition of grace, the distinction between *naturalia* and *gratuita*, the efficacy of infant baptism, the ground of merit, and the relation of grace and freedom remained unsolved puzzles."[26]

## The Lombard on the States of Man

In terms of speculative boldness and intellectual acuity, the Lombard's *Sentences* retreats from the Anselmian frontier. Its "quite solid" achievements in collecting and organizing the theological patrimony were, according to Lonergan, "not very brilliant."[27] Anselm "tried to make grace and freedom coherent by force of subtlety," while "the Lombard innocently lays bare the incoherence" by bringing together in one place various and seemingly contradictory strands of authoritative teaching. For Lonergan, however, the recession from the speculative challenges of the Anselmian phase of development evinced by the *Sentences* nevertheless "unconsciously suggests the lines along which deliverance was to be found."[28] Those lines of suggestion are organized around four states of human liberty. For the Lombard, these states follow the dynamics of creation and salvation. They conceive of liberty in relation to prelapsarian freedom, the Fall, the redemption, and the consummation, and they offer the first approximation of a theorematic perspective beyond the medicinal, psychological concept of grace.

The first state, the earthly paradise, is one in which liberty is ordered such that the human being has "no difficulty doing good" and "no impulsion to evil."[29] In the second state, that of liberty under the constrictions of the Fall, one is not able not to sin ("*non posse non peccare etiam damnabiliter*").[30] But through the economy of salvation, a third state of liberty is made possible, one in which a redeemed human being "can avoid mortal sin but also can commit it."[31] And while the third state of liberty characterizes the Christian life *in via*, it has its fulfillment in a fourth and final state of liberty, the life of the saints *in patria*, wherein there is "confirmation in grace" that "gives impeccability" to the redeemed.[32]

Grace, then, is located principally in the transition from the second to the third state. It is operative "inasmuch as it causes this efficacious good will, making what was already a will into a good and right will."[33] Operative grace, in other words, transforms *non posse* into *posse*. It alters the capacity and range of the will's possibility. But while this expansion includes the possibility of good actions, it does not itself secure their enactments. Cooperative grace, then, "aids the good will to execute good intentions."[34]

This division of grace follows the established Augustinian pattern but sets it within a broader analytic scheme. It does not begin with *non posse non peccare* but with the liberty of a created nature that is subsequently corrupted by sin. Though sin binds human freedom, it does not reduce freedom to illusion or elevate it to mystery, because, as the first state indicates, liberty belongs to the nature of created humanity. Furthermore, its conception of grace in the transition between the third and fourth states of liberty connects grace to merit and ultimately to salvation.

This nascent distinction between the nature of liberty and the grace of merit represents "an entirely new conception of the issue."[35] This new conception establishes "a direction of thought that only has to be pushed to its logical conclusion" in order for the theorem of the supernatural to emerge.[36] The Lombard, though, did not himself realize its emergence. Despite his coordination of liberty with nature and of merit with grace, his work "represents no more than an effort, a direction. Ultimately, a very real antinomy remains."[37]

## Philip the Chancellor, Supernatural Habit, and the Discovery of the Theorem

The basic difficulty at the root of twelfth-century speculations about grace and its relationship to liberty, according to Lonergan, can be summed up in the following question: since every created order and entity is a gratuitous, freely given gift, why is not everything grace?[38] The answer, he argues, lies ultimately not in some fresh exegetical insight or in the discovery of a cache of dogmatic teaching heretofore unavailable, but in a repatterning of the entire speculative tradition according to a new principle, a theorem. By "theorem," Lonergan means "a mental perspective" or "basic coordinates" that intervene upon a set of data in order to grasp from within it an explanatory pattern or nexus, one that can be generalized, transposed across contexts, and applied to any corresponding set of data.

His analogy, as discussed previously, is mathematical. The differential equation for acceleration adds nothing to the data of "going faster." But by applying it to any particular experience of going faster, one can explain just what is going on. One can eliminate the experiential ambiguities that make one vulnerable to illusion. And one can generalize from any particular experience of going faster to any and every such experience. But, as Lonergan writes, "just as one can apprehend the going faster without understanding the calculus, so also the theologians of the twelfth century and earlier could apprehend globally the supernatural character of grace without suspecting the theorem that regards the relationship between nature and grace."[39] Absent the requisite theorematic perspective, the antinomies of post-Augustinian speculative efforts could be shuffled around, but they could not be resolved. In service of grace's gratuity, theologians shifted liberty, reason, virtue, and love into the realm of divine mystery, and in so doing compounded the ambiguities of grace and freedom by leaving undefined and opaque what, in fact, a human being is. But in the thirteenth century, Philip the Chancellor discovered what proved to be the decisive tool for understanding grace and freedom in a more coherent way.

As Stebbins observes, "Before Philip came on the scene, no theologian had articulated with sufficient precision what it is that constitutes human being as human, and how grace supervenes on and perfects those constitutive elements; as the history of the early scholastics shows, until one knows what human nature is, one cannot say exactly why grace is an utterly gratuitous gift."[40] Philip's goal was to explain the relationship between excellencies that belong to the human person by virtue of their created integrity and those higher, "supernatural" excellencies possessed by human persons solely by means of grace. Where earlier theologians tended to deny the possibility of virtue among the unregenerate and, with it, the possibility of a natural love of God, Philip argued that such a love, "a natural *amor amicitiae erga Deum* quite distinct from charity" exists as a natural human virtue.[41] For Philip, this affirmation is the appetitive corollary to the traditional assertion that natural reason can know the existence of God as highest good. Because any *appetitus sequens cognitionem* does so according to the mode of knowledge that informs it, natural knowledge of God as highest good motivates a corresponding natural love of God as highest good.

Furthermore, because in addition to reason's natural knowledge there is also faith's supernatural knowledge, "there must be a corresponding duality in our love of God."[42] Natural knowledge motivates natural love. But faith, because it is a supernatural knowledge, motivates a supernatural love, or charity. For Philip, then, the relationship governing "the familiar series of grace, faith, charity, and merit" and "nature, reason, and the natural love of God" is a theory of entitative disproportion between the order of nature and the order of supernature.[43]

This allowed for a different dimension of grace to come into focus. Because the natural love of God was an entailment of the natural knowledge of God, it is a love that belongs to the human being by nature. Because participation in divine life is not an end owed to nature, then natural operations—even if they are executed without the noetic and volitional effects of sin—cannot merit eternal life. For human operation to be meritorious, it must have a supernatural principle under the aspect of which its operation results not merely in a good life but in the life of the blessed. "The theorem of the supernatural," writes Stebbins, "expresses an incapacity of human nature that is due not to sin but to our nature's intrinsic limitations. Even if we were in the state of innocence, we would need to be elevated by grace in order to attain the knowledge of faith and the love of charity."[44] By showing how grace has both a healing and an elevating function with respect to a human being, "Philip the Chancellor's notion of a grace that is explicitly supernatural represents a decisive advance beyond the traditional position that saw grace as performing only a psychological function."[45]

This breakthrough "set in motion a transformation of the entire speculative enterprise with respect to the doctrine of grace. The seemingly intractable difficulties of the earlier period began to give way, and within just a few decades Aquinas was able to propose the elegant and comprehensive synthesis of his *Prima secundae*."[46] But there is a further significance to the theorem of the supernatural. It represents "not just a plausible explanation of the gratuity of grace but also the foundation of a new and powerful methodological orientation."[47] By positing "the validity of a line of reference termed nature," Philip clarified that theological and philosophical methods of inquiry can be distinguished according to their respective domains of terms.[48] But those domains, like the "line of reference" itself, are abstract. They lie in human thinking and thus against any "two-tiered" ontologizing of speculative method. As Lonergan writes, "In the long term and in the concrete the real alternatives remain charity and cupidity, the elect and the *massa damnata*."[49] According to Lonergan,

> The fallacy in earlier thought had been an unconscious confusion of the metaphysical abstraction 'nature' with the concrete data which do not quite correspond; Philip's achievement was the creation of a mental perspective, the introduction of a set of coordinates, that eliminated the basic fallacy and its attendant host of anomalies.[50]

The theorem of the supernatural, then, does more than express the specific speculative nexus between the terms pertaining to grace and freedom, it also makes explicit a method of analysis adequate for speculative theology in general.

## GENERALIZING THE THEOREM OF THE SUPERNATURAL

### The Notion of Transcendence

The intellectual viability of the theorematic lies in the mobility of its scheme of explanatory relations to diverse sets of concrete data. That physical force, for example, is said to be the product of mass and its rate of acceleration would be a thin insight if it applied only to Harley Davidsons, only on Wednesdays, and only in Milwaukee. Like the theorem of force, the theorem of the supernatural has a generalized domain of applicative mobility. Though its emergence owes to the speculative pursuit of specific questions concerning the doctrines of grace and freedom, its significance outstrips the exigencies of that originating context. As an explanation of relation between distinct and disproportionate entitative orders, the theorem of the supernatural has its most generalized form of application in the notion of transcendence itself. To that notion we now turn.

Transcendence is the relation between terms when those terms are organized according to a proportional hierarchy of formal intelligibilities. Any higher term can be said to transcend the lower inasmuch as its intelligibility exceeds the formal proportion of the lower term. Biology transcends chemistry insofar as it treats of the higher integration of chemical compounds that is vital process, and thereby anticipates an intelligibility quite distinct from what is intended when those compounds are interrogated and explained solely in terms of their lower chemical elements and the physical laws that govern elemental interaction. Biology thus relatively transcends chemistry. However, while the whole of proportionate being can be understood in terms of the interactions of different levels of intelligibility relatively transcendent to one another, there is a further, fuller, and more definitive notion of transcendence that anticipates not merely the relative disproportion of some spheres of intelligibility to others within a given hierarchical frame but the absolute transcendence of the infinite to the finite.

Because the infinite absolutely transcends the finite, "it follows that the divine order is beyond the proportion of any possible creature and so is absolutely supernatural."[51] And in like manner to the way the meaning of the supernaturality of grace is controlled by the theorematic elaboration of its transcendental exceeding of the natural, so the absolute transcendence of divine supernaturality can be expressed in terms controlled by the same theorem of disproportionate entitative relation. Thus, analogous to the manner in which charity is absolutely transcendent of natural *amor*, God can be said to absolutely transcend the world.

Yet, clarifying that in which "the distinction" between God and the world consists—and, just as importantly, that in which it does not consist—is a fraught task.[52] Too often and too easily extroverted imagination proffers images of absolute transcendence couched in spatial and temporal terms. God, we like to say, is "beyond" or "outside" the world. But any Hegelian worth their salt knows that to recognize a limit is already to have transgressed it. God is not a thing that exists at the boundary of some extension or in the happening of some duration. God's transcendence cannot be measured by degrees of proximity and remove or by counting links in a Great Chain of Being. Instead, God is said to transcend the world in terms best understood by the interplay of discrete, disproportionate manners of relation between essence and existence—and so ultimately in a nondualist manner.

## From Substance to Existence: A Gilsonian Trajectory

To conceive of being in terms derived from asymmetrical modalities of relation between essence and existence is to involve oneself in a tradition of thought that stretches back to fourth-century Athens and to Aristotle's criticism of his teacher's doctrine. Though sharing Plato's desire for a philosophical explanation of identity in the midst of change, Aristotle denied that that explanation must ultimately have recourse to the realm of Ideas and its corresponding doctrine of participation. He argued instead that a nature is an immanent principle of operation, while an essence is that same formality grasped "as a possible object of intelligible definition."[53] And because form is an operative principle and an object of intellect only through the individuation accomplished by its union with matter, forms indwell the determinate data of the sensible world, while knowledge of the form is the presence of the known in the knower. This isomorphism between knowing and known is the ground of philosophical realism. Understanding is the act of organizing intelligence that grasps essence inasmuch as that essence subsists in the data that provoke intelligent inquiry. Forms, then, can be said to reside both in things (as a principle of operation) and in minds (as the content of an act of understanding).

Such an approach to ontology, however, does not resolve the ambiguity that is Aristotle's notion of substance. Aristotle's basic assertion is that reality is substantial: individual natures are substances that subsist inasmuch as they inform matter. Absent the union of form and matter, natures do not subsist at all. Yet, this assertion proves a difficult one to maintain. Gilson recognizes a seemingly inexorable pull back to the Platonic scheme of eternal ideas and participating natures. If first philosophy is a matter of possible intelligibilities or essences, then knowledge of essences is the philosopher's aim. The concrete world the philosopher thus investigates "remains the substantial world of Aristotle," but it "can be safely dealt with as if it were the ideal world of Plato."[54] Gilson argues that this reversion to the Platonic mean is evidenced in Avicenna's postulation of the *in se* neutrality of essences vis-à-vis universality and existence. "The essences of Avicenna," he charges, "are so many ghosts of Plato's Ideas."[55] Because of the neutrality of essence, it cannot be said to prefer actuality to potency, for in both it is the selfsame, neutral essence, and by being one or the other, it undergoes no change in what it is or even in the manner of its being what it is. A conception of being which foregrounds essence is thus a conception of being that cannot be said to include existence as part of its immanent intelligibility, a conception of being in which the act of existence is merely accidental, in which existence is something that happens to essence.

This sets up a zero-sum relation between essence and existence. As Gilson notes of Avicenna's view, "Actual being can no more be without its existence than it can be without its unity. Yet, since actual being is primarily its essence, even while a being actually is it *has* its existence, it *is* not it. It *is* not it because, were it its existence, then it could have no essence."[56] For this reason, the God of Avicenna is a God who is his existence at the cost of being a God who has no essence. For Avicenna, "The First, the Necessary Being, that is, God Himself, is the pure act of existence, and nothing can be superior to it."[57] Because God exists necessarily, God is identical with God's existence. As pure and necessary existence, God can have no quiddity logically prior to his act of existing. Existence cannot be "something *attributed* to the necessary existent."[58] And so while Avicenna's express concern is to foreground the identity of God with God's existence, his essentialist approach to the *ordo* of metaphysics leaves him open to Averroes's charge that he conceives of existence as accidental, as something that "'comes to' (*advenit, accidit*) the essence (or quiddity)."[59] Though Averroes mischaracterizes Avicenna's intention, the doctrine of essences proves itself to be an unstable ground as the first and basic element of a realist metaphysics and so insufficient for a fully generalized theory of transcendence.

Despite this difficulty, Avicenna is the first to conceive of the real distinction between essences and their existence. He observes that the "nature which is proper to each thing (*haqiqa*: lit., its truth) is other than [its] existence (*al-wujud*), which is synonymous with affirming it to be the case (*al-ithbat*)."[60] And it is this distinction that illuminates the path toward a fully generalized theory of transcendence. Walking that path, though, requires re-posing the question of metaphysics not as a formal question about essences (*quid sit?*) but rather as an existential question about what, in fact, is the case (*an sit?*). Furthermore, it is not enough that those questions and the answers they intend be disaggregated in philosophical analysis, they must also be reordered in significance. But this reordering requires a focused consideration of a basic question: "How can one hope to formulate what our ordinary ways of knowing must take for granted—the fact of existence?"[61] Since existence is not a predicate, the distinction between existence and nonexistence is not a distinction between different kinds or classes of things. Yet the distinction between existence and nonexistence is one manifestly observable in the world, even though it is not a distinction among entities within it. As Burrell notes, it is precisely this kind of distinction—one that appears in the world but does not obtain among beings within it—that one needs in order to distinguish God from the world.[62]

One need only shift the metaphysical accent from essence to existence for Avicenna's distinction to at last reach its explanatory potential. And it is precisely this shift that Aquinas achieved in his account of being in terms of the *actus essendi*. In his early philosophical work, *De ente et essentia*, Aquinas proposes an analogy by which to relate and order the terms relevant to metaphysical inquiry. Matter, he argues, bears a relationship to form analogous to that obtaining between essence and existence. And, furthermore, essence has a relationship to existence like that between potency and act. Following the Aristotelian contention that, for composite creatures, an essence is a form's subsistence in matter, "Aquinas could indicate—via the next couplet—that *esse* would bear an intelligibility with respect to essence analogous to that which form conveys to matter."[63] The dissimilarity that makes the analogy analogous, however, is that while matter is *in se* unintelligible, essence is "the commensurate object of human understanding."[64] Aquinas thus qualifies the analogy with a third couplet—the relation between potency and act. Unlike that of accident to substance, the relation between potency and act is not one between entities. Matter and form constitute an essence, but an essence is only a possible intelligibility whose actuality is determined by *esse*. It is in this respect that *esse* stands to essence as form to matter. This delicate analogical dance is required because, for Aquinas, intelligibility always pertains to essence, meaning that *esse* is not directly intelligible but is rather the act of existence of some intelligibility. As Burrell notes, "The intelligibility proper to *esse* must remain metaphorical, as a sign of the transcendence of the relation which it helps to formulate: that of creator to creature."[65]

The metaphorical intelligibility of *esse* is expressed as the *actus essendi* and as participation. Burrell writes, "The being which is subsistent in divinity is to be construed then, as though it were in act, and furthermore an act in which created things—even spiritual creatures—participate as 'having *esse* rather than being their own to-be.'"[66] And in this we have the means of articulating in just what the general notion of transcendence consists.

God can be said to absolutely transcend the world insofar as God is that unity of identity whose essence is *to be*. The divine essence is not in potency to divine actuality. The divine essence simply *is* divine actuality. This modality of relation between essence and existence transcends that mode of relation in which essence is a possible intelligibility related to existence as potency to act. This means that God transcends the world not because he is bigger, older, or more powerful, but because his essence is to exist. The world, on the other hand, has its existence not by its own essence, but as borrowed, gifted, and created. It is thus that the theorem of the supernatural's positing of an entitative disproportion between orders of existence is fully articulated.

In God there is no real distinction between essence and existence (nor between understanding and judgment). God's act of existing is not contingent; his essence not in potency. So disproportionate is this modality of relation to that of the kind with which we are more familiar (namely, our own), that it requires no special philosophical acumen to assert that between these modalities of relation there is a qualitative, not merely a quantitative, distinction. But because the distinction is qualitative, it can—and indeed must—be expressed in terms purified from the imagistic dualism that accompanies intramundane comparatives. Created *esse*, insofar as it is not its own principle, bears a relationship to uncreated *esse* that Sara Grant describes as a "non-reciprocal dependence relation."[67] According to Grant, this technical phrase denotes in broadly Thomistic terms what the Hindu philosophical theologian Adi Shankara understands to be the meaning of *advaita* or nonduality. If this is correct, then we should interpret the theorem of the supernatural not as an equator dividing up territories respectively called nature and supernature but rather as the structural insight into the nonduality entailed by divine transcendence. Yet, this entire approach to the generalization of the theorem of the supernatural is predicated on theology in ways not yet acknowledged. Created *esse* more than suggests a creation. But creation is a theological, not a philosophical, doctrine.

## Creation and Transcendence

What Avicenna (and Moses Maimonides) began and Aquinas completed was a theological transfiguration of Aristotelian substance. For all three thinkers, the doctrine of creation—shared by all Abrahamic faiths—exercises a governance over the adequacy of any metaphysical scheme. It is not enough that the first mover be unmoved. That mover must also be free. The necessity of that freedom is neither syllogistic nor axiomatic. It is the teaching of Holy

Writ. And yet, the strangeness such teaching imposes upon traditional philosophy leaves many matters opaque. "The very notion of creation," Burrell writes, "is notoriously difficult to clarify, for it contains scriptural as well as metaphysical elements and does so in a fashion in which they are quite impossible to disentangle."[68] Even for Aquinas, creation exercises a kind of subterranean influence over his account of philosophic rationality, so much so that Josef Pieper famously referred to creation as "the hidden key" in Thomas's philosophy.[69]

But it is not only the complexity of the commerce between scripture and metaphysics that pushes the doctrine of creation underground in Christian reflection. In the Christian tradition, in a manner distinct from Jewish and Islamic traditions, creation is often decentered, even crowded out by other doctrines. "For despite the fact that Christians confess their faith in 'one God, creator of heaven and earth,' a set of factors have worked in a cumulative fashion over time to eclipse that faith in creation as the initial gift of God in favor of the divine self-gift in Jesus. Redemption, in short, has so overshadowed creation in the Christian sensibility that Christians generally have little difficulty adopting a naturalistic attitude toward the universe. Rather than approaching it and responding to it as *gift*, they can easily treat it simply as *given*."[70] Among this "set of factors," Burrell identifies at least three principal perpetrators. First, the Christian transfiguration of the Sabbath gave liturgical primacy to the Day of the Lord and the redemption of Easter morning over the creative rest of the seventh day.[71] Second, inheritors of the theorem of the supernatural misunderstood and misused its central insight. Instead of following Philip and Thomas in asserting the analytic utility of "nature" as a line of reference in speculative thinking, lesser minds imagined a clean and concrete metaphysical separation between the natural and the supernatural, which they identified with nature and grace, the secular and the sacred. The result was "to imply that the natural order was not a grace, not a gift."[72] Finally, Burrell notes that in the nineteenth century's distinction of nature from history, the *ad extra* agency of God was located exclusively in the historical—*Heilsgeschichte*. This left nature wholly within the ambit of natural science, with the result that "our belief in creation as a divine gift is largely 'notional' in character."[73] These tendencies led to not only a devaluation and so a forgetting of the doctrine of creation among Christians but also a misremembering of creation's irreducible significance in the Christian theological imagination.

But the theological question at the heart of so much medieval philosophical speculation remains: Why is there something rather than nothing? Any adequate answer must square itself soberly to the "arresting note" entailed in that question, that of "absolute beginning."[74] But how can or ought one think of an absolute beginning? In medieval philosophy, two strategies predominated. There was a broadly Neoplatonist impulse that imagined creation as an eternal emanation from the One, existing dependently, but also existing necessarily according to the logical determinations of the One's own nature. Others saw the emanation scheme as incompatible with divine freedom and insisted on a conception of creation that viewed it as the temporal effect of a divine act, something that has a determinate beginning in time. Moses Maimonides championed this latter view, arguing that it seemed to be the plain meaning of the biblical creation narratives, though he was quick to qualify that if Aristotle had succeeded in giving a philosophical demonstration of the eternity of the world, such a cosmology could nevertheless be integrated with the metaphysical implications of divine freedom suggested by the biblical text. But since this demonstration did not exist and was not forthcoming, Maimonides insisted on the plain sense of the *bereshith bara elohim*.[75] With these words, the Priestly author provides scriptural scaffolding for the doctrine of *creatio ex nihilo*, an interpretation that directly informs Robert Sokolowski's notion that part of the positive content of the term "creation" is the understanding that the world possesses no formal necessity and therefore might possibly not have existed at all.[76]

For Maimonides (and for Aquinas), the freedom entailed in the doctrine of creation demands creative intention behind the existence of the world that goes a step beyond the assertion of the world's relation of dependence upon God. His criticisms of the emanation scheme coalesce on this principle. For while emanations from the One have a relation of dependence upon the One, their existence is the effect not of an intention but of the nature of the One. The emanations exist insofar as the One exists. But they require no "let there be." As Burrell summarizes,

> Creation means the free origination of all from the one God, who gains nothing thereby. Moreover, what the notion of *free* primarily concerns is the lack of any constraint, even a *natural* constraint; so it need not involve *choice*, as it spontaneously tends to for us, except quite secondarily. That creating fills no need in God and so is an utterly spontaneous and gratuitous act: that is the cumulative message of the scriptures appropriated by Maimonides and Aquinas.[77]

The spontaneity and gratuity of divine action in causing the existence of what is not divine to be rules out the spatial, picture-thinking that commonsense notions of transcendence invite. But in order not to be reduced to silence, a strategy or method of predication is required, one carefully purged of contrastive or competitive images. As we will see, the theorem of the supernatural itself can be reassigned precisely to this purpose. But first, we must examine the way in which the notion of transcendence not only arises from and informs a theology of creation but emerges in a special way in the theology of incarnation. For while the distinction between exegesis and doctrinal formulation considerably lowers the existential stakes concerning the "literal" meaning of Genesis 1:1–2, it is important to recognize how that text itself is significantly reimagined in light of the Christian affirmation that Jesus of Nazareth is God incarnate.

## Incarnation and Transcendence

Robert Sokolowski notes that "[T]he Christian notion of God as creator was most completely disclosed in the life of Jesus and in the church's understanding of who and what Christ was."[78] The process by which this understanding developed is, of course, a point of perennial debate among New Testament exegetes and scholars of early Christianity. But it is also a process that can be traced in distinct registers. One can follow the development of a theoretical account of the ontological and psychological constitution of Christ from Nicaea to Chalcedon and focus on the ways philosophical terms are repurposed and redefined in order to lend explanatory precision to scriptural, creedal, and homiletical teaching. But one can also trace development within that teaching itself. The experience of the collapse of the nation, the destruction of the temple, and the corruption of the priesthood motivated the reinterpretation of Torah in accord with distinct ideological strategies of exilic and second temple theologies, each with its own etiological explanation of creation and evil.[79] In analogous fashion, the historical experience of Jesus of Nazareth—his teaching, his death, and the testimony of his resurrection—led early Christians to reinterpret the Torah in its light. The prologue to the Gospel of John offers perhaps the most obvious example. Structurally parallel to Genesis 1:1–2, the Johannine author locates "the beginning" with the Word, the one who both is and is with God, the one through whom all things were made and apart from whom nothing was made, and the one who became flesh and dwelt among us. And while this reinterpretation of Genesis is presented progressively from eternity to history, its theology is developed analytically from the historical experience of Christ and the incarnation to the transcendent eternality of the Word and God's free creative act through the Word that results not only in all that is but also, significantly, in *nothing* else.

Sokolowski argues accordingly that "the Christian distinction between God and the world, the denial that God in his divinity is part of or dependent upon the world, was brought forward with greater clarity through the discussion of the way the Word became flesh."[80] Incarnation, for Sokolowski, is the privileged theological disclosure of the meaning of divine transcendence, for it is by God becoming what is not God that the theologian is invited to consider what transcendence would mean if the metaphor of spatial distance were ruled out by definition. And given the affirmation of the incarnation of the Word of God in Jesus Christ, what becomes clear in a developed Christology is that "clarifying the 'ontological constitution' of Jesus will help us to articulate that ever-mysterious relationship of creator to creation."[81] Because of incarnation and redemption, the distinction between God and the world "becomes more fully visible to us."[82]

But if the doctrine of the incarnation gives new and expanded significance to the doctrine of creation, it remains that "the new significance is always reciprocal."[83] Not only does each doctrine recast the meaning of the other, but apart from such a hermeneutics of reciprocity, "each will be misunderstood."[84] As Burrell puts it, "One cannot speak of redemption without presuming creation, nor can one speak properly of creation without the idiom supplied by revelation. Indeed, the operative faith of Christians has always presumed this inner connection; the task of theologians is at best not to betray it."[85] Thus, the theorem of the supernatural, an articulation of "the distinction" opaquely traced in creation and fully disclosed in the incarnation, both clarifies the noncontrastive relation of transcendence between God and the world and organizes the intellectual procedures in which the *nexus mysteriorum* can be thought. As we will see, there is a double significance to this organization. The theorem establishes two domains of reference from which analogical terms for speculative understanding of the *nexus mysteriorum* can be drawn. It also functions dialectically to regulate the results of speculative endeavors by coordinating the complementary and diagnosing the contradictory. And in so doing, the generalized theorem of the supernatural has an even more generalized significance: it is the basic dialectical element of speculative pluralism.

## DIALECTICAL APPLICATION AND THE THEOLOGY OF THEOLOGIES

### The Theorematic as Methodical

The foregoing considerations of Lonergan's historical reconstruction of the theorem of the supernatural and its generalization to the notion of transcendence have not been undertaken for their own sake. The ulterior motive throughout has been to assemble from these interrogations the basic elements required for a repurposing of the theorem of the supernatural to the modern speculative question of the theology of theologies. With the historical and metaphysical elements in place, this motive can now be made explicit. The theorem of the supernatural, as we have seen, denotes, in both its historical and generalized metaphysical registers, an entitative disproportion between the natural and supernatural orders. This disproportion is neither spatial nor temporal and so cannot be expressed in terms like "beyond," "outside," "before," or "prior." No, the disproportion pertains to the act of existence itself and to whether that act is consequent to any particular essence, dependent upon a prior act, or is identical with essence itself. God is that unity of identity between essence and existence, that one who *is* by virtue of himself—not as self-caused, but rather as uncaused—whose name is "I AM that I AM." Regardless of how we refer to it—"the world," "creation," "the natural order," "the universe of proportionate being"—that which is not God is a structure of entitative relation between whose essence and existence there is a real distinction, and thus whose *esse* depends upon a causally prior, unrestricted act of existence. Simply put, "nature" is whatever exists that cannot truthfully be called the reason for its own existence. God, on the other hand, is not only his own existence but also the reason for the existence of anything that exists which is not God.

But this metaphysical articulation of the theorem of the supernatural has a further methodical function that Lonergan's historical reconstruction helps to bring into focus. Because the entitative disproportion is an intelligible relation and not some already-out-there-now real, its significance lies in thought, in the ordering of thinking, and in the coordination of that which is the subject of thought. The theorem of the supernatural clarifies the formally disproportionate from the formally proportionate and organizes possible terms of inquiry into distinct theorematic domains. These domains are not ontological buckets or regions on a map. They are lines of reference within thinking itself. Thus, those terms which are formally disproportionate to created natures and are knowable solely on the basis of divine revelation are distinguished intellectually from those terms that belong to the line of reference termed nature.

Much of what is known on the basis of revelation, it must be said, does not belong to the realm of technical, metaphysical language. Despite the utility the analogy of habit provided to the articulations of the theological virtues or the notion of consubstantiality to the unity of *ad extra* operations, it remains that many, even most of the contents of Christian belief lack a metaphysical explanation, let alone an explanation that has moved from a speculative hypothesis to a church doctrine. As Robert Doran notes, "The element of mystery extends beyond what has been or perhaps ever will be formulated in explicit dogmatic pronouncements. Systematic theological understanding must find a way to include these elements."[86] But if the theorem of the supernatural clarifies the domain of thinking in which disproportionate terms of intelligible relations are given as revelations of divine meaning in history, then the historical *ordo* of salvation becomes not only a question for speculative theology (there is as yet no term that stands to the *pro nobis* as the *homoousion* stands to inseparable operations) but also a source of meaning, perhaps even a source of analogies, which might be brought to bear upon other speculative questions.

But if such a theorematic domain were to be a lively, fruitful source of analogical mediation, then the theologian must contend with the fact that

> the affirmed truth of the redemption, the doctrine of redemption, lies rather in the domain of permanently elemental meaning. That is to say, it is possible that its meaning will always be better expressed in the symbolic, aesthetic, and/or dramatic terms of scripture, literature, and drama, and be lived forward from the narrative, than it will be formulated in the quasi-technical type of formulation that most dogmas provide.[87]

If these symbols are to be analogical structures, then there must be "some kind of explanatory employment of symbols themselves through a further immersion into the symbols that enables one *to grasp in their relations to one another first the symbolic meanings, and through those meanings the elements of the drama that are affirmed precisely by employing these symbols.*"[88] Such immersion in the symbolic is not without risk. To speculate at all, however, is always risky.

Part of the difficulty in admitting of explanatory methods of symbolization in speculative theology is the fact that speculation's hard-won and well-worn path to progress in theological understanding has been charted through metaphysical, technical, and "natural" analogies. And certainly one should not wager those gains lightly. Yet, we can—and indeed should—ask with Doran, "Must all systematic theological construction eventually take a metaphysical turn?" If we answer in the negative, there is a consequent question, "Where are the analogies to be found through whose help the mysteries of faith are understood?"[89] While Doran poses this question with an eye toward an aesthetic-dramatic modality of speculative analysis to be deployed in the examination of the *pro nobis*, one can equally ask whether an aesthetic-dramatic modality of speculative analysis might employ the terms of the *pro nobis* in the speculative examination and explanation of the *in se*. And it is precisely this kind of speculative directionality that is opened up when the theorem of the supernatural is allowed to both clarify its domains of inquiry and elucidate the relations between them.

Doran points to a little-noticed passage in the epilogue of Lonergan's *Insight* that is instructive. "[T]he theologian," writes Lonergan, "is under no necessity of reducing to the metaphysical elements, which suffice for an account of this world, such supernatural realities as the Incarnation, the indwelling of the Holy Spirit, and the beatific vision."[90] Consequently, "there is nothing to prevent the analogies that would enable a properly theological understanding of at least some of these mysteries of faith from being aesthetic and dramatic analogies."[91] The contention offered here is that the "nothing to prevent" is an effect of a properly generalized and methodically applied theorem of the supernatural. For not only does the theorem classify, organize, and correlate terms of inquiry into distinct theorematic domains, it also invites speculative interrogations to make use of those terms and (as we will see) also provides the regulative, dialectical means of controlling the fruits of their analogical deployment (be they sweet or sour). For Doran, the possibility of an aesthetic-dramatic method of analogical predication must wrestle with a fundamental question, *"Whence the analogies that will render such technical discourse possible?"*[92] A generalized, repurposed theorem of the supernatural offers the beginnings of an answer: a theorematically controlled deployment of the symbols of revelation themselves.

## Nature and Supernature as Theorematic Domains

The question of analogical predication is a famously vexed one, ostensibly pitting Thomas Aquinas against both later scholastics and his own interpreters. As Burrell wryly notes, "Aquinas is perhaps best known for his theory of analogy. On closer inspection, it turns out he never had one."[93] The traditional "Thomist" theory of analogy is actually that of Cajetan, who proposed a doctrine of formal analysis of "proper proportionality" wherein the relation of A to B is identical to that of C to D.[94] But if there is an entitative disproportion between the relations of terms, then there can be no straightforward predication in the manner of formal analysis. And so, for Aquinas, a full-blown theory of analogical relations will not be of much use in speculative theology. Burrell even suggests that "'dialectical' offers a useful rendering of 'analogous,' as Aquinas himself employs analogous discourse."[95] A theological analogy, then, is not a relationship of proper proportionality. Burrell writes,

> Indeed for Aquinas [analogy] seems to refer to any manner of establishing a notion too pervasive to be defined or too fundamental or exalted to be known through experience. More often than not, this is accomplished via examples designed to point up enough relevant aspects of these notions to use them responsibly. The word coined for this technique was *manuductio*.[96]

An analogical term is thus more than a mere similitude or *vestigium* but less than a formal proportion.

If analogical predication cannot be a strictly controlled procedure of formal analysis, then analogical understanding will prove difficult without examples. These examples function as phantasms for the intellectual grasp of the intelligibility of analogical predication, like the images Socrates sketched in the sand for the benefit of Meno's servant. And yet, if the theorem of the supernatural has the expanded significance that has been claimed for it in this chapter, one must clarify the domains of analogical reference at work in a given theological discourse and examine the relationship that obtains between those domains of reference. Insofar as the theorem of the supernatural clarifies the properly theological domain of terms from the line of reference termed nature, it becomes the controlling theorematic term for two domains of intellectual reference: one delimited by the proportionality of a term to human understanding, and another formally disproportionate to understanding and yet revealed to it through the absolutely supernatural self-communication of God in history.

T understand how the *pro nobis* can be a source of analogical terms for the , it is worth repeating once again the basic insight of the theorem of the supernatural and the consequences that follow from it. "The theorem of the supernatural," writes Doran, "names what it is that makes a question and a discussion distinctly theological. It gave theology access to what Lonergan would later call its special categories, those categories that are proper to theology."[97] This access is what allowed Thomas Aquinas to locate human freedom in human nature and merit in the elevated life of grace, thereby eliminating the mistaken view that because freedom is difficult to understand, it must be a divine mystery, and that merit, because it accrues on the basis of acts, must owe to some native capacity of human willingness and operation. As a consequence of correlating terms with their entitative orders, the theorem also "freed human speculation to investigate what is not supernatural, what belongs to the domain of 'nature'—to investigate it in its own right, and to relate it to the realities that could be included under the rubrics of the supernatural."[98] Because speculative method requires analogs as intellectual pivots between any series of affirmed mysteries and the nexus of relations that must be grasped to understand their affirmation, such a method, when informed by the theorem of the supernatural, looks to *both* the natural and the supernatural orders for such analogs and the theorematic domains that organize them. The natural order that is clarified by the theorem of the supernatural and that corresponds to its general form makes available to speculative theology the analogs whose basic intelligibility is knowable by reason *per se* and whose analogical intelligibility is capable of occasioning an imperfect but highly fruitful understanding of the *nexus mysteriorum*. The supernatural order, whose terms are knowable solely on the basis of divine revelation, also serves as a theorematic domain for speculative analogies inasmuch as the formal intelligibility of the analogical term is *de facto* revealed in the *ordo* of salvation history.

Since the theorem of the supernatural, in both its general and specific forms, regards one and the same structural insight into entitative disproportion, and because grace is not contrary to nature, one should anticipate a complementarity between speculative theological products effected through the mediation of analogs from both orders of terms. This position has numerous consequences for contemporary and future speculative theologies. Much of the contemporary disdain for the psychological analogy for the Trinitarian processions, for example, is motivated by a sense that this classical achievement of speculative theology is severed from the revelatory sources that compel Trinitarian belief in the first place—namely, the incarnation, crucifixion, and resurrection of Jesus of Nazareth. As Anne Hunt notes,

> In our prayer, *lex orandi*, the cross and the Trinity are in this very concrete way intimately and inextricably connected and yet, when we turn to the study of classical expressions of trinitarian theology, the *credenda*, as expressed in the Augustinian-Thomistic synthesis at the apogee of Latin trinitarian theology, we find no direct or explicit connection at all between the Trinity and the Easter events of Jesus' death and resurrection, even though it was through precisely those events that Jesus' disciples came to proclaim that Jesus is Lord and that God is Father, Son, and Holy Spirit.[99]

One can, and should, take umbrage with many of the modern characterizations of the Augustinian-Thomist tradition of Trinitarian reflection.[100] However, such rebuttals should not obscure a fundamental insight in the critique. Hunt writes, "The *redemptive* significance of Jesus' death and resurrection was clearly recognized, but not its *revelatory* significance."[101] From within the bounds of speculative method, one might say that the analogs for the Trinitarian processions favored, developed, and advanced by Augustine, Aquinas, and Lonergan had their central intelligibility in the line of reference termed nature. The fruits of such speculation could be deployed in an effort to further explore the meaning of Christ's life, death, and resurrection, but those events themselves are not generally used *as the analogical means* for understanding the immanent constitution of divine life itself. And yet, if one follows the path marked out by the theorem of the supernatural, one can say that there need not be a competitive relationship between natural and supernatural analogies for the Trinity any more than there needs to be a competitive relationship between charity and *amor*.

The Augustinian-Thomist analogy for the processions (which the next chapter will explore in detail) belongs properly to the theorematic domain that is the line of reference termed nature. Other analogies, however, are on offer. As the life of Christ in all its historical specificity discloses or reveals the supernatural order, so too can it be a source of analogies for understanding further that which is revealed but not fully understood, including the divine processions themselves.

The Trinitarian theology of Hans Urs von Balthasar exemplifies this latter strategy. It looks to the theorematic domain that the theorem of the supernatural clarifies as the properly theological domain for revealed analogs that can further illuminate what has been revealed. Whether a particular analog is drawn from the natural or the supernatural theorematic domain, the same theorem of entitative disproportion regards the intelligibility of any speculative result. Thus, if a speculative theology confuses, violates, or undoes the entitative disproportion that makes analogical understanding analogous, it should be regarded as the negative pole of a dialectic of contradictories and set aside on the basis of the theorem of the supernatural's regulative function.

## The Regulative Function of the Theorematic

According to Lonergan, dialectic "deals with conflicts."[102] In theology, these conflicts "may regard contrary orientations of research, contrary interpretations, contrary histories, contrary styles of evaluation, contrary horizons, contrary doctrines, contrary systems, contrary policies."[103] Speculative pluralism is, in a rather narrow sense, an attempt to come to terms with the diachronic and synchronic facts of contrary systems of speculative thought in the Christian religion. It takes as its point of departure the notion that theology is the mediator between a religion and its significance and role in a culture and that there are as many cultures as there are sets of meanings and values incarnated in the shared lives of people. Such plurality rules out any singular theological mediation and places organic limits on the time any particular mediation is capable of doing its work. But rather than considering material transmission of the past in research, interpretation, and history; the conflictual horizons of foundations; or fundamental doctrinal disagreements about what has truly been revealed by God, speculative pluralism deals with conflicts in contrary systems, in contrary patterns of intellectual labor in pursuit of the coherence of faith.

The efforts of this chapter to retrieve and generalize the theorem of the supernatural have had as their main goal to equip the dialectical element of speculative pluralism with a theorematic tool for its work of addressing the genetic, complementary, contrary, and contradictory relationships between and among speculative understandings. The repurposed theorem of the supernatural clarifies the intellectual lines of reference or theorematic domains in which speculative, analogical structures are born. It coordinates the relationships obtaining between structures that arise from distinct domains, and it dialectically discerns the resulting plurality of speculative understandings, be it genetic, complementary, contrary, or contradictory. The theorem of the supernatural thus exercises a regulative function in theological science.

As Kathryn Tanner notes, "A rich diversity in theological forms of Christian self-expression has always existed; orthodoxy in the sense of limits to acceptable Christian statement has never demanded uniformity."[104] The fact of such diversity is no guarantee of coherence. To the contrary, incoherence is to be expected. For Tanner, "the coherence of Christian theology hinges on principles that regulate the construction of theological statements *whatever* the particular vocabulary or conceptuality or metaphysical substrate of beliefs about human beings and the world."[105]

Two such principles predominate in Tanner's account: "God transcends the world; God is directly involved with the world as its creator."[106] These two principles are maintained through the observance of two rules that help form a deep grammar for coherent Christian speech. First, the theologian must "avoid both simple univocal attribution of predicates to God and the world and a simple contrast of divine and non-divine predicates."[107] Second, she must also "avoid in talk about God's creative agency all suggestions of limitation in scope or manner. The second rule prescribes talk of God's creative agency as immediate and universally extensive."[108] These rules proscribe contrastive or competitive modes of predication and make possible the counterintuitive but theologically compulsory assertion that "God's transcendence alone is one that may be properly exercised in the radical immanence by which God is said to be nearer to us than we are to ourselves."[109]

Despite the uniformity that a focus on "rules" would suggest, Tanner argues that "major divergent theological strands within the Christian tradition will be considered as functional complements in virtue of such differences of emphasis in their utilization of the same basic rules for coherent Christian discourse."[110] These rules constitute "a force for theological diversity" both across epochs and within them "because they have two sides."[111] The positive side of this grammar broadly corresponds to the theorem of the supernatural's clarification of the line of reference termed nature. Because God's creative act establishes a relation rather than occasions an event, its application is universal, and thus capable of a methodical bracketing in the investigation of created causes and their effects. Such investigations yield knowledge of natural structures, which, in turn, become the reserve of analogs for speculative theologies that turn to the natural theorematic domain for analogical pivots to understanding. But Tanner also notes a negative side to her rules, which stress the radical, universal dependence of all created things upon God, and so highlight the divine goodness, mercy, and initiative in both creation and redemption. This negative side corresponds to the theorem of the supernatural's clarification of the properly theological, of the mystery of God made known through the communication of the divine nature in history. Tanner writes, "Some theologians emphasize the negative side, some the positive, depending upon the intellectual climate, their method of exposition, the theological topics of special importance to them, and their practical agendas."[112]

This unity-in-diversity is characteristic of genetic, complementary, and even contrary varieties of speculative pluralism. But theology is not immune from conflicts of a deeper sort, conflicts born not of ignorance of relevant data or "the complexity of historical reality" but rather of "an explicit or implicit cognitional theory, and ethical stance, a religious outlook."[113] Such conflicts yield contradictory theologies that cannot be coordinated in an integral pluralism. Taken as a regulative structure, the theorem of the supernatural helps the community of theological inquiry to identify these contradictories and apply the techniques by which the advancement of the positive pole and reversal of the negative becomes more probable. Many such conflicts arise not accidentally but by design. Tanner notes that "modern theologians tend to *form* their statements about God and the world in violation of our rules."[114] They do not find themselves innocently or unwittingly in violation of the regulative grammar. They style themselves rather as outlaws. Tanner offers many examples, including Gabriel Biel's exaggerated account of autonomous human agency and the *de auxiliis* debate about divine and human freedom. To these, more could be adduced. What unites these examples is their inability to hold divine transcendence and the universal immediacy of creative relation together in a coherent whole. Put another way, they fail to maintain the theorematic perspective that grasps the entitative disproportion between lines of reference and the nonreciprocal relation of dependence obtaining between them. The result is either contrastive, zero-sum relations or some franchise of monism.

A theorematic perspective has a further benefit. Beyond bringing to light the conflicts imbedded in contradictory forms of speculative pluralism and providing the basic technique for reversing the negative pole, it also brings with it the bedrock principle of speculative theology, that because such theology is in the order of understanding while doctrine is in the order of existence, speculative failure is not the same as heresy. This principle considerably lowers the stakes concerning the speculative task. To risk speculation need not mean risking salvation. A theorematic and dialectical approach to speculative pluralism can help identify dead ends, promote integral, constructive plurality, and keep always in view the finite, imperfect, fruitful, and ultimately temporary nature of the speculative task.

## CONCLUSION

This chapter has attempted to articulate a starting point in the open-ended frame of speculative pluralism. Toward that end, it has charted a path through Lonergan's historical reconstruction of the theorem of the supernatural within the context of the theologies of grace and freedom. It has labored to generalize the theorem out of its specific context regarding the debates around those specific historical theologies and into the notion of transcendence itself. Finally, it has tried to show that such a generalized notion of transcendence can function as a dialectical theorem for speculative pluralism by opening up distinct lines of intellectual reference, populated by distinct nexuses of terms, some of which are capable of bearing the weight of analogical disclosure in the speculative task. Beyond clarifying these domains of reference, the generalized theorem of the supernatural can take on a regulative function of directing the flow of speculative thinking, identifying the places in which the regulative structure has been violated with contradictory results, and providing the techniques by which the positive pole of the dialectic can be advanced and the negative pole reversed. The final chapter will attempt to show how these methodical clarifications can function in at least one speculative locus: the theology of the divine processions. It will demonstrate how the repurposed theorem of the supernatural can aid in the generation of distinct theologies of the processions, how those theologies can develop in both orders of analogs, and ultimately, how the resulting plurality, contrary to all appearances, can evince an authentic unity-in-diversity in the mission of theological understanding.

## NOTES

1. See Lonergan, "Doctrinal Pluralism," CWL 17, 77–81, 86–88.
2. Lonergan, *Grace and Freedom*, CWL 1, 4.
3. Lonergan writes, for instance, of Anselm that "the brilliance of his work is a monument to his genius; its almost complete unsatisfactoriness is an illuminating instance of the difficulty there was in evolving the method and technique of theological speculation." See Lonergan, *Grace and Freedom*, CWL 1, 8.
4. Lonergan, *Grace and Freedom*, CWL 1, 17.
5. This is the systematic thesis of Eric Mabry's historical reconstruction and interpretation of Thomas Aquinas's existential Christology. See Mabry, "*Inquantum est Temporaliter Homo factum*: Background, Reception, Meaning, and Relevance of the Hypothesis of *esse secundarium* in the Christology of Thomas Aquinas," PhD dissertation, University of St. Michael's College, 2018.
6. As Lonergan summarizes the matter, "The division of grace into operative and cooperative arose not from a detached love of systematization but to meet the exigencies of a controversy." See Lonergan, *Grace and Freedom*, CWL 1, 4.
7. Lonergan, *Grace and Freedom*, CWL 1, 4.
8. Lonergan, *Grace and Freedom*, CWL 1, 5.
9. Lonergan, *Grace and Freedom*, CWL 1, 5.
10. Lonergan, *Grace and Freedom*, CWL 1, 6.
11. Lonergan, *Grace and Freedom*, CWL 1, 7.
12. See Stebbins, *The Divine Initiative*, 67.
13. Lonergan, *Grace and Freedom*, CWL 1, 7.
14. Lonergan, *Grace and Freedom*, CWL 1, 6.

15. Stebbins, *The Divine Initiative*, 70.
16. Lonergan, *Grace and Freedom*, CWL 1, 8.
17. Lonergan, *Grace and Freedom*, CWL 1, 8.
18. Lonergan, *Grace and Freedom*, CWL 1, 8.
19. Lonergan, *Grace and Freedom*, CWL 1, 10.
20. Lonergan, *Grace and Freedom*, CWL 1, 10.
21. Lonergan, *Grace and Freedom*, CWL 1, 10.
22. Lonergan, *Grace and Freedom*, CWL 1, 10.
23. Critics of Vatican I's teaching often fail to grasp the difference between order of thinking and the order of being. They imagine the Council fathers are describing a "t tiered" universe of hermetically sealed domains of truth and so a view of "nat. is self-justifying and self-sufficient.
24. Lonergan, *Grace and Freedom*, CWL 1, 10.
25. Lonergan, *Grace and Freedom*, CWL 1, 10.
26. Stebbins, *The Divine Initiative*, 68.
27. Lonergan, *Grace and Freedom*, CWL 1, 11.
28. Lonergan, *Grace and Freedom*, CWL 1, 11.
29. Lonergan, *Grace and Freedom*, CWL 1, 11.
30. Lonergan, *Grace and Freedom*, CWL 1, 11.
31. Lonergan, *Grace and Freedom*, CWL 1, 11.
32. Lonergan, *Grace and Freedom*, CWL 1, 11.
33. Lonergan, *Grace and Freedom*, CWL 1, 12.
34. Lonergan, *Grace and Freedom*, CWL 1, 12.
35. Lonergan, *Grace and Freedom*, CWL 1, 12.
36. Lonergan, *Grace and Freedom*, CWL 1, 12.
37. Lonergan, *Grace and Freedom*, CWL 1, 13.
38. Lonergan, *Grace and Freedom*, CWL 1, 15.
39. Lonergan, *Grace and Freedom*, CWL 1, 15.
40. Stebbins, *The Divine Initiative*, 79–80.
41. Stebbins, *The Divine Initiative*, 79.
42. Stebbins, *The Divine Initiative*, 79.
43. Lonergan, *Grace and Freedom*, CWL 1, 17.
44. Stebbins, *The Divine Initiative*, 81.
45. Stebbins, *The Divine Initiative*, 81.
46. Stebbins, *The Divine Initiative*, 68.
47. Stebbins, *The Divine Initiative*, 68.
48. Lonergan, *Grace and Freedom*, CWL 1, 17.
49. Lonergan, *Grace and Freedom*, CWL 1, 17.
50. Lonergan, *Grace and Freedom*, CWL 1, 17.
51. Lonergan, "Mission and the Spirit," in *A Third Collection*, ed. Robert M. Doran and John D. Dadosky, CWL 16 (Toronto: University of Toronto Press, 2017), 25.
52. On "the distinction," see Robert Sokolowski, *The God of Faith and Reason: Foundations of Christian Theology*, repr. ed. (Washington, DC: Catholic University of America Press, 1995).
53. Gilson, *Being and Some Philosophers*, 74.

54. Gilson, *Being and Some Philosophers*, 74–75.
55. Gilson, *Being and Some Philosophers*, 76.
56. Gilson, *Being and Some Philosophers*, 80 (emphasis original).
57. Gilson, *Being and Some Philosophers*, 81.
58. Burrell, *Knowing the Unknowable God: Ibn-Sina, Maimonides, Aquinas* (Notre Dame: University of Notre Dame Press, 1986), 26 (emphasis original).
59. Burrell, *Knowing the Unknowable God*, 26.
60. Avicenna, *Shifa* I.5; Anawati trans., 108. Cited in David Burrell, *Knowing the Unknowable God*, 19.
61. Burrell, *Knowing the Unknowable God*, 21.
62. Burrell, *Knowing the Unknowable God*, 20: "To respect the reality proper to creator and creature alike, as well as to try to articulate the relation between them, i.e., creation, one needs a distinction which makes its appearance within the world as we know it yet does not express a division *within* that world."
63. Burrell, *Knowing the Unknowable God*, 29.
64. Burrell, *Knowing the Unknowable God*, 30.
65. Burrell, *Knowing the Unknowable God*, 30.
66. Burrell, *Knowing the Unknowable God*, 30 (citing Thomas Aquinas, *Q. D. De anima*, 1.3.4).
67. Sara Grant, *Toward an Alternative Theology: Confessions of a Non-Dualist Christian* (Notre Dame, IN: University of Notre Dame Press, 2002).
68. Burrell, *Freedom and Creation in Three Traditions* (Notre Dame: University of Notre Dame Press, 1993), 7.
69. Josef Pieper, *The Silence of St. Thomas*, trans. John Murray and Daniel O'Connor (New York: Pantheon, 1957), 47.
70. Burrell, *Freedom and Creation*, 3.
71. Burrell, *Faith and Freedom*, 235.
72. Burrell, *Faith and Freedom*, 235.
73. Burrell, *Faith and Freedom*, 235.
74. Burrell, *Freedom and Creation*, 7.
75. Burrell, *Freedom and Creation*, 8–9.
76. Sokolowski, *The God of Faith and Reason*, 23.
77. Burrell, *Freedom and Creation*, 8.
78. Sokolowski, *The God of Faith and Reason*, xi–xii.
79. Different approaches to the ideological diversity of the Second Temple period yield different understandings of the specific etiologies evinced by Genesis. Gabriele Boccaccini offers a heuristic typology that divides the intellectual climate of the Second Temple into Enochic, Sapiential, and Zadokite strands of theology, each with its own exclusive understanding of true Torah, true priesthood, sacred geography, and the etiology of evil. The Priestly author's creation account falls within the Zadokite ideology insofar as Genesis 3's explanation of evil assigns its origin to human rebellion. Yet, Genesis 6 retains some elements of the Enochic etiology that designates angelic rebellion and the impartation of forbidden knowledge to human beings as the origin of evil. Levenson's interpretation moves the Genesis account out of the Zadokite worldview. It presents a different etiology altogether, a *tehomic* etiology that pictures evil

as the chaos always threatening to break forth. For the development of the major ideologies, see Gabriele Boccaccini, *Roots of Rabbinic Judaism: An Intellectual History from Ezekiel to Daniel* (Grand Rapids: Eerdmans, 2002). In addition to the Adamic and Enochic etiologies (and hybrids of them in, for instance, *The Life of Adam and Eve*), Hermann Gunkle's 1895 work, *Schöpfung und Chaos*, highlights the importance of God's ongoing battle with various chaos monsters as a major theme from Genesis all the way to Revelation. Building on Gunkle's work, subsequent scholars recognize a chaos/Leviathan etiology distinct from the Adamic and Enoch strands. All this suggests that Genesis itself contains multiple etiologies, and so cannot be totally subsumed within a single revisionary paradigm. See Gunkle, *Creation and Chaos in the Primary Era and the Eschaton: A Religio-Historical Study of Genesis 1 and Revelation 12*, trans. K. William Whitney (Grand Rapids: Eerdmans, 2006). Yet, Levenson argues that the process of priestly redaction demythologized the chaos monster, and such demythologization is evident in the text of Genesis 1 (save the reference to the "great sea monsters" in 1:21), and represents a step of development toward the *ex nihilo* doctrine beyond even that of Psalm 104, which depicts Leviathan as a creature created for YHWH's amusement rather than as a preexistent oppositional foe. See Jon Levenson, *Creation and the Persistence of Evil: The Jewish Drama of Divine Omnipotence* (Princeton, NJ: Princeton University Press, 1994). This developmental move away from chaotic preexistence, toward human rebellion as the *ratio* of sin and evil comports with the Zadokite ideology that Boccaccini describes.

80. Sokolowski, *The God of Faith and Reason*, 37.
81. Burrell, *Faith and Freedom*, 236.
82. Sokolowski, *The God of Faith and Reason*, 40.
83. Burrell, *Faith and Freedom*, 235.
84. Burrell, *Faith and Freedom*, 236.
85. Burrell, *Faith and Freedom*, 240.
86. Doran, *What Is Systematic Theology?*, 23.
87. Doran, *What Is Systematic Theology?*, 22.
88. Doran, *What Is Systematic Theology?*, 24 (emphasis original).
89. Doran, *What Is Systematic Theology?*, 24.
90. Lonergan, *Insight*, CWL 3, 756. Cited in Doran, *What Is Systematic Theology?*, 25.
91. Doran, *What Is Systematic Theology?*, 25.
92. Doran, *What Is Systematic Theology?*, 26 (emphasis original).
93. Burrell, *Aquinas, God and Action*, 3rd ed., ed. Mary Budde Ragan (Eugene, OR: Wipf & Stock, 2016), 62.
94. There is voluminous literature on Aquinas's theory of analogy and its relationship to Cajetan's interpretation. For a helpful overview, see the John R. Betz's Translator's Introduction to Erich Przywara, *Analogia Entis: Original Structure and Universal Rhythm*, trans. John R. Betz and David Bentley Hart (Grand Rapids, MI: Eerdmans, 2014), 37–46.
95. Burrell, *Aquinas, God and Action*, 64.
96. Burrell, *Analogy and Philosophical Language*, repr. ed. (Eugene, OR: Wipf & Stock, 1973), 122.

97. Doran, *What Is Systematic Theology?*, 83.
98. Doran, *What Is Systematic Theology?*, 83.
99. Anne Hunt, *The Trinity and the Paschal Mystery: A Development in Recent Catholic Theology*, New Theology Studies 5 (Collegeville: Liturgical Press, 1997), vii–viii.
100. For a helpful rejoinder to various modern critiques, see Neil Ormerod, *The Trinity: Retrieving the Western Tradition* (Milwaukee: Marquette University Press, 2005).
101. Hunt, *The Trinity and the Paschal Mystery*, viii.
102. Lonergan, *Method in Theology*, CWL 14, 220.
103. Lonergan, *Method in Theology*, CWL 14, 220–221.
104. Tanner, *God and Creation in Christian Theology*, 4.
105. Tanner, *God and Creation in Christian Theology*, 7.
106. Tanner, *God and Creation in Christian Theology*, 38.
107. Tanner, *God and Creation in Christian Theology*, 47.
108. Tanner, *God and Creation in Christian Theology*, 47.
109. Tanner, *God and Creation in Christian Theology*, 79.
110. Tanner, *God and Creation in Christian Theology*, 104.
111. Tanner, *God and Creation in Christian Theology*, 105.
112. Tanner, *God and Creation in Christian Theology*, 120.
113. Lonergan, *Method in Theology*, CWL 14, 221.
114. Tanner, *God and Creation in Christian Theology*, 122.

*Chapter 5*

# Speculation, Procession, Collaboration

Early on in *Insight*, Lonergan reminds his readers that the primary concern of his philosophy is not with the contents of knowing but rather with knowing itself. The former are extensive, diverse, specialized, incomplete, and subject to radical revision. Their sheer volume and ongoing production outpace the philosopher's investigations and offer her no hope of catching up. Knowing, however, is invariant. It is dynamic but also structured. It is the activity of knowers, and knowers are the source of all accumulations, revisions, and the questions upon which accumulations and revisions follow. For all its interdisciplinary complexity, *Insight* is an investigation not of disciplines but of inquiry itself. Its objective contents are no more than a series of examples. Examples, however, are important. Knowing cannot be without its content. Knowing is intentional. And intentions intend objects.

This study has so far been concerned with knowing. It has sought to recover and renew the structure of speculative theological operation. And while examples, mainly historical ones, have been adduced along the way, the methodical questions guiding the forgoing have been the following: What am I doing when I speculate? Why do I speculate? How do differences in one's historical-cultural matrix inform speculation? What are the theorematic coordinates of thought by which a plurality of speculations might be dialectically ordered? And while answers have been ventured, it remains that a sustained application of the methodical elements of this work to a speculative *locus* has yet to be attempted. This chapter is such an attempt. Its aim is twofold. First, it shows how the systematic exigence for speculative Trinitarian theology arises from the doctrinal matrix of Christian belief about God *in se* and explores how distinct patterns of analogy can meet the determinations of that exigence. Second, it explains how the repurposed theorem of the supernatural dialectically orders the resulting plurality of speculative theologies. This chapter is thus both an interpretation of two different analogical strategies for a speculative theology of the divine processions and an exploration of the theology of theologies within the determinate context of Trinitarian theory.

A speculative theology of the divine processions has as its first and primary task the elucidation of an analogical conception of the processions that is adequate to the specific doctrinal determinations of simplicity and procession, while also effectuating an intellectual grasp of the intelligibility of those doctrines from within the horizon of meaning of a given age, culture, life, or orientation. This chapter looks at two such theologies, paying special attention to the entitative orders from which analogs are drawn, the methods of speculation deployed, and the dialectical comportment among this plurality of theologies. Given these restrictions, this chapter aims at little more than a "proof concept" for the more substantial methodical proposals offered in the first four chapters, proposals that, I hope, will find a far wider range of application than the modest one attempted here.

In applying the method of speculative pluralism, this chapter looks at two apparently incongruous approaches to the theology of the divine processions and shows how that apparent incongruity resolves into authentic plurality through methodical analysis. It looks first to the often-pilloried tradition of analogical reflection associated with Augustine and Aquinas and evoked by the term "psychological analogy." The chapter examines the genetic structure of the various theologies within this tradition, beginning with the ongoing explorations of Augustine's *De Trinitate*, developing through Aquinas's *Summa* to Lonergan's *De Deo Trino*, before coming to rest in the present with Robert Doran's *Trinity in History*. In tracing the development of this tradition, the chapter explores the entitative order of the analogy of spirit, the genetic plurality that attaches to developments in meaning over time, the centrality of self-appropriation as the term underlying all psychological analogs, and the possibilities for an analogical conception of the divine processions drawn from the divine indwelling and its supernatural elevation of spiritual acts.

Second, the chapter examines the Trinitarian theology of Hans Urs von Balthasar, which emphasizes the divine kenosis as revealed in the incarnation, cross, and resurrection as an analog for the divine processions themselves. In so doing, the chapter examines the respect in which the *mysterium salutis* is an analogical domain controlled by the theorem of the supernatural in the same way as the line of reference termed nature. It explores the immanent and economic functions of kenosis as an analogical linkage between procession and mission. And it draws out the hidden analogy of spirit that unifies the various strands of kenotic analogy.

By showing how the theorem of the supernatural controls the analogical domains of these distinct speculative approaches and the relations obtaining between them, this chapter provides one basic example of how the methodical elements of speculative pluralism can be deployed to promote the integral plurality of theological understandings in the hope that further, more significant examples could be added by others.

## COORDINATING ANALOGICAL LINES OF REFERENCE

### The Systematic Exigence and Theorematic Domains

The basic problem of Trinitarian theology, according to Lonergan, is that, in their respective and distinct ways, the Son and the Spirit both are and are not *a se*.[1] To put the matter in creedal language and in an interrogative form, how can there be, in the "one God" a term that is "begotten" and another that "proceeds"? For Thomas Aquinas, this is the first question in a *systematic* theology of the Trinity—is there procession in God? The aporia that establishes the systematic exigence for speculative understanding lies at the conjunction of divine simplicity and the divine processions. Both elements are matters of binding Catholic faith, but the apparent contradiction of one by the other demands an intellectual intervention of a theoretical sort. The speculative theology of the divine processions is that intervention. It seeks to offer a hypothetical, analogical, imperfect, but fruitful way of understanding how it can be true that divine life is perfectly simple while being constituted by internal processions, relations, and persons.

But finding the analogical means by which to grasp the meaning of procession within simplicity is a major intellectual project, one fraught with traps, tripwires, and dead ends. For Aquinas, the archetypal heresies of the Christian faith have in common (though each in its own way) a notion of procession that, because it is *prima facie* irreconcilable with divine simplicity, involves one form or another of denying true divinity to the Son or the Spirit.[2] Arius, Thomas notes, understands the biblical language of procession to denote the relation an effect has to its cause. Thus, to say that the Son proceeds from the Father is to say that the Son is the effect of the Father's causal act. But whatever is caused is also created. Therefore, the Son proceeds in the mode of a creature, not as *true* God.

Procession can also be understood as the impression of a likeness of the cause to an effect. It is thus, according to Thomas, that Sabellius interprets the language of procession to assert that God is to be called "Son" only insofar as he takes on flesh, and "Spirit" inasmuch as he sanctifies the creature. Both the Arian and Sabellian notions of procession are united around a common conception—namely, that a procession implies a movement from some interior principle to some other external term and is thus an outward act. So long as procession is understood as an outward act, the relationship obtaining between principle and term will always be one of cause to effect, and while true divinity can be predicated of the cause, it cannot be so predicated of the effect without violating the principle of divine simplicity, and, with it, the notion of divinity itself. And for all their errors, neither Arius nor Sabellius had any confusion about divine simplicity and the strictures it places upon what can meaningfully be called "God."

For Lonergan, the problem at the source of the various contestations over the meaning of divinity in early Christianity is one of competing conceptions of the real. "Insofar as Christianity is a reality," writes Lonergan, "it is involved in the problems of realism."[3] He identifies three modalities of this involvement: a remote involvement that concerns problems that "have not yet appeared," a proximate involvement wherein the problems "gradually manifest themselves and meet with implicit solutions," and an explicit involvement that attaches to the vexed question of the possibility of a distinctly Christian philosophy.[4] The remote involvement follows upon Christianity's mediation in the meanings communicated by its preachers, believed by its faithful, and enacted by its saints. But these mediations of Christian meaning do not exhaust the Christian world. Immediacy is also part of the remote involvement. This immediacy is conversion. And conversion is "primarily, not the product of the preacher, not the fruit of one's free choice, but the effect of God's grace."[5] As such, Christian constitutive meaning is affected by "the ambiguity of realism," by the immediacy of the meanings effectuated by grace, meanings which, as experienced, are conscious, but not known—not understood, not verified by reflexive insight, and therefore not affirmed.[6]

While the remote involvement of Christianity in the problem of realism owes to the duality of consciousness and knowledge in the experience of grace, the proximate involvement pertains to the historical, dialectical process of development in Christian understanding. Lonergan notes three historical examples that represent stages in the development of Christian doctrine, and, by extension, stages in the development of the notion of the real. He considers the Stoic materialism of Tertullian, the Platonic idealism of Origen, and the nascent critical realism of Athanasius.

One of the first luminaries of the Latin church, Tertullian engaged in an apologetic dispute with Praxeas concerning the relation between the Father and the Son. For Praxeas, the absolute identity between Father and Son results in a kind of transitive property between what is predicated of the one and the other. Thus, for Praxeas, insofar as it is true to say that the Son was crucified on the cross, it is true to say that the Father was crucified on the cross. Tertullian argues, on the basis of Scripture and early creedal dogmatics, that the Son of God is "both real and really distinct" from the Father.[7] While the thrust of the argument is doctrinal, Lonergan argues that there is a philosophical notion of the real beneath the argument that leads to a decidedly materialist interpretation of the Trinity. Following Zeno and Cicero, Tertullian asserts that the real is the corporeal, that whatever has existence exists as a body. What it means, then, that the Son is real is that the Son has a body or shape. The Son's distinction from the Father is likewise a distinction between corporalities. The Father possesses his Wisdom eternally, but when the Father creates, he utters that eternal Wisdom as his Word, as the Son. The Son as Son, therefore, is not created, but is nevertheless Son only in and through the creative act. The Son is the root's shoot, the spring's stream, the sun's ray.[8] As such, God is three according to sequence, aspect, and manifestation.[9]

Against the notion of the real as the corporeal, Origen argued for "the strict immateriality of both the Father and the Son."[10] For Origen, the real is the ideal, and thus the same idea of eternality and divinity that governs the affirmation of the Father as God governs that of the Son as God. At the same time, however, the distinction of the Father from the Son must, accordingly, be a distinction between ideas. So while Origen has no trouble affirming that the Son is no less eternal than the Father, that divine generation *cannot* be according to the manner of that of animals, that the Son proceeds spiritually by means of the volition of the divine mind, he nevertheless must distinguish the divinity of the Son from that of the Father by means of a doctrine of participation. The Son—as eternal, as divine—participates in the pure idea of divinity that is the Father. The Son as Son is true light, true wisdom, truth itself, life itself, but beyond all these, the Father is still the unthinkable, mysterious source and fullness of each.[11] The Son is the Father's image, "an image in which participation reaches its supreme perfection for it consists in the Son's eternal contemplation of the Father and his constant acceptance of the Father's will."[12]

The issue at the core of the difference between Tertullian and Origen, according to Lonergan, is their respective, diametrically opposed notions of reality. But as neither Tertullian nor Origen managed to articulate an interpretation of the data of faith and reason in a manner that accords entirely with the later, fully-formed pro-Nicene understanding of consubstantiality, it is worth questioning whether either the extroverted materialism that stands behind Tertullian's apologetics or the idealism undergirding Origen's doctrine of perfect participation are sufficient philosophical positions with which to interrogate the relation of the Father and the Son. But if Tertullian's extroversion conceives of divinity on an analogy with the corporeality of the world of immediacy and Origen's strict immateriality of divinity with the world mediated by meaning, it remains that "there is a third possibility,"[13] one "in which one's apprehension of reality is in the world mediated by meaning, where the meanings in question are affirmations and negations, that is, answers to questions for reflection."[14] It is thus that Athanasius put forward his "fundamental little rule" that "all that is said of the Father also is to be said of the Son except that the Son is Son and not the Father."[15]

If reality is known through the affirmation of correct understanding, then the systematic exigence that calls for speculative theory consists in the questions for understanding that follow upon the affirmation of the truth of God as one, of the Son as begotten, and of the Spirit as proceeding. If all are true God, then the relevant aspect of "procession" cannot be the movement from interior principle to external term. It cannot be a relation of cause to effect. It cannot be a matter of spatially distinct corporalities or spiritually distinct ideas. Procession in God, as procession, must be an act. But procession in God, as God, must be an internal, intelligent act that remains within the agent. As Thomas notes, while we should not understand God according to the mode of bodies, we must also recognize that even the likeness between divine procession and intellectual substances "falls short in representation of divine objects."[16]

This matrix of doctrinal determinations concerning simplicity and procession, the entitative disproportion between the finite and the infinite, and the intellectual—even spiritual—demand to understand these doctrines in a way that avoids heretical errors all create the conditions for an analogical conception of the divine processions. And as we have already seen in the previous chapter, there are multiple analogical domains that correspond to the intellectual coordinates of the theorem of the supernatural, and thus there are multiple analogical structures which can be deployed in the development of a theology of the processions. This chapter will look at two such structures, their respective analogical domains, and the possibilities they evince for an integral speculative pluralism.

## Two Analogical Structures

Any adequate theory of procession, if it is to emerge successfully from the critical press of dogmatic formulation, must offer an understanding of how it can be true that procession exists within divinity itself, not merely as divinity's self-communication in creation but as the immanent constitution of divine life. Such a theory requires an analog, known to human understanding either by reason or by revelation, which can serve as the intellectual pivot between the truth affirmed and the truth understood. That pivot must meaningfully signify the intelligibility of a divine procession—an intelligibility beyond the proportion of created intellect—while also, and more fundamentally, signifying some proportionate or revealed human reality. As Thomas notes, "Whatever is said both of God and creatures is said in virtue of the order that creatures have to God as their source and cause in which all the perfections of things pre-exist transcendently."[17]

For Aquinas, once one rules out any meaning of procession in God that involves the movement toward external matter (like that of Arius or

Sabellius), one is left searching for a corresponding mode of procession by which what proceeds from the agent has its term also within the agent. He finds precisely this kind of procession in created intellect itself. He writes, "procession always implies action; and as there is an outward procession corresponding to the act tending to external matter, so there must be an inward procession corresponding to the act remaining within the agent. This applies most conspicuously to the intellect, the action of which remains in the intelligent agent."[18] But what is this intellectual procession? For Aquinas, such a procession is the *emanatio intelligibilis* that is the word of concept that proceeds from the act of understanding. He writes, "For whenever we understand, by the very fact of understanding there proceeds something in us, which is a conception of the thing understood, a conception issuing from our intellectual power and proceeding from our knowledge of that thing."[19] From this natural act-from-act spiritual procession, Thomas concludes, "Procession, therefore, is not to be understood from what it is in bodies. . . . Rather it is to be understood by way of intelligible emanation, for example, of the intelligible word which proceeds from the speaker, yet remains within him. In that sense the Catholic Faith understands procession as existing in God."[20]

The *emanatio intelligibilis* is a natural analog. It belongs among those data whose immanent intelligibility can be known through the application of human reason. And while such knowledge, as we will see, requires philosophic differentiation and self-interrogation, the term in question does not *per se* require the light of faith to be known, even if, *de facto*, religious conversion precedes intellectual conversion in the ordinary course of human living.

But what of revelation? If, in fact, there is a word from God, should not that word make visible to human eyes, if only through a mirror dimly, what is the truth, structure, and being of divine life? What, after all, would a word from God reveal if not God himself? In the wake of Karl Rahner's *Grundaxiom*, many theologians have sought to recover the revelatory elements of the paschal mystery. Perhaps no Catholic theologian looms as large in this arena as Hans Urs von Balthasar. And yet, while many (maybe most) postconciliar theologies have taken Rahner's insight to entail a rejection of all speculation regarding the immanent Trinity, Balthasar's consistent thesis is that if the life of God is revealed in the *mysterium salutis*, then the immanent constitution of divine life is "the ever-present, inner presupposition of the doctrine of the Cross."[21]

The resulting speculative approach argues that the kenosis made manifest on the Cross has its foundation and possibility in an eternal kenosis. Balthasar argues that "the Father's self-utterance in the generation of the Son is an initial 'kenosis' within the Godhead that underpins all subsequent kenosis."[22] The divine kenosis, by definition, is not a natural human reality and therefore not a likely candidate to serve as the analogical base for a theology of the divine processions. Yet, if the *mysterium salutis* is understood in revelatory and not only redemptive terms, one can say that inasmuch as the mystery of salvation is made known to the world through the events of the paschal mystery, God has revealed God's own life to human understanding through those events. If kenosis tells us the structure of the divine missions, then, in Thomistic fashion, it can also tell us of the structure of the divine processions. The kenotic analogy for the processions is, as we have said, a supernatural analogy, one whose prime referent lies within the economy of revelation and hidden in the mystery of God. But as the theorem of the supernatural indicates, the specifically theological, supernatural elements communicated through the economy of revelation, inasmuch as they are understood through the eyes of faith and faith's illumination of reason, can shed further analogical light on the mystery of God in God's self. In what follows, both of these analogical structures will be treated in greater, though by no means comprehensive, detail.

## THE PSYCHOLOGICAL PROCESSION

Any modern exploration of the psychological model of the divine processions must contend with three inconvenient facts: the near complete misunderstanding of the psychological analogy from the late medieval period down to the modern era, the postconciliar rejection of the psychological analogy on the basis of that misunderstanding, and the ongoing influence that rejection still exercises in contemporary Catholic thought. While it is tempting to attack each in turn, it is not the purpose of this section, nor of the chapter as a whole, to provide a comprehensive response. They are already available.[23] Instead, the procedure in what follows is more positive. It aims to replace misunderstanding with understanding by walking the reader down the path illuminated by the psychological analogy. Most of all, it clarifies for the confused what, in fact, the psychological analogy is.

But this section aims at more than an exposition of the psychological model of the divine processions. Its larger goals are to demonstrate how the methodical tools proffered by the theorem of the supernatural inform the conception of the analogical domains from which the psychological analog is drawn, to propose a clarification of that analog, and to show how the basic structure of the psychological analogy can be found in multiple theorematic domains, thereby offering at least one instance of an integral speculative pluralism.

## Nature, Action, and the Analogy of Spirit

In the aftermath of Karl Rahner's influential 1967 essay "Der dreifaltige Gott," an ecumenical cohort of theologians have sought to purchase a postconciliar renewal of Trinitarian theology with a critical currency. The main object of that criticism has been the Augustinian-Thomist tradition. Rahner, for his part, famously observed that most modern Christians are "mere monotheists," for whom the hypothetical falsification of the doctrine of the Trinity would have no measurable practical or spiritual effect.[24] Rahner diagnosed the isolation of the Trinity from Christian living as an illness caused by the doctrine of appropriations, the division between the *De Deo Uno* and *De Deo Trino* schemes of scholastic *summae*, and the "mere hypothesis" of the psychological analogy for the divine processions. So long as these elements of the so-called western tradition endure, the Trinity remains ever behind the veil of methodical abstraction from salvation history, from creation, fall, and redemption, from sin, grace, and glory, and thereby ever at a remove from the lives of the faithful. And so, into the chasm between speculative notions of divine aseity and the drama of salvation, Rahner posited his *Grundaxiom* that the economic Trinity is the immanent Trinity and vice versa.[25]

This claim, at once obvious and opaque, has been at the center of Trinitarian thinking ever sense. Owing in no small part to its inexactness, the axiom has been interpreted in various and contradictory ways, from speculations about divine futurity and self-realizing negativity in the theologies of Moltmann, Jüngel, Pannenberg, and Jenson, to Roger Haight's rejection of all theologies of aseity, to Catherine Mowry LaCugna's positing of a real relation between God and the world, such that God simply is his *pro nobis*.[26] What unites these revisionary proposals—from Rahner's relatively mild criticisms of the concept of person to Moltmann's social trinitarianism—is the shared belief in the illegitimacy of the psychological analogy and the deleterious effects of speculative theologies built upon it.[27]

But the psychological analogy has the distinction of being misunderstood by its champions and detractors alike. The reason is simple. As Lonergan notes of the strange, widespread misunderstanding of Thomas's theology of the divine processions and the psychological analogy that lies at its center, "Its simplicity, its profundity, and its brilliance have long been obscured by interpreters *unaware of the relevant psychological facts* and unequal to the task of handling merely linguistic problems."[28] The key to understanding the significance of the psychological analogy is also the key to understanding the analogy itself; namely, a personal experience, understanding, and affirmation of oneself as intelligent and of one's operations as intelligible. But before those relevant psychological facts can be properly investigated, it is beneficial to clarify the theorematic domain of the psychological or spiritual analogy and to offer a few comments on the notion of action.

As discussed in the previous chapter, for Aquinas, the act of existence rather than essence receives the accent in metaphysical analysis, even while essence remains ever the object of understanding. While this allowed Thomas to overcome Avicenna's problem of a zero-sum relation of essence to existence, and thus of a denial of essence to divinity, it also meant that existence, particularly the *act* of existence would serve as the foundational notion for conceiving of divinity in itself. It is thus that Thomas famously refers to God as *pure act* in question 3 of the *Prima Pars*. But this assertion contains a twofold difficulty. First, God as God is not knowable by his essence (which is his act of existence), so it is not immediately clear what aspect of *actus* is relevant to analogical affirmation. Second, even proportionate *actus* is only intelligible analogically, since, by definition, proportionate act is distinct from the proportionate essence that is the content of understanding. As it relates to divine realities, Aquinas makes this one term, *actus*, the central analogy for three distinct aspects of the divine reality: the divine act of existence (*ipsum esse subsistens*), the divine processions (*emanatio intelligibilis per modum operati*), and the divine *ad extra* agency (*creare*). What *actus* means in all these senses (and, indeed, even in its created, proportionate sense) can only be glimpsed through examples.[29]

For Aquinas, the paradigm for understanding *actus* is the act of understanding itself. So effective is this strategy that Thomas applies it to all three major contexts of divine *actus*. Most significant to the present argument, however, is Thomas's notion that the controverted matter of the divine processions can be resolved through recourse to the act of understanding not only as a predicate of the divine name (*ipsum intelligere*), but as an analogy drawn from ordinary human intellectual life. It is in this respect that the psychological analogy can be said to be both natural and spiritual. Its analogical base lies with the relation between intellectual consciousness, the light of agent intellect, and the uncreated light of being. Its analogical structure, though, centers on the determination that the act of understanding adds to that base, for from the act of understanding, "there proceeds within our intellectual consciousness a conception or definition of the reality understood."[30] Foundational to the psychological theory of the Trinitarian procession of the eternal Word, then, is the theorematic control whereby the natural terms and relations of understanding and intellectual procession are distinguished from among the various data of proportionate being, clarified as themselves proportionate to reason, affirmed as a participation in uncreated light, and investigated accordingly as a means of understanding the divine processions themselves.

Intelligible emanation, then, as Lonergan argues, "is the conscious origin of a real, natural, and conscious act from a real, natural, and conscious act, both within intellectual consciousness and also by virtue of intellectual consciousness itself as determined by the prior act."[31] According to this definition, "act" is not defined through genus or species but is rather "clarified by a familiar proportion, namely, act: form: potency:: seeing: eyesight: eye:: hearing something: the faculty of hearing: the ear:: understanding something: the intelligible species: the possible intellect:: willing: willingness: will:: existence: substantial form: prime matter."[32] That this act is "real" means that the act is, in fact, the case. And that the act is "natural" means that it belongs to intelligence as such (not merely to intelligence as intentional).

So defined, the act-from-act procession of the inner word from the act of understanding that is the ordinary process of human intellection can serve as an analog for the procession of the eternal Word. But this analogy did not fall fully formed from heaven. It is the fruit of centuries of biblical interpretation, doctrinal clarification, and speculative exploration. Distinguishing the *meaning* of the psychological analogy from its various verbal formulae, then, benefits from some rudimentary familiarity with that development. Such development, moreover, provides an example of diachronic or genetic speculative pluralism.

## The Genetic Pluralism of the Analogy of Spirit

### Biblical Foundations

While popular convention assigns to Augustine credit (or blame) for the psychological analogy's genesis, Lonergan argues that there is a biblical basis for the notion that often goes unexamined. "The psychological analogy," he writes, "is not only a theory but is rooted deeply in both the New Testament and tradition."[33] Lonergan organizes the biblical data under three main rubrics: the Word of God, the missions of the Son and Holy Spirit, and the eternal processions and persons themselves. The Word of God includes not only such biblical actions as speaking, listening, hearing, but also "the notions of gospel, commandment, precept, testimony, truth, to observe, to keep, to believe, to accept, and so on."[34] What unites this nexus of terms is an affirmation of the word by which humanity is addressed as "the word of God, of the Lord, of Christ, of the kingdom, of salvation, of grace, of truth."[35] The truth of this word, moreover, is not its objective contents alone, but the subjective truthfulness of the speaker and the trusting receptivity of the hearer. It is a word that is believed. Because the word of truth is also the word of salvation, it "regards values, expresses them, and commends them."[36] The word as practical, as a judgment of value means that the "one who hears this word of life (1 John 1.1) in the fuller sense experiences a manifest and radical religious conversion."[37] Because an intelligible emanation is "nothing other than what begins to be known by anyone who has reached the age of reason, what even a child discovers within himself as soon as he is able to say sincerely, 'This is not true,' and 'It's not my fault,'" then one must say that insofar as the apostles in their sincerity "proclaimed a word as true," there is "an intelligible emanation by way of truth."[38] Furthermore, insofar as the first Christians in their moral integrity "accepted a word as good," there proceeds within them "an intelligible emanation by way of goodness."[39]

Besides the notion of intelligible emanation that one discovers in the word of truth believed and proclaimed and in the word of value willed or acted upon as good, the notion of intelligible emanation is found in the biblical testimony to the missions of the Son and Holy Spirit. The Johannine testimony is especially insistent that the Son is the one who has been sent by the Father. He speaks not his own word but only the Father's word. He was born to testify to the truth. That word of the Father that is not only spoken but is also heard, however, is the work of the Spirit who is also sent. The Spirit teaches even what the apostles cannot bear. The Spirit abides in truth. The Spirit is sent, poured out, given to the human heart. The truth of God is spoken through the sending of the Son. The divine affirmation of value is heard through the Spirit that is sent.[40] From the testimony of these sendings, Lonergan concludes,

> With this we have reached our objective. For the intelligible emanation by way of truth that we acknowledged in the apostles as preaching we must similarly acknowledge in the Son as man, since he said, 'We speak of what we know and testify to what we have seen' (John 3.11). And the intelligible emanation by way of goodness that we acknowledged in the first Christians hearing the word, we must also acknowledge in the Spirit who is sent, not only inasmuch as he makes others hear, but also formally as he himself really and truly, albeit analogously, hears.[41]

Lonergan traces the residues of the emanation by way of truth and the emanation by way of goodness not only through the preaching of the apostles, the religious conversion of the early Christians, and the missions of the Son and the Spirit, but also in the persons themselves in their eternal proceeding. His approach is deductive. According to John 16:13, the Spirit does not speak on his own. Rather, the Spirit hears the Word that is spoken by the Father. As eternal, simple, and immutable, what is predicated of the Spirit is predicated eternally. Thus, the emanation by way of goodness traced to the Spirit's mission is the temporal determination of the Spirit's eternal emanation by way of goodness. The Spirit's hearing, then, "signifies the procession of love, the intelligible emanation by way of goodness."[42] But when he turns to examine the procession of the Son, Lonergan notes that here the deduction is not so straightforward. For the Son is both human and divine, and therefore, "one cannot conclude to the eternal procession by way of truth from the fact that his temporal mission is by way of truth."[43] Yet, Lonergan goes on to argue that when one takes the Johannine "word" in its totality and leaves out those elements that belong to the materiality of the created order, one can conclude "that the Word is the Father's and from the Father, not by being created or made (for he is God), but by the intelligible emanation that is by way of truth."[44] Furthermore, there is a mutual relation between these processions. The Father eternally speaks the Word. The Word is eternally spoken and heard. The Spirit eternally hears what the Father speaks. Once the material elements are bracketed, there remains only the spiritual elements, which "are nothing other than the intelligible emanations by way of truth and by way of goodness."[45]

*Augustinian Experimentations*

The opening sentences of Augustine's *De Trinitate* stand as a permanent caution to anyone daring to speak of God as triune. The Trinity, Augustine tells us, is the starting point of faith. And yet, its mysterious nature, its unthinkability and so unspeakability invite sophistries of various kinds—procedures of reason that, owing to their disordered affections, irrationally distort the triune mystery into alluring but mundane forms of sensation and imagination. He writes of the tendency of those that use reason "to transfer what they have observed about bodily things to incorporeal and spiritual things, which they would measure by the standard of what they experience through the senses of the body or learn by natural human intelligence, lively application, and technical skill."[46]

Corporality—even in its most concrete biological valence—can exert so great a force upon the imagination that "the body" can become the criterion of the real. This was the mentality, Augustine recounts, that so dominated his thinking prior to his encounter with Platonism.[47] God's reality, he thought, must be of a piece with God's corporality. "Hence," he writes, "although I did not think of you as being in the shape of a human body, I was forced to think of you as something corporeal, existent in space and place, either infused into the world or even diffused outside the world through infinite space."[48] Augustine's notion of truth, and so his notion of God, was undermined by an all-too-common tendency to think of the real as the already-out-there-now.[49]

And while his own thinking underwent a radical conversion as he came to realize that *veritas* intends not corporality but reality, Augustine quickly cautions that the return to a biologically extroverted theological mentality is an ever-present danger for those trying to comprehend divinity in terms borrowed from human experience, however much augmentation the terms undergo. Augustine's counsel of caution, though, does not prevent him from speaking of God; it is not a false humility that uses pious silence as a cloak for ignorance. It is, rather, precisely this risk of bodily confusion that establishes the exigence for a theology that moves beyond the sensorial and imaginal. If Christians are not to be reduced to a laconic agnosticism toward the object of their adoration, then a theology of the triune God is required.

In *De Trinitate*, Augustine searches for structures of human knowledge that, when purified of all bodily determination, might illuminate the mystery of Trinity. In Book VIII, he considers how the triadic relations of a lover, a beloved, and the love between them might be an *imago* in the creature. In Book IX, however, he moves to exclude from his analysis any residual corporality that might corrupt his results. He thus delimits the generic relations of the original triad to the specific case of the mind's love of itself. This specification leads to an augmentation of the triad, which is now considered as mind, knowledge, and love (IX.1). Vital to Augustine's experiments with spiritual analogy, however, is not only that the terms of the triad undergo the purgation of corporeal division, but that they be related, one to another to another, so as to demonstrate their oneness and uniqueness. Thus, while still considering the *imago* as mind, knowledge, and love, Augustine takes up the question of whether and in what way knowledge and love are *verba mentis*, inner words. The mind, he argues, perceives in temporal things the form by which they are, and "by this form we conceive true knowledge of things, which we have with us as a kind of word that we beget by uttering inwardly, and that does not depart from us when it is born."[50] And while this process of conceptualization obtains in all circumstances of coming-to-know, the theological application of this structure requires the unity of the act as directed to itself. Augustine writes,

> From this we can gather that when the mind knows and approves of itself, this knowledge is its word in such a way that it matches it exactly and is equal to it and identical, since it is neither knowledge of an inferior thing like a body nor of a superior one like God. And while any knowledge has a likeness to the thing it knows, that is to the thing it is the knowledge of, this knowledge by which the knowing mind is known has a perfect and equal likeness. And the reason it is both image and word, is that it is expressed from the mind when it is made equal to it by knowing it; and what is begotten is equal to the begetter.[51]

In Book X, Augustine aims "to remove some of the knots and polish some of the roughness out of our draft presentation of these matters."[52] His worries about the problem of self-knowledge and self-presence lead him to modify his triad one last time. He moves to the indubitable structures of mind: memory, understanding, and will. Through his examination, he shows that these three are one with regard to life, mind, and substance, and are three as they regard one another. They are terms that have their distinction through their relations. In those relations, they can be said to contain each other: memory remembers memory, understanding, and willing. Understanding understands memory, understanding, and willing. And willing wills memory, understanding, and willing. Each term, then, is said to contain all the others through the unique relations that obtain among them. After a thorough discrediting of all material triads, Augustine returns to this mental triad in Book XIV. There, he concludes that in the operation of memory, understanding, and will in self-knowledge, the image of God is manifest in the human soul. But this remains an imperfect manifestation until those same operations operate with regard to their divine source. The full image of God in the human person, then, is the person remembering, understanding, and willing God. This, Augustine tells us, is wisdom.[53]

## *Thomistic Synthesis*

Through the iterative process of Augustine's experiments with mental triads, one can detect the various elements that, in the hands of Aquinas, will become the full articulation of a systematic treatment of the Trinity: relations of opposition, the *verbum mentis*, etc. Yet, it remains that Augustine's approach and, in fact, his aims are distinct from those of the *Summa Theologiae*. But even granting those distinctions, there is an integral genetic relation—both historically and intellectually—between *De Trinitate* and the *Summa*. As Burrell states,

> In his *de Trinitate*, Augustine carried the issue beyond the spare logic of relations to the region of intentional activity. This domain is rich with analogies, and any activity which qualifies as intentional is *ipso facto* a relating as well. What Aquinas added to Augustine's triad of *memoria*, *intelligentia*, and *amor*, was a cognitional analysis which showed how *verbum* and *amor* each represent activities within divinity. More exactly: how the activity generating an interior word goes on to elicit a loving assent.[54]

Furthermore, one can detect in Aquinas a keener and clearer sense than one finds in Augustine of just how and why the systematic exigence emerges within theological reflection and why *analogia* (as a strategy of reason beyond similitude or the search for *vestigia*) is the proper tool to meet it. And one suspects (though proving the case materially is difficult) that Aquinas's procedure in the context of Trinitarian theory is made possible by the same theorematic breakthrough regarding the line of reference termed nature that made possible his synthetic elaboration of the speculative reconciliation of grace and freedom. We have already seen how Thomas's treatment of the matter is illustrative of his conception of speculative theology as a whole. But now we can look more singularly at his account of the psychological analogy for its own sake.

To understand how Thomas augments the Augustinian framework, one must begin with his thorough appropriation of the Aristotelian maxim that knowing is identity in act. To know something is to reproduce its act. When an act of understanding achieves the reproduction of the intelligible species of the thing understood, understanding, in fact, occurs. "Nothing more is required."[55] The act of understanding is thus conscious. It is not the passive impression or intuition of externalities upon the intellect. Knowing, as Lonergan often remarked, is not like taking a good look. Furthermore, if knowing is identity in act, then to know is to be really related to the known.[56]

As even Augustine saw, the immediacy of understanding is little more than the affectivity of what Lonergan calls the release of the tension of inquiry. It is the nexus of feelings resulting from the flash of insight. For insights to be useful, applicable, or even available, they must be expressed. By this expression a knower is sustained in real relation to the known. Burrell summarizes, "The act of understanding something makes over the one knowing by really relating him to what he knows. If the new relation is to last, however, and have a chance to alter his comportment, he must be able to express this new understanding."[57] Such expression is the inner word, and such expressing is the act by which the inner word is produced. For Thomas, this production is immanent to consciousness, to the operative structure of intelligence as such. He thus refers to the production of an inner word as an intelligible emanation (*emanatio intelligibilis*). As intelligible, the inner word is more like a "ratio or logos" than it is a "nomen."[58] It is not the "private language" so criticized by Wittgensteinians.

The foregoing is indicative of Thomas's overall conception of word and idea, of cognitional structure, of the rational soul. But how is any of this an analog for the divine procession of the eternal Word? For Thomas, the proceeding inner word attains a likeness according to species between the thing understood and the expression of that understanding. There is, furthermore, a second procession, a movement of the will that loves what is known and expressed because it is good and loveable. Thus, while the first procession pertains to the likeness of the intellect, the second procession pertains to the will's inclination to what is loveable.

The Word of God, by analogy, proceeds in the mode of an intelligible emanation from the Father as *Dicens*. This procession, like its analog, is natural, autonomous, and spiritual. It is an act proceeding logically and causally from an act. It is a perfect expression of the identity, fullness, and totality of that from which it proceeds. The Holy Spirit, by analogy, proceeds in the mode of an intelligible emanation of love from the judgment of value that affirms what is known to be loveable. Inasmuch as that emanation of love regards what is expressed in the Word, the procession of the Spirit is co-principled, even while remaining a single procession. The Spirit proceeds from the Father and the Son.

By situating and augmenting Augustine's mental triads within a more differentiated rational psychology and by putting the resulting transformation to explicitly speculative use, Thomas resolved the tension long detected at the intersection of simplicity and procession, and, with it, showed how hard-won doctrinal achievements can be reconciled with each other through the application of theorematic control. It remains, however, that Thomas's version of the psychological analogy is limited by the metaphysical approach to the study of the soul (faculty psychology). In the twentieth century, Lonergan transposed the Thomistic achievement by both rigorously retrieving Thomas's doctrine of *Verbum* and renewing it on the basis of a modern, empirical cognitional theory.

## Lonerganian Transpositions

The relative neglect of Bernard Lonergan's unique contributions to Trinitarian theology has two main sources. First, Lonergan's two principal texts: *The Triune God: Doctrines* and *The Triune God: Systematics* were, like most of Lonergan's dogmatic works, written in Latin as textbooks for scholastics at the Gregorian University in Rome in the midst of the reforms of the Second Vatican Council, and so were largely ignored during their initial rounds of publication. Second, the tradition of Trinitarian reflection within which Lonergan worked was the Augustinian-Thomist line of psychological analogical reasoning, a tradition of theological thinking much maligned during the renaissance Trinitarian theology has enjoyed in the decades following the publication of Rahner's "Der dreifaltige Gott." This comes despite the numerous references to Lonergan's text throughout that work. As a result, the linguistic and intellectual trends within modern systematics have set conditions under which a theology student is unlikely to encounter Lonergan's work and, if they do, is unlikely to recognize it as a unique or groundbreaking text.

The foundational work in Lonergan's development of the psychological analogy is the collection of five *Theological Studies* articles published from 1946 to 1949 compiled in book form as *Verbum: Word and Idea in Aquinas*. In *Verbum*, Lonergan endeavors to retrieve Thomas Aquinas's theory of knowledge, especially in his articulation, explanation, and expansion of Augustine's proceeding "inner word." For Lonergan's Aquinas, there are two proceeding inner words that are the immanent terminal objects of intellectual operation corresponding to the two principal intellectual operations in human knowing: understanding and judging.

The first operation, understanding, is the operation by which one answers the question *quid sit*? ("What is it?"). Understanding (*intelligere*) is intelligence coming to possess some intelligible species immanent to the manifold of sensation or consciousness through insight into phantasm or image. Understanding is not satisfied with imaginal objects, and so consequent upon its own actuality, the act of understanding makes for itself an inner word, a concept, a formulation, a definition, a *quod quid est*. The actuality of the inner word *proceeds* from the actuality of the act of understanding. What proceeds from the act of understanding is an *emanatio intelligibilis* (intelligible emanation). The intelligibility of the *emanatio intelligibilis* is active and actual not passive and potential, because it is the intelligibility of the act of understanding acting, as understanding itself. "It is native and natural," Lonergan writes, "for the procession of the inner word to be intelligible, actively intelligible, and the genus of all intelligible process; just as heat is native and natural to fire, so is intelligible procession to intelligence in act."[59] As the active, intelligible effect of an active, intelligible cause, the *emanatio intelligibilis* of the procession of the inner word in human understanding is a created base and fruitful analogical term in the human mind that images the triune constitution of divine life, wherein the divine Word proceeds natively, naturally, actively, and intelligibly from the Father.

Many of the disagreements among Thomists about the nature of Aquinas's Trinitarian theory stemmed, Lonergan argues, from an almost universal failure to grasp both the meaning and importance of Thomas's notion of the act of understanding (*intelligere*) for both his psychology and for his Trinitarian theology. Lonergan argues that Thomas's notion of *intelligere* differs drastically from most accounts of his intellectual psychology. On the basis of this recovery of Thomistic *intelligere*, Lonergan argues that Thomas's principal natural analogy for the Trinitarian procession of the Word, *emanatio intelligibilis*, can only be understood adequately as the act of the proceeding inner word of concept from the prior act of *intelligere*. If, in human intellectual and rational psychology, there proceeds something both real and nonmaterial that proceeds as act from a prior act, then it may prove a fecund place from which, however dimly and with the caution of Lateran IV always in mind, to conceive of the act-from-act procession of the Son from the Father and of the Spirit from the Father and the Son.

What the *Verbum* articles already gesture toward is a transformation of the Thomistic inner word beyond the strictures of Aristotelian faculty psychology so as to grasp more completely not just a theory of *knowledge* predicated on a metaphysics of the soul and its powers, but a theory of *consciousness* predicated on the structured operational performance of the knower. Such a theory is articulated in Lonergan's 1957 philosophical masterpiece, *Insight*. In it, Lonergan is able to propose a reordering of all of human inquiry on the basis of the self-appropriation of one's conscious performance of knowing. Understanding, he argues, is the supervening of intelligence upon experience, it is a cluster of operations in the subject that emerge in consciousness as answers to questions. Questions themselves spontaneously arise on the basis of experience and act as operators moving the conscious subject from one class of operations to another. From the acts of understanding proceed concepts, formulations, expressions, and definitions. These are the articulations of the answers grasped by intelligence to the interrogation of experience. Yet, at the level of understanding, these answers remain only hypothetical and potential. Some intelligible form has been understood, but the human knower wants to know if what has been understood is, in fact, true. And so, questions for intelligence (what is it?) give way to questions for rational reflection (is it so?), and acts of understanding give way to acts of judgment. The operations of rational consciousness weigh the evidence, evaluate, grasp the conditions of understanding's truthfulness, and judge whether or not those conditions have been fulfilled. Only after grasping both the conditions of a concept's veracity and the fulfillment of those conditions can one reasonably affirm as true any particular insight, and only then can one truly be said to know.

Lonergan's achievements here are twofold. He both sets the natural ground of the psychological analogy on the firmer footing of empirical cognitional theory—thereby making the natural terms and relations clearer, more concise, and more available to philosophical inquiry—and brings to the service a correlated and essential fact: the natural analog underlying the psychological analogy is not an already-out-there-now object of the natural world but the theologian's own appropriation of themselves as intellectual, rational, volitional, and loving actors in an intelligible and loveable universe.

## Self-Appropriation as Analog

Few theologians today express much affection for the psychological analogy. Even those who are otherwise defenders of Thomas's teaching on Trinity often express misgivings about the analogy.[60] This was not always so. But even when it enjoyed the cultural and intellectual superstructure of neoscholastic hegemony, Lonergan argued that few Thomists had anything more than a conceptual grasp of Thomas's doctrine. "Not a few vigorously affirm [the psychological analogy]," he writes, "and yet clearly have never attended to that root from which this whole theory proceeds."[61] Lonergan contends that such opinions are "poorly propounded" in that they "employ the psychological analogy, but in a way that overlooks to some extent the proper force and efficacy of the analogy."[62] This oversight of insight may entail an affirmation of the likeness between the divine processions and those of human intelligence, but mere verbal ascent to this likeness differs in kind from understanding it.

For Lonergan, this difference is explained by distinguishing between two models of understanding. In the first model, understanding is the intelligent grasp of the intelligible through the act of organizing insight. It is an answer to a question. In the second model, intelligence is conceived on an analogy with sensibility, especially the sensible act of vision. To "understand" the psychological analogy, according to the second model, is to utter its verbal expressions with accuracy. It is to know how to use a word. Procession, accordingly, is "from external words to universal concepts . . . from the corporeal act of seeing to some simple apprehension whereby concepts become known to us."[63] But insofar as sensation is not yet intellectual, processions from sensation are not yet intelligible. And a procession that is not intelligible cannot serve as the basis for an analogical conception of the divine processions.

"Therefore," Lonergan concludes, "not only should the psychological analogy be employed, it must also be understood in such a way that the likeness is not sought between the sensitive part of our nature and the triune God."[64] To avoid this error, Lonergan encourages us to "attend even for a few moments to our own internal and intellectual experiences."[65] When we do, we make three discoveries: (1) When we understand anything, something proceeds in us as the definition or concept of what we understand; (2) love proceeds only from such concepts; (3) perfect procession perfectly is one with that from which it proceeds. These discoveries, in turn, are the heart of the psychological analogy.[66] But the key to these discoveries is the pattern of attention in the inquirer and the success the inquirer has in interrogating their own conscious operations.

The functions of human consciousness may be empirical, but the only data set to which an inquirer has empirical access is their own. The data of consciousness are only experienced in the first person. The natural analog for the divine processions is therefore not just the intelligible emanation, but *my* experience, understanding, and affirmation of a proceeding inner word *in me* that proceeds from *my* act of understanding. This is the process that Lonergan refers to as self-appropriation. Not only is self-appropriation the key to solving the entrenched philosophical problems Lonergan addresses in *Insight*, it is also the key to the psychological analogy. It is, in fact, the natural term underlying the psychological analogy itself.

## Divine Indwelling and the Supernatural Elevation of Spiritual Acts

The theorem of the supernatural, insofar as it clarifies the intellectual coordinates of the line of reference termed nature, sets the speculative conditions for the disengagement of a natural analogy for the divine processions. Those conditions have been fulfilled by a tradition of speculative rationality that has its material origins in scripture, its historical origins in Augustine, its refinements and perfections in Aquinas, and its transposition from soul to subject in Lonergan. But it remains a tradition quite consciously and intentionally wedded to the line of reference termed nature in order to secure its control of meaning. But what of the supernatural term? Recent speculative theology demonstrates that one can take the basic structure of the natural analogy found in human conscious operation and refound it as a supernatural analogy, where the analogs are not the operations of consciousness as naturally operative but those operations as operative under the principle of sanctifying grace and charity, which is to say, to operate under the new conditions of consciousness made possible by the historical missions of the Son and the Holy Spirit. There is, thus, an incipient authentic speculative pluralism, constituted by both natural and supernatural analogies, within the psychological analogy itself—analogies controlled by the dialectical operation of the theorem of the supernatural.

In *The Trinity in History*, Robert Doran argues that "the trinitarian structure of created grace provides a psychological analogy for understanding Trinitarian life, an analogy whose structure is isomorphic with the analogies suggested by Augustine, Aquinas, and Lonergan. There is thus established an analogy for understanding Trinitarian processions that obtains in the supernatural order itself."[67] Following Lonergan's lead, Doran takes the implications of the transposition from soul to subject all the way to their conclusion, asking after the cognitional/conscious correlates to the metaphysical doctrines of sanctifying grace and the habit of charity, absolutely supernatural created terms that have their Trinitarian base in the uncreated relations of active and passive spiration.

In scholastic theology, sanctifying grace is an entitative habit, an accidental formal cause that is posited in the essence of the soul. Its effects flow through the natural structure of relations between the essence, the powers, habits, and acts. It is thus the root and source of the habit of charity in the will. In Doran's transposition, the conscious correlate to sanctifying grace as accidental form is the retrospective recollection of being on the receiving end of unrestricted love. The love is unrestricted because it is God's own love. It has neither conditions nor limitations. As such, it is known only through retrospective recollection, or what Lonergan called an undertow in retrospect. Between retrospection and Augustinian *memoria*, there is an obvious affinity. It is thus that Doran argues that the retrospective interpretation of being on the receiving end of unrestricted love is *memoria* as an operative cognitional act when that act occurs under the principle of sanctifying grace.

*Memoria*, however, is not an *emanatio intelligibilis*. Or, in Doran's gloss, it is not an autonomous spiritual procession. And yet, insofar as the retrospective interpretation of being on the receiving end of unrestricted love is an acknowledgement of that experience, it grasps the sufficient evidence for the judgement of value that assents to that love—specifically that such love is good—and does so in faith. That judgment of value is an inner word. It proceeds from *memoria*'s grasp of sufficient evidence. As Doran summarizes, there are two steps: "The gift itself recollected and acknowledged in *memoria* and the inner word of a judgment of value that proceeds from the evidence of *memoria* and acknowledges the goodness of the gift."[68] These two steps, in turn, together constitute the "conscious manifestation" of the active spiration by which the Holy Spirit proceeds from the Father and the Son. From this, Doran synthesizes the whole,

> Thus it may be said that the three divine persons dwell in us and among us, are present to us, precisely as the uncreated terms of created supernatural relations: supernatural, because their subjects are created participations in divine life, namely, sanctifying grace (gift and word, *notionaliter diligere*) and charity (*amor proceedens*). Sanctifying grace and charity, thus conceived, are the special basic relations that ground the derivation of special categories in theology.[69]

The supernatural analogy for the psychological procession, as Doran articulates it, represents a development from within the speculative tradition of the psychological analogy that looks for its prime referent in the supernatural rather than the natural order. Because of the theorem of the supernatural, this development can be classified as an integral, diachronic, but also dialectical development (in the precise sense described in the previous chapter). Yet, the supernatural analogy is not exhausted with consciousness and grace. As we will see in the next section, a supernatural analogy for the divine processions can be found within the *mysterium salutis* not only in the invisible missions but the visible missions as well. In particular, we will see how Balthasar's kenotic analogy both issues from the revelation of God in the visible mission of the Son—his life, death, and resurrection—and backs its way into its own psychological conception of kenosis and thus of the divine processions.

## THE KENOTIC PROCESSION

No traditional Trinitarian axiom is as central to Hans Urs von Balthasar's kenotic analogy as the Thomistic teaching that the missions are the processions, that the former relate God to history as the latter relate God to God's self. In contrast to the social trinitarians with whom his thought is sometimes (and mistakenly) linked, Balthasar's fundamental speculative Trinitarian question is not one of personal *vestigia* but of procession and its economic correlate—mission. But while Thomas begins his speculative theology of the Trinity with the processions, Balthasar, in ways both converging and diverging with and from Doran, begins his speculative theology with the missions—without ever forgetting the identity between the two.

But how can a divine mission, which has as its constitutive condition the eternal self-communication of divine life, be a source for the analogical, intellectual mediation of that life? The missions presume the processions. And the processions are made known only through revelation. If revelation reveals the formally disproportionate reality that is divine life, how can what it reveals also be a source of analogs for speculative theology? Can the historical missions, which have as their purpose the redemption of the world, also be analogs for the processive life of God? As we saw with Doran's account of the supernatural elevation of spiritual acts, a speculative theology drawn from a supernatural analog is possible because the theorem of the supernatural controls the meaning of both natural and supernatural intellectual domains. As we will see, that same theorematic control governs the relationship between the historical mission of the Word, its kenotic modalities, and its formal condition in the eternal divine self-communication. First, this section clarifies how the *mysterium salutis* can be both soteriological and theorematic. Second, it charts Balthasar's theology of the processions from its Christological manifestation in the *Aesthetics*, to its kenotic content in the *Dramatics*, to its expression in a modified analogy of spirit in the *Logic*. This triad—manifestation, content, expression—is Balthasar's characteristic manner of theologizing.

### The *Mysterium Salutis* and Analogical Disclosure

Analogical mediation, whether considered as a formal metaphysical relation or as an intellectual interval of semantic predication has at its core the notion of disproportion. In the context of theology, the disproportion is between the finite and the infinite, wherein the former refers to the mode of existing in which the cause, reason, and explanation of a thing is independent of the essence of the thing itself, and the latter refers to the identity of essence and existence. This disproportion is absolute. It admits of no gradation according to magnitude. Yet, fundamental to theology is the affirmation that even so absolute a disproportion between *relata* contains a relation. The formally unconditioned, theology claims, reveals itself in and among the conditioned. As the previous chapter outlined, the theorem of the supernatural governs the intellectual structure of this relation. It represents the coordination of properly theological terms and relations with the supernatural order, thereby clarifying by contrast those terms and relations whose intelligibility is, in principle, explicable according to "the line of reference termed nature." The repurposing of the theorem proposed in this work suggests that that intellectual frame not only clarifies and relates terms and relations with their proper *ordo essendi* and the two *ordines* to one another, but it also disengages the theorematic domains from which terms can be selected and applied in the speculative pursuit of analogical mediation.

The psychological analogy, at least as it has been articulated from Augustine to Lonergan, finds its analog (*emanatio intelligibilis*) in the line of reference termed nature. But clarification of that line of reference has the further entailment of correlating properly theological terms with the supernatural order. But once the theorem is operative and the properly theological elements are grasped and distinguished from the natural elements, speculative theology can utilize one theological element as an analog for understanding others. The reason for this intra-theological analogizing owes to the *revelatory* character of the underlying data of theology. The basic claim of Christianity is that God, unknowable in himself, makes himself known (through a mirror dimly) in the law, the prophets, the incarnation, and the divine indwelling. Once what God reveals is known to those to whom it is revealed, it enters into the fund of insights through which the intellectual and practical lives of Christians are lived.

Soteriology, as Katherine Sonderegger has argued, is not all of theology.[70] Furthermore, soteriology itself is more than soteriological. Inasmuch as it names the economy of divine self-communication in history through creation and redemption, it also names the economy of revelation itself. As revelatory, the *mysterium salutis* is a theorematic domain of special terms and relations revealed through the visible and invisible missions of the Son and the Spirit. With the theorem of the supernatural as its control of meaning, the *mysterium salutis* itself provides a basic set of terms and relations for an analogical conception of the divine processions. Furthermore, as a theorem of disproportion, the theorem of the supernatural allows for a precise interpretation of the regulative function that dissimilitude exercises (according to Lateran IV) over speculative relations of analogy.

For Balthasar, the visible mission of the Word, the incarnation—and with it the full arc of Christ's life, death, and resurrection—is not merely soteriological. It is also revelatory. What Christ's life reveals progressively through the various modalities of his obedience to the Father is the processive life of God. By linking Christic authority, obedience, poverty, expropriation, and self-abandonment with historical kenosis, Balthasar shows how the economic unity of Christ's historical life discloses the intra-divine kenosis, and with it, the processive life of God's immanent constitution. Christ's form is "the revelation of [God's] absolute freedom, as this is *in God himself*, the freedom of eternal self-giving out of unfathomable love."[71] Such unrestricted self-giving and the freedom according to which it proceeds eternally "is poured out over the entire form of revelation, gives it its being and structure, and is present in it."[72]

## Kenosis as Explanatory Term

While the *locus classicus* of Balthasar's theory of kenotic relations is volume 4 of his *Drama*, the grounding for that content is the manifestation of ristic obedience in the concluding volume of the *Aesthetics*. In it, Balthasar attempts to synthesize the whole of history's manifestation of uncreated glory into the *Gestalt* of Christ's historical life. In his examination of the gospels, especially the gospel of John, Balthasar characterizes Christ's manner of being in the world through three seemingly contradictory descriptors: authority, poverty (obedience), and self-abandonment. His authority owes to his relation to the Father as the Father's Word. As the one sent from the Father, Christ is possessed of the Father's authority. But the content of the Father's Word and thus of the Word's authority is poverty—dependence, obedience, prayer, faith, and Spirit. In Christ's historical mission there is thus a "paradox" in which Jesus "makes his absolute claim [to authority] in equally absolute poverty, in the renunciation of all earthly power and every earthly possession."[73] And as "perfect poverty is one with perfect obedience," so "Jesus himself is the one who is *absolutely poor.*"[74]

The contradiction between Christic authority and poverty is transposed into a higher synthesis in Christic self-abandonment, which clarifies that both authority and obedience are functions of freedom, of self-giving. But sublimating the paradox of authority and obedience in this way does not yet reach the ground of their possibility. As Balthasar writes, "For such obedience, a divine decision must truly be required, a decision that as such implies the 'surrender' of the *forma Dei*."[75] Readers of the Vulgate can already see where he is going. *Forma Dei* is how the Vulgate translates the Pauline phrase, *morphe theou*, in the kenotic Christ hymn of Philippians 2:6–11. But unlike many kenotic theologians of the nineteenth century and their twentieth-century heirs, Balthasar insists that Christic kenosis, inasmuch as it is the kenosis of the divine person, "cannot postulate any alteration as this is found in creatures, nor any suffering and obeying in the manner proper to creatures."[76] Divine self-divestment, then, has to be proper to divine life itself in order to be economically extended.

Divine selflessness, "pure relations of love within the Godhead" is "the basis of everything," including creation (the first kenosis) and the cross (the second kenosis).[77] Balthasar explicitly connects the pure relation of kenosis to the Son's eternal "being begotten." When Christ surrenders the *forma Dei*, he "translates his being begotten by the Father (and in this, his dependence on him) into the expressive form of creaturely obedience."[78] In the act of Christic surrender, "the whole Trinity remains involved."[79] The Father sends, the Son surrenders, and the Spirit unites and expresses their relation.

By surrendering the *forma Dei*, Christ manifests economically the immanent, processive relation of the Father to the Son. The kenotic existence of Jesus, Balthasar concludes, "was an existence of expectation and of readiness for the 'hour,' condensed in the unity of claim, poverty, and self-abandonment." In the *Aesthetics*, kenosis is the explanatory term that organizes the seemingly contradictory affirmations of Christic authority, poverty, and self-abandonment. It names the modalities of appearance of the processions in the historical appearance of Christ. But in the *Dramatics*, kenosis is also the explanatory term that unites Christ's mission with the Word's eternal procession. It is the content of what Christ manifests. The transition from one to the other entails a transition from a focus restricted to the economic appearance of Christ's mission to a focus dilated to include a formal description of the immanent Trinity.

In the *Aesthetics*, divine freedom is the exigence that leads Balthasar to use kenosis as unifying term for Christ's authority, obedience, and self-abandonment. In the *Dramatics*, the relation of divine to human freedom is the central matter. For Balthasar, the economic appearance of Christ's form and mission is unthinkable apart from the "inner presupposition" of Trinitarian doctrine.[81] But a one-sidedly economic account of the Trinity cannot be that inner presupposition. "Many theologians," Balthasar writes, "in attempting to establish the relationship between immanent and economic Trinity, seem to lay such weight on the latter that the immanent Trinity, even if it is still distinguished from the other, becomes merely a kind of precondition for God's true, earnest self-revelation and self-giving."[82] In reaction to Rahner and Moltmann, Balthasar argues that the immanent Trinity "must be understood to be that eternal, absolute self-surrender whereby God is seen to be, in himself, absolute love; this in turn explains his free self-giving to the world as love, without suggesting that God 'needed' the world process and the Cross in order to become himself (to 'mediate himself')."[83] The dramatic soteriology considers the Trinity not just in terms of the *pro nobis* but goes on to speculatively explore the ways in which the *pro nobis* sheds light on the inner life of God *in se*.

Kenosis is the analogical pivot for this speculative exploration. From the kenotic structure disclosed in the modalities of Christ's historical form, Balthasar considers kenosis as the Ur-act that throws light on the mystery of simplicity and procession. In the procession of the Son, the Father surrenders the fullness of divinity. But because the procession is eternal, the full surrender does not rob the Father of divinity but rather demonstrates his constitutive attribute as the One who, by love, begets the Son. "The Son's answer to the gift of Godhead (of equal substance with the Father)" writes Balthasar, "can only be eternal thanksgiving (*eucharistia*) to the Father, the Source—a thanksgiving as selfless and unreserved as the Father's original self-surrender."[84] And as if to prove that the kenotic act by which the Son is can be fully expressed only by a correlative act of kenotic love, there proceeds from the Father and the Son the Spirit, who "as the essence of love, he maintains the infinite difference between them, seals it and, since he is the one Spirit of them both, bridges it."[85]

With a control of meaning supplied by the theorem of the supernatural, Balthasar is able to risk the *pro nobis* starting place of Rahnerian and post-Rahnerian Trinitarian theology without letting the immanent Trinity fade into apophatic silence. Through the kenotic analogy drawn out of the historical Christ form, Balthasar repurposes soteriology in service of a speculative theology of the divine processions. In so doing, he draws a line in the sand beyond which such a theology must not cross. His theory of kenotic relation is the eternal relations of love that constitute divine life. They are extended temporally in the missions of the Son and Spirit, but that extension does not alter, enhance, or sublate the eternal processions. Rather, the processive life of God is the *sine qua non* of creation, revelation, and salvation. But to claim as Balthasar does that the content of what appears in Christic kenosis is the eternal relations of love in God still must be expressed. If the kenotic analogy effectuates an intellectual grasp of the coherence of procession in a perfectly simple God, it remains that apart from an articulation of that intelligible content, the immediacy of understanding is just a feeling that the tension of inquiry is resolved. In the *Theo-Logic*, Balthasar provides the expression for the speculative theology of the processions, and he does so by articulating how kenotic love—as an operation of consciousness—illumines the mystery of the processions and makes possible the self-appropriation of the mystery.

## *Imago, Kenosis,* and a Hidden Analogy of Spirit

In the second volume of the *Theo-Logic*, Balthasar offers some of his most in-depth engagements with Augustinian and Thomistic Trinitarian theology.[86] And while his analyses are not without hesitations and even some criticisms, one should not conclude from them that his intention is to reject that tradition. What is more surprising, however, is that despite those hesitations and cautious critiques, Balthasar elaborates, perhaps without realizing it, a modified psychological analogy—taken from the supernatural order—that sets his speculative theology of kenosis into the terms and relations of consciousness. The central question, both in his critique and his articulation, is what it means for the Logos to have been spoken not by some anonymous speaker but rather by a father. For the father to speak there is presumed "a corresponding power and a corresponding will at the base of one's utterance and communication. In the present case, what 'motivates' the will can only be love."[87] The Father thus speaks the Word not out of silence but out of love. But the love that motivates the Father's utterance is also the substance of what is communicated in the utterance. The Word is the expression of the love of the Father, out of which the Father speaks the Word.

If the Word expresses the Father in the Father's self-expressing, groundless love, then the expression of the Father in the Word must itself be in its own mode, as Word, an expression of self-expressing groundless love. As Balthasar writes,

> Precisely for this reason, since it is not the mere objectification of a subjective principle but also co-represents this principle in its mirroring or imaging, it cannot content itself with merely being an expression; it must likewise image, that is, coexecute, the movement of groundlessly loving self-expression, and do so, indeed, together with the source and ground that produces the Logos. This means that the Logos has a 'toward' together with his 'from': the groundlessly loving production of the one whom we call, for want of a clearer term, the Holy Spirit.[88]

With this statement, we have an initial approximation of a Balthasarian scheme for the immanent constitution of divine life. And from this approximation, Balthasar can then work out the analogical correlates whereby the operational structure of loving can manifest, even through the dim mirror of the ever-greater dissimilarity, the truth of that immanent constitution. He writes, "We can say that truth belongs primarily to the Son, both within God and in the economy, but that theologically it rests upon the wonder of the Father's generative act, which, considered from the standpoint of the hypostasis of the Logos, is groundless love."[89] This groundless love is thus the "from which" of the Word's procession, and so an analogical term for the Father from whom the Word proceeds. But if what proceeds from the Father is truth, then the Son can be analogically conceived in terms of an eternal judgment that means or expresses the total self-giving of groundless love. The analogical term for the Son is thereby the true expression of groundless love. And because the character of groundless love is complete self-giving in processive expression, the Word only expresses groundless love insofar as it is itself a coprinciple of expressing groundless love. The Word as the truth of groundless love transcends itself together with the Father into the Holy Spirit, who, as Balthasar writes, "is neither the Father nor the Son but exposits into infinity their hypostatic sphere—the love that belongs to each (Jn 16:13–15)."[90] And with this we have the analogical term for the third person of the Trinity. Thus, the Father as groundless love expresses that love truly and without remainder in the Word. The Word as true expression of groundless love must itself groundlessly love, together with the Father, as expression. The groundless loving between the Father and the Word is the Holy Spirit, who subsists as coprincipled loving. And so, as the Word truly expresses the groundless love of the Father, so the Holy Spirit exposits the love between the Father and the Father's Word.

The compactness of Balthasar's presentation leaves its technical and existential brilliance vulnerable to being overlooked. However, a comparison between Balthasar's account of the divine processions in terms of groundless love and Lonergan's so-called "later" psychological analogy helps bring clarity to what Balthasar accomplishes here. Readers of Lonergan's essay "Christology Today" will recognize a structural similarity between Lonergan's analogy and what Balthasar elaborates in the *Theo-Logic*. Whereas Lonergan's early writings, both in *Verbum* and in *The Triune God: Systematics*, work out a Thomistic psychological analogy in terms of the inner word of concept that proceeds causally and logically from a prior act of understanding, "Christology Today" insists that the starting point of the psychological analogy is the "higher synthesis of intellectual, rational, and moral consciousness that is the dynamic state of being in love."[91] The dynamic state of being in love truly expresses itself as a judgment of value, and the sincerity of the judgment is enacted in acts of loving. Now, regardless of whether or not the dynamic state here refers to natural love or Christian charity, the operational structure itself remains a created base for conceiving of the processions, relations, and persons of the divine Trinity.

Drawing from the Johannine assertion that the Father is love, Lonergan shows that the Word that proceeds from the Father is accordingly a *verbum spirans amorem*, a judgment of value, a judgment that affirms the truth of the love on the basis of the evidentiary grasp of that love's worth. The judgment, in turn, grounds the act of loving that is the Holy Spirit. The structure of the later analogy unfolds in the same *ordo disciplinae* as the earlier one, in which the correlates of the two analogical terms are the processions of the Word and the Holy Spirit respectively. An analogical grasp of the two processions makes possible a shift in perspective that allows the mutually opposed directionality of the processions to be conceived as four real relations, three of which are really distinct not only relationally but also in their mode of subsisting. These three distinct subsistents can thus be understood as three persons.[92]

Lonergan's more systematic presentation can help to organize Balthasar's scheme. The same Johannine conviction leads both Balthasar and Lonergan to affirm, on the basis of revelation, that God the Father is love. Lonergan specifies that love as "originating," while Balthasar calls it "groundless." But both modifiers attest to the unoriginated character of the Father. In both cases, eternal, groundless, originating love expresses itself completely and without remainder in a proceeding word. For Lonergan the proceeding word is a judgment of value that communicates the truth of originating love. Balthasar argues that the Word is the true expression or image or communication of groundless love in its totality, including groundless love as self-gift (kenosis). And for both Lonergan and Balthasar, the true expression of groundless love itself becomes a principle of proceeding loving expression together with the groundless love that is the Father. And in this way, the Spirit is the active, proceeding loving between the Father who speaks and the Word that is spoken.

But there is another important element of congruence between these two accounts of proceeding love. Because both Balthasar and Lonergan affirm with Thomas that the divine missions have as their constitutive condition the divine processions, it becomes possible and necessary to verify the *a priori* speculative structure of intra-divine life in light of the economic communication of that life in salvation history. And thus neither Lonergan nor Balthasar can be legitimately implicated in Rahner's criticism of the divorce between the immanent and the economic Trinity.

Recognizing the structural correspondence between Balthasar's notion of the situatedness of the Logos in divine life and Lonergan's later psychological analogy has several small advantages and at least one very significant one. First, it helps to complicate our picture of Balthasar's place within post-Rahnerian revisionary theologies. If Balthasar elaborates his own psychological analogy based in loving that emphasizes that God in God's self is eternally love in act, then he can hardly be the Catholic Moltmann. And, further, highlighting Balthasar's point-by-point correspondence with Lonergan on this issue might have some apologetic value for convincing skeptical Balthasarians to take the psychological analogy more seriously. But beyond these gains, there is a much larger, but also more provisional and tentative possibility. If what I've described as Balthasar's psychological analogy shares with Lonergan's analogy the same explanatory *ordo*, then we have in Balthasar's psychological analogy a systematic framework for interpreting some of the more provocative, imaginative, and dramatic imagery that populates the first two panels of the trilogy, imagery that on first blush seems to violate the metaphysical principles much more clearly indicated in this later scheme.

The vexed issue of kenosis that haunts the interpretations of the Trinitarian theology of the *Theo-Drama* become explicable when placed within the immanent scheme of the *Theo-Logic*. Balthasar seizes upon the Pauline image of the Son's self-emptying as an analogical term for the intra-divine processions. And because it is an analogy for the processions, it is also an analogy for the missions. And as a result, the *Theo-Drama* tends to understate the contingency of the missions. It is clear about the constitutive condition of the mission (namely, the procession and nothing else) but is unclear about the contingency of the consequent condition that makes it true to say that the mission is the procession. But if we interpret kenosis as a specification of self-expressing love, then we can differentiate different senses of kenosis in accord with the different elements of love: the groundless love's self-communication in a true expression, the active loving between the Father and the Word that proceeds from them as the decision to love. Further, mapping kenosis onto the analogy can help make the vital distinctions between kenosis as immanent constitution and kenosis as the missions in history.

## CONCLUSION

This chapter has attempted to provide one example of how speculative pluralism, informed by the application of the repurposed theorem of the supernatural, can provide the means for comparing, correcting, and, ultimately, mutually affirming speculative theologies whose analogs are drawn from distinct theorematic domains. In the course of that pursuit, the philosophical contours of the speculative terrain have been clarified, the psychological theory of the divine processions has been explained, and the kenotic structure of intra-divine love has been articulated.

While the details of these two approaches to the theology of the divine processions have been explored at some length, the overriding and undergirding intention of the foregoing expositions has been to show how the repurposed theorem of the supernatural can function in a particular speculative context. In the course of executing that intention, this chapter has provided an analysis of how the natural and supernatural theorematic domains relate to one another. It has presented both a developmental and a synthetic account of the psychological analogy for the divine processions—from Augustine and Aquinas to Lonergan and Doran—and it has confronted and complemented that tradition with the supernatural, kenotic analogy evinced in the work of Hans Urs von Balthasar. These two approaches, like the theorematic domains from which their prime analog is drawn, are distinct, but not separate, from one another.

In the Middle Ages, the Augustinian-Aristotelian debates brought hard-won achievements of the medieval synthesis under suspicion. In the centuries since, these two legitimate expressions of Christian theology have developed at a safe distance from one another. But, as this chapter has shown, this distance can be overcome when these traditions are placed within an adequate methodical frame. But while the disputes of postconciliar Trinitarian theology are ripe for the application of speculative pluralism, more pressing applications lay in the future.

## NOTES

1. ˋergan, *The Triune God: Systematics*, CWL 12, 127.
2. ˋ ıas Aquinas, *ST* I.27.1
3. Lonergan, "The Origins of Christian Realism (1972)," CWL 13, 206.
4. Lonergan, "The Origins of Christian Realism (1972)," CWL 13, 206–207. In a 1961 essay by the same name, Lonergan treats of the Francophile debate among Gilson, Blondel, and Emile Bréhier over Christian philosophy in more explicit terms. See Lonergan, "The Origins of Christian Realism (1961)," in *A Second Collection*, ed. Robert M. Doran and John D. Dadosky, CWL 6 (Toronto: University of Toronto Press, 2016), 81–82. See also, Gregory A. Sadler, ed. and trans., *Reason Fulfilled by Revelation: The 1930s Christian Philosophy Debates in France* (Washington, DC: Catholic University of America Press, 2011).
5. Lonergan, "The Origins of Christian Realism (1972)," CWL 13, 207.
6. Lonergan, "The Origins of Christian Realism (1972)," CWL 13, 207.
7. Lonergan, "The Origins of Christian Realism (1972)," CWL 13, 208.
8. Lonergan, "The Origins of Christian Realism (1972)," CWL 13, 209.
9. Lonergan, "The Origins of Christian Realism (1972)," CWL 13, 209.
10. Lonergan, "The Origins of Christian Realism (1972)," CWL 13, 210.
11. Lonergan, "The Origins of Christian Realism (1972)," CWL 13, 210.
12. Lonergan, "The Origins of Christian Realism (1972)," CWL 13, 211.
13. Lonergan, "The Origins of Christian Realism (1972)," CWL 13, 211.
14. Lonergan, "The Origins of Christian Realism (1972)," CWL 13, 211.
15. Lonergan, "The Origins of Christian Realism (1972)," CWL 13, 212.
16. Thomas Aquinas, *ST* I.27.1.
17. Thomas Aquinas, *ST* I.13.5.
18. Thomas Aquinas, *ST* I.27.1.
19. Thomas Aquinas, *ST* I.27.1.
20. Thomas Aquinas, *ST* I.27.1.

21. Hans Urs von Balthasar, *Theo-Drama: Theological Dramatic Theory, Volume 4: The Action*, trans. Graham Harrison (San Francisco: Ignatius Press, 1994), 319.
22. Balthasar, *Theo-Drama 4: The Action*, 323.
23. See Ormerod, *The Trinity: Retrieving the Western Tradition*, 2005.
24. Karl Rahner, *The Trinity*, trans. Joseph Donceel (New York: Herder & Herder, 1970), 10–11.
25. Rahner, *The Trinity*, 22.
26. See Jürgen Moltmann, *The Crucified God: The Cross of Christ as the Foundation and Criticism of Christian Theology*, trans. R. A. Wilson and John Bowden (Minneapolis: Fortress Press, 1993); idem, *The Trinity and the Kingdom: The Doctrine of God*, trans. Margaret Kohl (Minneapolis: Fortress Press, 1993); Eberhard Jüngel, *God's Being Is in Becoming: The Trinitarian Being of God in the Theology of Karl Barth*, trans. John Webster (London and New York: Bloomsbury T&T Clark, 2014); Wolfhart Pannenberg, *Systematic Theology, vol. 1.*, trans. Geoffrey W. Bromiley (Grand Rapids: Eerdmans, 1991); Robert Jenson, *Systematic Theology, vol. 1: The Triune God* (Oxford: Oxford University Press, 1997); Roger Haight, *Jesus Symbol of God* (Maryknoll, NY: Orbis, 1999); Catherine Mowry LaCugna, *God for Us: The Trinity & Christian Life* (San Francisco: Harper Collins, 1991). For an account of the various interpretations of the relationship between the immanent and economic trinities, see Chung-Hyun Baik, *The Holy Trinity—God for God and God for Us: Seven Positions on the Immanent-Economic Trinity Relation in Contemporary Trinitarian Theology*, PTMS (Eugene, OR: Wipf & Stock, 2011). For an account of the promises and perils of interpreting Rahner's *Grundaxiom*, see David Bentley Hart, *The Beauty of the Infinite: The Aesthetics of Christian Truth* (Grand Rapids: Eerdmans, 2003), 155–175.
27. A possible exception is Robert Jenson, who maintains that the psychological analogy is the greatest achievement of Augustine's Trinitarian theology, even though Jenson strongly opposes the doctrine of appropriations. His own theology is an attempt to "rescue" the psychological analogy from the rest of Augustinian theology. See Jenson, *The Triune God*, 123: "The position here developed . . . allows preservation—indeed, rescue—of a chief achievement of Augustinianism, the 'psychological' explication of the triune life."
28. Lonergan, *Verbum*, CWL 2, 11 (emphasis mine).
29. See Burrell, *Aquinas, God and Action*, 131–133.
30. Lonergan, *The Triune God: Systematics*, CWL 12, 139.
31. Lonergan, *The Triune God: Systematics*, CWL 12, 141.
32. Lonergan, *The Triune God: Systematics*, CWL 12, 141.
33. Lonergan, *The Triune God: Doctrines*, ed. Robert M. Doran and H. Daniel Monsour, trans. Michael Shields, CWL 11 (Toronto: University of Toronto Press, 2009), 717.
34. Lonergan, *The Triune God: Doctrines*, CWL 11, 717.
35. Lonergan, *The Triune God: Doctrines*, CWL 11, 717.
36. Lonergan, *The Triune God: Doctrines*, CWL 11, 717.
37. Lonergan, *The Triune God: Doctrines*, CWL 11, 717.
38. Lonergan, *The Triune God: Doctrines*, CWL 11, 719.

39. Lonergan, *The Triune God: Doctrines*, CWL 11, 719
40. Lonergan, *The Triune God: Doctrines*, CWL 11, 723.
41. Lonergan, *The Triune God: Doctrines*, CWL 11, 723.
42. Lonergan, *The Triune God: Doctrines*, CWL 11, 725.
43. Lonergan, *The Triune God: Doctrines*, CWL 11, 725.
44. Lonergan, *The Triune God: Doctrines*, CWL 11, 727.
45. Lonergan, *The Triune God: Doctrines*, CWL 11, 727.
46. Augustine, *The Trinity (De trinitate)*, trans. Edmund Hill, The Works of St. Augustine: A Translation for the 21st Century, vol. 5 (Hyde Park, NY: New City Press, 1991), 65; I.1.1.
47. The exact nature of this encounter is not at all straightforward. Much of Augustine's initial knowledge of Platonism seems to be derived from his encounters with so-called "Christian Platonists" like Ambrose of Milan. Only subsequent to his conversion to Christianity did Augustine seriously read many of the actual texts of the middle and neo-Platonic traditions so evident in his accounts of Plotinus and Porphyry in *The City of God*. See Lewis Ayres, *Augustine and the Trinity* (Cambridge: Cambridge University Press, 2010), 13–20. Ayres demonstrates that Augustine's engagement with the constellation of texts and traditions of interpretation that constitute "middle" and, later, "neo" Platonisms was a long, complicated process, and not a matter of Augustine's being converted first from Manicheism to Platonism, only subsequently from Platonism to Christianity. As Ayres shows, Augustine's habit of engagement with Platonic doctrines places him not within any "school" of non-Christian Platonism (about which his knowledge is often lacking) but rather within the tradition of Christian writers taking doctrines out their native contexts in Platonic texts and recontextualizing them in service of Christian theological rationality.
48. Augustine, *The Confessions of St. Augustine*, trans. John K. Ryan (New York: Image Books, 1960), 157; VII.1.1.
49. See Lonergan, *Insight: A Study of Human Understanding*, CWL 3, 275–279.
50. Augustine, *De Trinitate*, IX.2.12., 277–278.
51. Augustine, *De Trinitate*, IX.2.16., 280.
52. Augustine, *De Trinitate*, X.1.1., 286.
53. Augustine, *De Trinitate*, XIV.4.15., 383.
54. Burrell, *Aquinas, God and Action*, 161.
55. Burrell, *Aquinas, God and Action*, 163.
56. Burrell, *Aquinas, God and Action*, 163.
57. Burrell, *Aquinas, God and Action*, 167.
58. Burrell, *Aquinas, God and Action*, 170.
59. Lonergan, *Verbum*, CWL 2, 47.
60. See D. Stephen Long, *The Perfectly Simply Triune God: Aquinas and His Legacy* (Minneapolis: Fortress Press, 2016).
61. Lonergan, *The Triune God: Doctrines*, CWL 11, 715.
62. Lonergan, *The Triune God: Systematics*, CWL 12, 131.
63. Lonergan, *The Triune God: Systematics*, CWL 12, 133.
64. Lonergan, *The Triune God: Systematics*, CWL 12, 133.
65. Lonergan, *The Triune God: Systematics*, CWL 12, 133.

66. See Lonergan, *The Triune God: Systematics*, CWL 12, 133–135; Thomas Aquinas, *ST* I.27.1–3, *SCG* 4.11.1–8.

67. Robert M. Doran, *The Trinity in History: A Theology of the Divine Missions, Volume One: Missions and Processions* (Toronto: University of Toronto Press), 33.

68. Doran, *Trinity in History*, 34.

69. Doran, *Trinity in History*, 35.

70. This thesis is a key feature of the argument in Katherine Sonderegger, *Systematic Theology, Volume 2: The Doctrine of the Holy Trinity: Processions and Persons* (Minneapolis: Fortress Press, 2020).

71. Hans Urs von Balthasar, *The Glory of the Lord: A Theological Aesthetics, Volume 7: The New Covenant*, trans. Brian McNeil, ed. John Riches (San Francisco: Ignatius, 1989), 17.

72. Balthasar, *Glory of the Lord 7*, 17.

73. Balthasar, *Glory of the Lord 7*, 131.

74. Balthasar, *Glory of the Lord 7*, 132–133.

75. Balthasar, *Glory of the Lord 7*, 213.

76. Balthasar, *Glory of the Lord 7*, 213.

77. Balthasar, *Glory of the Lord 7*, 213–214.

78. Balthasar, *Glory of the Lord 7*, 214.

79. Balthasar, *Glory of the Lord 7*, 214.

80. Balthasar, *Glory of the Lord 7*, 217.

81. Balthasar, *Theo-Drama 4*, 319.

82. Balthasar, *Theo-Drama 4*, 320.

83. Balthasar, *Theo-Drama 4*, 323.

84. Balthasar, *Theo-Drama 4*, 324.

85. Balthasar, *Theo-Drama 4*, 324.

86. For an account of the underappreciated Thomistic valences of Balthasar's theology, see Anne M. Carpenter, *Theo-Poetics: Hans Urs von Balthasar and the Risk of Art and Being* (Notre Dame: University of Notre Dame Press, 2015).

87. Hans Urs von Balthasar, *Theo-Logic: Theological Logical Theory, Volume 2: The Truth of God*, trans. Adrian J. Walker (San Francisco: Ignatius, 2004), 152.

88. Balthasar, *Theo-Logic 2*, 152.

89. Balthasar, *Theo-Logic 2*, 155.

90. Balthasar, *Theo-Logic 2*, 155.

91. Lonergan, "Christology Today: Methodological Reflections," in *A Third Collection*, ed. Robert M. Doran and John D. Dadosky, CWL 16 (Toronto: University of Toronto Press, 2017), 91.

92. Lonergan, "Christology Today," CWL 16, 91–92.

# Conclusion

## DEMOCRATIZING THE REGAL SCIENCE

This book opened with a counterintuitive claim. It asserted (and with any luck has by now demonstrated) the strange thesis that speculative theology's renewal in modern theology requires a commerce with the revolutions in modern thought that led to its decline. Prosecuting that case has followed a curious route from scholastic retrievals of Thomas Aquinas; to the empirical turn in philosophy, science, and culture; to the development and repurposing of the theorem of the supernatural; to the theology of the divine processions. Now, at the end of that case, the whole brief must be recapitulated in a closing argument that concludes the succession of individual theses that have been articulated and advanced in this work, along with the structural architecture that ties each element to the others in a synthetic whole. But it is also time to venture guesses and cast visions. About the opportunities for renewal in the present. About the possibilities for emergences in the future. And about what is demanded of us by both.

Speculative theology, like all forms of inquiry, finds its exigence in the existential horizon of an inquirer. It is the method—the road, way, path—that the *eros* of intellectual desire follows as the mind migrates from wonder's immediacy to the articulation of questions, to the fantastic, irreducible delight of discovering answers and sharing them with others. But questions are specifications of intellect's *eros* to circumstance. They arise as logical emanations not from universal *eros* but from the slings and arrows of living in a world. Speculation is a tool of understanding. And understanding is the answer to questions that arise in someone, at some time, in some place, about something. Abstract too far from the concrete contexts of its exigence, and speculation becomes a method for answering questions that no one is asking.

The tortured pluralism of the late patristic and early medieval world was the consequence of a shared existential circumstance that desired, desperately, to know what it meant to be free in a world of sin and grace. Everyone knew what the Catholic faith proclaimed, but no one seemed able to explain how such a proclamation could be reconciled with the demands of intellectual consciousness. It was only by adopting a new mentality, by mapping the coordinates of the problem onto that mentality, and by holding relevant mental distinctions in a theorematic frame that high medieval theology found its footing on centuries of nettlesome questions and at long last made progress on answering them. Through such a mentality, theology became a *scientia*—the *regina scientiarum*. The flowering of speculative theology in the soil of thirteenth-century thought is an inflection point in the development of Christian (indeed, human) intellectual life, but that life itself was held aloft by a superstructure of cultural and social institutions whose hegemony has long since passed into the realm of memory.

Today, modern empirical methods are legion. Having subordinated the abstract rigor of logic and metaphysics to the canons of empirical science, philosophy, theology, and the notion of culture itself have been remade, each according to the determinations of their respective objects of inquiry. Contemporary theologians—if they are to be truly contemporary—must set their faces toward the complexity, growth, transpositions of context, and dynamism of spirit that establish the exigence for authentic pluralism. This self possessed spiritual dynamism is more than the condition of possibility for authentic theological performance. It is also an analogy for the speculative theology of the divine procession of the eternal Word.

Where theology goes in the future will in large part be determined by decisions made in the present. If today's revanchist forces prevail—even in the short term—understanding will suffer. Their capacity for curiosity is meager. And their hunger for certainty (especially for the sort that can be weaponized) is profound. The integralist fantasy is that—by hook or by crook—classicist culture will reassert itself through the machinations of strongmen and strong gods. But the flight from understanding, even in its gilded forms, has the liability of lionizing stupidity. No serious revanchist thinks their scheming will win the day. They cast their vituperations only to be heard, with the hope that in being heard, their voices matter and won't be forgotten. But they are cursing into the wind. They can stand athwart history shouting "stop" until they are hoarse, but history's momentum will be conserved. Time marches on. And their time is over.

Speculative theology is both local and global. Its geography still encompasses the institutions and legacies of the medieval world. But it extends to those places in which the systematic exigence is only now beginning to emerge (and in response to a quite distinct set of concrete questions). The paradigmatic question for contemporary theology is not whether and where a new Aquinas will arise. Contemporary methods do not admit of a singular genius. Instead, the question is how speculative mediations that come to the fore of theology in distinct places, cultures, and times will be related, one to the other, in an authentic whole—a *Catholica*.

Speculative pluralism is one answer to that question. It is a form of catholicity that responds to the emergence of the systematic exigence in new cultural, religious, and intellectual situations. It is a realist, liberal rejection of the romantic, integralist fantasy. It is a declaration that power is an effect of cooperative thinking, not the cause of what one should think or how one should live. A perceptive critic might ask how demonstrating the compatibility of two storied theologians of the previous century (and even then on only one particular question) proves the validity of speculative pluralism's methodical frame for the less familiar, less conventional—to be frank, less white—theologies of the future. All I can say in response is that any future theology, if it is to be Catholic, must reconcile itself not only to its present but also to its past. As such, the "proof" offered here is meant only as an initial step in a much longer journey, one that will be trod only by those who believe that in authentic understanding lies liberation.

# Bibliography

Ahmari, Sorhab. *The Unbroken Thread: Discovering the Wisdom of Tradition in an Age of Chaos*. New York: Convergent, 2021.

Augustine. *The Confessions of St. Augustine*. Translated by John K. Ryan. New York: Image Books, 1960.

———. *The Trinity (De trinitate)*. Translated by Edmund Hill. The Works of St. Augustine: A Translation for the 21st Century 5. Hyde Park, NY: New City Press, 1991.

Aristotle. *Posterior Analytics, Topica*. Translated by Hugh Tredennick and E. S. Forster. Loeb Classical Library 391. Cambridge: Harvard University Press, 1960.

Ayres, Lewis. *Augustine and the Trinity*. Cambridge: Cambridge University Press, 2010.

———. "The Memory of Tradition: Postconciliar Renewal and One Recent Thomism." *The Thomist* 79 (2015): 511–550.

———. *Nicaea and Its Legacy: An Approach to Fourth-Century Trinitarian Theology*. Oxford: Oxford University Press, 2004.

Baik, Chung-Hyun. *The Holy Trinity—God for God and God for Us: Seven Positions on the Immanent-Economic Trinity Relation in Contemporary Trinitarian Theology*. Princeton Theological Monograph Series. Eugene, OR: Wipf & Stock, 2011.

Balthasar, Hans Urs von. *Cosmic Liturgy: The Universe according to Maximus the Confessor*. Translated by Brian Daley. San Francisco: Communio and Ignatius Press, 2003.

———. *Epilogue*. Translated by Edward T. Oakes. San Francisco: Ignatius Press, 2004.

———. *Explorations in Theology, Volume 1: The Word Made Flesh*. Translated by A. V. Littledale and Alexander Dru. San Francisco: Ignatius Press, 1989.

———. *Explorations in Theology, Volume 2: Spouse of the Word*. Translated by A. V. Littledale, Alexander Dru, Brian McNeil, John Saward, and Edward T. Oakes. San Francisco: Ignatius Press, 1991.

———. *Explorations in Theology, Volume 3: Creator Spirit*. Translated by Brian McNeil. San Francisco: Ignatius Press, 1993.

———. *Explorations in Theology, Volume 4: Spirit and Institution*. Translated by Edward T. Oakes. San Francisco: Ignatius Press, 1995.

———. *The Glory of the Lord, Volume 1: Seeing the Form.* Translated by Erasmo Leiva-Merikakis. Edinburgh: T&T Clark, and San Francisco: Ignatius Press, 1982.

———. *The Glory of the Lord, Volume 2: Studies in Theological Style: Clerical Styles.* Translated by Andrew Louth, Francis McDonagh, and Brian McNeil. Edinburgh: T&T Clark, and San Francisco: Ignatius Press, 1984.

———. *The Glory of the Lord, Volume 3: Studies in Theological Style: Lay Styles.* Translated by Andrew Louth, John Saward, Martin Simon, and Rowan Williams. Edinburgh: T&T Clark, and San Francisco: Ignatius Press, 1986.

———. *The Glory of the Lord, Volume 4: In the Realm of Metaphysics in Antiquity.* Translated by Brian McNeil, Andrew Louth, John Saward, Rowan Williams, and Oliver Davies. Edinburgh: T&T Clark, and San Francisco: Ignatius Press, 1989.

———. *The Glory of the Lord, Volume 5: In the Realm of Metaphysics in the Modern Age.* Translated by Oliver Davies, Andrew Louth, Brian McNeil, John Saward, and Rowan Williams. Edinburgh: T&T Clark, and San Francisco: Ignatius Press, 1991.

———. *The Glory of the Lord, Volume 6: Theology: The Old Covenant.* Translated by Brian McNeil and Erasmo Leiva-Merikakis. Edinburgh: T&T Clark, and San Francisco: Ignatius Press, 1991.

———. *The Glory of the Lord, Volume 7: Theology: The New Covenant.* Translated by Brian McNeil. Edinburgh: T&T Clark, and San Francisco: Ignatius Press, 1989.

———. *Mysterium Paschale.* Translated by Aidan Nichols. Edinburgh: T&T Clark, 1990; Second Corrected Edition. Grand Rapids, MI: Eerdmans, 1993.

———. *Presence and Thought: An Essay on the Religious Philosophy of Gregory of Nyssa.* Translated by Mark Sebanc. San Francisco: Communio and Ignatius Press, 1995.

———. *Theo-Drama: Theological Dramatic Theory, Volume 1: Prolegomena.* Translated by Graham Harrison. San Francisco: Ignatius Press, 1988.

———. *Theo-Drama: Theological Dramatic Theory, Volume 2: Dramatis Personae: Man in God.* Translated by Graham Harrison. San Francisco: Ignatius Press, 1990.

———. *Theo-Drama: Theological Dramatic Theory, Volume 3: Dramatis Personae: Persons in Christ.* Translated by Graham Harrison. San Francisco: Ignatius Press, 1992.

———. *Theo-Drama: Theological Dramatic Theory, Volume 4: The Action.* Translated by Graham Harrison. San Francisco: Ignatius Press, 1994.

———. *Theo-Drama: Theological Dramatic Theory, Volume 5: The Final Act.* Translated by Graham Harrison. San Francisco: Ignatius Press, 1998.

———. *Theo-Logic: Theological Logical Theory, Volume 1: The Truth of the World.* Translated by Adrian J. Walker. San Francisco: Ignatius Press, 2000.

———. *Theo-Logic: Theological Logical Theory, Volume 2: The Truth of God.* Translated by Adrian J. Walker. San Francisco: Ignatius Press, 2004.

———. *Theo-Logic: Theological Logical Theory, Volume 3: The Spirit of Truth.* Translated by Graham Harrison. San Francisco: Ignatius Press, 2005.

———. *Theology of History.* Second Edition. New York: Sheed & Ward, 1963.

———. *Truth Is Symphonic: Aspects of Christian Pluralism.* Translated by Graham Harrison. San Francisco: Ignatius Press, 1987.

Becker, Carl. *The Heavenly City of the Eighteenth Century Philosophers.* New Haven: Yale University Press, 1932.

Beumer, Johannes. "Konklusionstheologie?" *Zeitschrift für katholische Theologie* 63 (1939): 360–365.

———. *Theologie als Glaubensverständnis.* Würzburg: Echter-Verlag, 1953.

Blondel, Maurice. *The Letter on Apologetics & History and Dogma.* Translated by Alexander Dru and Illtyd Trethowan, Grand Rapids: Eerdmans Publishing Company, 1994.

Boccaccini, Gabriele. *Roots of Rabbinic Judaism: An Intellectual History from Ezekiel to Daniel.* Grand Rapids: Eerdmans, 2002.

Bouillard, Henri. *Conversion et grâce chez s. Thomas d'Aquin.* Paris: Aubier, 1944.

Brague, Rémi. *Curing Mad Truths: Medieval Wisdom for the Modern Age.* Notre Dame: University of Notre Dame Press, 2019.

Burrell, David. *Analogy and Philosophical Language.* Reprint Edition. Eugene, OR: Wipf & Stock, 1973.

———. *Aquinas, God and Action.* Third Edition. Edited by Mary Budde Ragan. Eugene, OR: Wipf & Stock, 2016.

———. *Freedom and Creation in Three Traditions.* Notre Dame: University of Notre Dame Press, 1993.

———. *Knowing the Unknowable God: Ibn-Sina, Maimonides, Aquinas.* Notre Dame: University of Notre Dame Press, 1986.

———. *Faith and Freedom: An Interfaith Perspective.* Oxford and Malaen, MA: Blackwell, 2004.

Butterfield, Herbert. *The Origins of Modern Science.* Revised Edition. New York: Free Press, 1997.

Candler, Peter. *Theology, Rhetoric, Manuduction, or Reading Scripture Together on the Path to God.* Grand Rapids: Eerdmans Publishing Company, 2006.

Carpenter, Anne M. *Theo-Poetics: Hans Urs von Balthasar and the Risk of Art and Being.* Notre Dame: University of Notre Dame Press, 2015.

Chenu, Marie-Dominique. *Introduction a l'étude de Saint Thomas d'Aquin.* Montreal: Institut d'études médiévales, 1950.

———. *St. Thomas d'Aquin et la théologie.* Paris: Les Editions du Seuil, 1959.

Coakley, Sarah. *God, Sexuality, and the Self: An Essay "On the Trinity."* New York: Cambridge University, 2013.

Congar, Yves. *A History of Theology.* Translated and edited by Hunter Guthrie. Garden City, NY: Doubleday, 1968.

Copeland, M. Shawn. *Enfleshing Freedom: Body, Race, and Being.* Minneapolis: Fortress Press, 2009.

Cowell, F. R. *Culture in Private and Public Life.* London: Thames and Hudson, 1959.

Crombie, A. C. *Augustine to Galileo: The History of Science, A.D. 400–1650.* Cambridge: Harvard University Press, 1953.

———. *Robert Grosseteste and the Origins of Experimental Science, 1100–1700.* Oxford: Clarendon Press, 1953.

Crowe, Frederick E. *The Lonergan Enterprise.* Cambridge, MA: Cowley Publications, 1980.

Daley, Brian. "Balthasar's Reading of the Church Fathers." In *The Cambridge Companion to Hans Urs von Balthasar*, 187–206, edited by Edward T. Oakes and David Moss. Cambridge: Cambridge University Press, 2004.

Davies, Brian. "Is *Sacra Doctrina* Theology?" *New Blackfriars* 71 (1990): 141–147.

Dawson, Christopher. *The Age of the Gods: A Study in the Origins of Culture in Prehistoric Europe and the Ancient East*. Works of Christopher Dawson. Washington, DC: Catholic University of America Press, 2012.

———. *The Historic Reality of Christian Culture: A Way to the Renewal of Human Life*. New York: Harper Torchbooks, 1960.

Deansley, Margaret. *A History of the Medieval Church, 590–1500*. Ninth Edition. London and New York: Routledge, 1969.

Desmond, William. *God and the Between*. Malden, MA, and Oxford: Blackwell, 2008.

Doran, Robert M. "Envisioning a Systematic Theology." *Lonergan Workshop* 20, 105–126. Edited by Frederick Lawrence. Boston College, 2008.

———. "A New Project in Systematic Theology." *Theological Studies* 76, no. 2 (2015): 243–259.

———. "*Intelligentia Fidei* in *De Deo Trino, Pars Systematica*: A Commentary on the First Three Sections of Chapter One." *Method: Journal of Lonergan Studies* 19, no.1 (2001): 35–84.

———. "The Starting Point of Systematic Theology." *Theological Studies* 67, no. 4 (2006): 750–776.

———. "System and History: The Challenge to Catholic Theology." *Theological Studies* 60, no. 4 (1999): 652–678.

———. *Theology and the Dialectics of History*. Toronto: University of Toronto Press, 1990.

———. "The First Chapter of *De Deo Trino*: The Issues." *Method: Journal of Lonergan Studies* 18, no.1 (2000): 27–48.

———. *The Trinity in History: A Theology of the Divine Missions, Volume One: Missions and Processions*. Toronto: University of Toronto Press, 2013.

———. *The Trinity in History: A Theology of the Divine Missions, Volume Two: Missions, Relations, and Persons*. Toronto: University of Toronto Press, 2019.

———. "The Truth of Theological Understanding in *Divinarum Personarum* and *De Deo Trino, Pars Systematica*." *Method: Journal of Lonergan Studies* 20, no.1 (2002): 33–76.

———. *What Is Systematic Theology?* Toronto: University of Toronto Press, 2005.

Drey, Johann Sebastian. *Brief Introduction to the Study of Theology with Reference to the Scientific Standpoint and the Catholic System*. Translated by Michael J. Himes. Notre Dame, IN: University of Notre Dame Press, 1994.

Eliot, T. S. *Notes towards the Definition of Culture*. London: Faber and Faber, 1948.

Faggioli, Massimo. *True Reform: Liturgy and Ecclesiology in* Sancrosanctum Concilium. Collegeville, MN: Liturgical Press, 2012.

Filser, Hubert. *Dogma, Dogmen, Dogmatik: Eine Untersuchung zur Begründung und zur Entstehungsgeschichte einer theologischen Disziplin van der Reformation bis zur Spätaufklärung*. Munster: LIT Verlag, 2001.

Fukuyama, Francis. *Liberalism and Its Discontents*. New York: Farrar, Strauss and Giroux, 2022.

Gadamer, Hans Georg. "The Problem of Historical Consciousness." In *Interpretive Social Science: A Second Look*, 82–140, edited by Paul Rabinow and William M. Sullivan. Berkeley, Los Angeles, and London: University of California Press, 1987.

Geertz, Clifford. "The Impact of the Concept of Culture on the Concept of Man." In *The Interpretation of Cultures: Selected Essays by Clifford Geertz*, 33–54. New York: Basic Books, 1973.

———. *The Interpretation of Cultures: Selected Essays by Clifford Geertz*. New York: Basic Books, 1973.

———. "On Deep Play: Notes on a Balinese Cockfight." In *The Interpretation of Cultures: Selected Essays by Clifford Geertz*, 412–454. New York: Basic Books, 1973.

———. "Religion as a Cultural System." In *The Interpretation of Cultures: Selected Essays by Clifford Geertz*, 87–125. New York: Basic Books, 1973.

———. "Thick Description: Toward an Interpretive Theory of Culture." In *The Interpretation of Cultures: Selected Essays by Clifford Geertz*, 3–32. New York: Basic Books, 1973.

Gilson, Etienne. *Being and Some Philosophers*. Second Edition. Toronto: Pontifical Institute of Medieval Studies, 1949 and 1952.

Gopnik, Adam. *A Thousand Small Sanities: The Moral Adventure of Liberalism*. New York: Basic Books, 2019.

Grant, Sara. *Toward an Alternative Theology: Confessions of a Non-Dualist Christian*. Notre Dame, IN: University of Notre Dame Press, 2002.

Gunkle, Hermann. *Creation and Chaos in the Primary Era and the Eschaton: A Religio-Historical Study of Genesis 1 and Revelation 12*. Translated by K. William Whitney. Grand Rapids: Eerdmans, 2006.

Haight, Roger. *Jesus Symbol of God*. Maryknoll, NY: Orbis, 1999.

Hart, David Bentley. *The Beauty of the Infinite: The Aesthetics of Christian Truth*. Grand Rapids: Eerdmans, 2003.

Hofstadter, Richard. *Hofstadter: Anti-Intellectualism in American Life, The Paranoid Style in American Politics, Uncollected Essays 1956–1965*. Library of America. New York: Library of America, 2020.

Hunt, Anne. *The Trinity and the Paschal Mystery: A Development in Recent Catholic Theology*. New Theology Studies 5. Collegeville: Liturgical Press, 1997.

Jacobs, Jane. *Dark Age Ahead*. New York: Random House, 2004.

———. *The Death and Life of Great American Cities*. Modern Library Edition. New York: Modern Library 1993.

Jaspers, Karl. *The Origin and Goal of History*. Translated by Michael Bullock. New York: Routledge, 2010.

Jenson, Philip Peter. *Graded Holiness: A Key to the Priestly Conception of the World*. Sheffield, UK: Sheffield Academic Press, 1992.

Jenson, Robert. *Systematic Theology, Volume 1: The Triune God*. Oxford: Oxford University Press, 1997.

Johnson, Elizabeth A. *She Who Is: The Mystery of God in Feminist Theological Discourse.* New York: Crossroad, 1992.

Jüngel, Eberhard. *God's Being Is in Becoming: The Trinitarian Being of God in the Theology of Karl Barth.* Translated by John Webster. London and New York: Bloomsbury T&T Clark, 2014.

Keller, Catherine. *Face of the Deep: A Theology of Becoming.* London: Routledge, 2003.

Kessler, Michael, and Christian Sheppard, eds. *Mystics: Presence and Aporia.* London and Chicago: University of Chicago Press, 2003.

Kluckhohn, Clyde. *Mirror for Man: The Relation of Anthropology to Modern Life.* New York: McGraw-Hill, 1959.

Kuhn, Thomas. *The Structure of Scientific Revolutions.* Third Edition. Chicago: University of Chicago Press, 1996.

LaCugna, Catherine Mowry. *God for Us: The Trinity & Christian Life.* San Francisco: Harper Collins, 1991.

Langer, Susanne K. *Philosophical Sketches: A Study of the Human Mind in Relation to Feeling, Explored through Art, Language, and Symbol.* Baltimore: Johns Hopkins University Press, 1962.

Latour, Bruno. *We Have Never Been Modern.* Translated by Catherine Porter. Cambridge, MA: Harvard University Press, 1993.

Lehner, Ulrich, Richard Muller, and A. E. Roeber, eds. *Oxford Handbook of Early Modern Theology.* Oxford: Oxford University Press, 2016.

Leinsle, G. "Sources, Methods and Forms of Early Modern Theology." In *Oxford Handbook of Early Modern Theology*, 25–42, edited by Ulrich Lehner, Richard Muller, and A. E. Roeber. Oxford: Oxford University Press, 2016.

Leo XIII. *Aeterni Patris.* Accessed August 28, 2020. Vatican.va.

———. *Providentissimus Deus.* Accessed August 28, 2020. Vatican.va.

Levenson, John. *Creation and the Persistence of Evil: The Jewish Drama of Divine Omnipotence.* Princeton, NJ: Princeton University Press, 1994.

Liddy, Richard. *Transforming Light: Intellectual Conversion in the Early Lonergan.* Collegeville, MN: Liturgical Press, 1993.

Lilla, Mark. *The Reckless Mind: Intellectuals in Politics.* Rev. ed. New York: New York Review Books, 2016.

———. *The Shipwrecked Mind: On Political Reaction.* New York: New York Review Books, 2016.

Lonergan, Bernard. "The Absence of God in Modern Culture." In *A Second Collection*, 86–98. Edited by Robert M. Doran and John D. Dadosky. Collected Works of Lonergan 13. Toronto: University of Toronto Press, 2016.

———. "The Analogy of Meaning." In *Philosophical and Theological Papers, 1958–1964*, 183–213. Edited by Robert C. Croken, Frederick Crowe, and Robert M. Doran. Collected Works of Bernard Lonergan 6. Toronto: University of Toronto, 1996.

———. "Aquinas Today: Tradition and Innovation." In *A Third Collection*, 34–51. Edited by Robert M. Doran and John D. Dadosky. Collected Works of Bernard Lonergan 16. Toronto: University of Toronto Press, 2017.

———. "Christ as Subject: A Reply." In *Collection*, 153–184. Edited by Frederick E. Crowe and R. Doran. Collected Works of Bernard Lonergan 4. Toronto: University of Toronto Press, 1988.

———. "Christology Today: Methodological Reflections." In *A Third Collection*, 70–93. Edited by Robert M. Doran and John D. Dadosky. Collected Works of Bernard Lonergan 16. Toronto: University of Toronto Press, 2017.

———. "Cognitional Structure." In *Collection*, 205–221. Edited by Frederick E. Crowe and R. Doran. Collected Works of Bernard Lonergan 4. Toronto: University of Toronto Press, 1988.

———. "De ente supernaturali." In *Early Latin Theology*, 53–255. Edited by Robert Doran and H. Daniel Monsour. Collected Works of Bernard Lonergan 19. Toronto: University of Toronto Press, 2011.

———. "De scientia atque voluntate Dei." In *Early Latin Theology*, 257–411. Edited by Robert M. Doran and H. Daniel Monsour. Collected Works of Bernard Lonergan 19. Toronto: University of Toronto Press, 2011.

———. "Dialectic of Authority." In *A Third Collection*, 3–9. Edited by Robert M. Doran and John D. Dadosky. Collected Works of Bernard Lonergan 16. Toronto: University of Toronto Press, 2017.

———. "Dimensions of Meaning." In *Collection*, 232–245. Edited by Frederick E. Crowe and R. Doran. Collected Works of Bernard Lonergan 4. Toronto: University of Toronto Press, 1988.

———. "Doctrinal Pluralism." In *Philosophical and Theological Papers, 1965–1980*, 70–104. Edited by Robert C. Croken and Robert M. Doran. Collected Works of Bernard Lonergan 17. Toronto: University of Toronto Press, 2004.

———. *Early Latin Theology*. Edited by Robert Doran and H. Daniel Monsour. Translated by Michael Shields. Collected Works of Bernard Lonergan 19. Toronto: University of Toronto Press, 2011.

———. *Early Works in Theological Method I*. Edited by Robert M. Doran and Robert C. Croken. Collected Works of Bernard Lonergan 22. Toronto: University of Toronto Press, 2010.

———. *Early Works on Theological Method II*. Edited by Robert M. Doran and H. Daniel Monsour. Translated by Michael G. Shields. Collected Works of Bernard Lonergan 23. Toronto: University of Toronto Press, 2013.

———. "Existenz and Aggiornamento." In *Collection*, 222–231. Edited by Frederick E. Crowe and Robert M. Doran. Collected Works of Bernard Lonergan 4. Toronto: University of Toronto Press, 1988.

———. "Faith and Beliefs." In *Philosophical and Theological Papers, 1965–1980*, 30–48. Edited by Robert C. Croken and Robert M. Doran. Collected Works of Bernard Lonergan 17. Toronto: University of Toronto Press, 2004.

———. "Finality, Love, Marriage." In *Collection*, 17–52. Edited by Frederick E. Crowe and Robert M. Doran. Collected Works of Bernard Lonergan 4. Toronto: University of Toronto Press, 1988.

———. "The Form of Inference." In *Collection*, 3–16. Edited by Frederick E. Crowe and Robert M. Doran. Collected Works of Lonergan 4. Toronto: University of Toronto Press, 1988.

———. "The Form of Mathematical Inference." In *Shorter Papers*, 3–12. Edited by Robert C. Croken, Robert M. Doran, and H. Daniel Monsour. Collected Works of Lonergan 20. Toronto: University of Toronto Press, 2007.

———. "The Functional Specialty 'Systematics.'" In *Philosophical and Theological Papers, 1965–1980*, 172–198. Edited by Robert C. Croken and Robert M. Doran. Collected Works of Bernard Lonergan 17. Toronto: University of Toronto Press, 2004.

———. "The Future of Thomism." In *A Second Collection*, 39–47. Edited by Robert M. Doran and John D. Dadosky. Collected Works of Lonergan 13. Toronto: University of Toronto Press, 2016.

———. "God's Knowledge and Will." In *Early Latin Theology*, 257–411. Edited by Robert M. Doran and H. Daniel Monsour. Translated by Michael Shields. Collected Works of Bernard Lonergan 19. Toronto: University of Toronto Press, 2011.

———. *Grace and Freedom: Operative Grace in the Thought of St Thomas Aquinas*. Edited by Frederick E. Crowe and Robert M. Doran. Collected Works of Bernard Lonergan 1. Toronto: University of Toronto Press, 2000.

———. "The *Gratia Operans* Dissertation: Preface and Introduction." *Method: Journal of Lonergan Studies* 3, no.2 (1985): 9–46.

———. "Horizons." In *Philosophical and Theological Papers, 1965–1980*, 10–29. Edited by Robert C. Croken and Robert M. Doran. Collected Works of Bernard Lonergan 17. Toronto: University of Toronto Press, 2004.

———. "Horizons and Transpositions." In *Philosophical and Theological Papers 1965–1980*, 409–432. Edited by Robert C. Croken and Robert M. Doran. Collected Works of Bernard Lonergan 17. Toronto: University of Toronto, 2004.

———. "The Human Good." In *Philosophical and Theological Papers, 1965–1980*, 332–351. Edited by Robert C. Croken and Robert M. Doran. Collected Works of Bernard Lonergan 17. Toronto: University of Toronto, 2004.

———. *Insight: A Study of Human Understanding*. Edited by Frederick Crowe and Robert M. Doran. Collected Works of Bernard Lonergan 3. Toronto: University of Toronto, 1992.

———. "Insight Revisited." In *A Second Collection*, 221–234. Collected Works of Lonergan 13. Edited by Robert M. Doran and John D. Dadosky. Toronto: University of Toronto Press, 2016.

———. "An Interview with Fr. Bernard Lonergan, S.J." In *A Second Collection*, 1176–1194. Edited by Robert M. Doran and John D. Dadosky. Collected Works of Lonergan 13. Toronto: University of Toronto Press, 2016.

———. "Is it Real." In *Philosophical and Theological Papers 1965–1980*, 119–139. Edited by Robert C. Croken and Robert M. Doran. Collected Works of Bernard Lonergan 17. Toronto: University of Toronto Press, 2004.

———. "The Mediation of Christ in Prayer." In *Philosophical and Theological Papers 1958–1965*, 160–182. Edited by Robert C. Croken, Frederick Crowe, and Robert M. Doran. Collected Works of Bernard Lonergan 6. Toronto: University of Toronto Press, 1996.

———. "Merging Horizons: System, Common Sense, Scholarship." In *Philosophical and Theological Papers 1965–1980*, 49–69. Edited by Robert C. Croken and

Robert M. Doran. Collected Works of Bernard Lonergan 17. Toronto: University of Toronto Press, 2004.

———. "Method in Catholic Theology." In *Philosophical and Theological Papers, 1958–1964*, 29–53. Edited by Robert C. Croken, Frederick Crowe, and Robert M. Doran. Collected Works of Bernard Lonergan 6. Toronto: University of Toronto Press, 1996.

———. *Method in Theology*. Edited by Robert M. Doran and John D. Dadosky. Collected Works of Bernard Lonergan 14. Toronto: University of Toronto Press, 2017.

———. "Method: Trend and Variations." In *A Third Collection*, 10–20. Edited by Robert M. Doran and John D. Dadosky. Collected Works of Bernard Lonergan 16. Toronto: University of Toronto Press, 2017.

———. "Mission and the Spirit." In *A Third Collection*, 21–33. Edited by Robert M. Doran and John D. Dadosky. Collected Works of Bernard Lonergan 16. Toronto: University of Toronto Press, 2017.

———. "The Natural Desire to See God." In *Collection*, 81–91. Edited by Frederick E. Crowe and Robert M. Doran. Collected Works of Bernard Lonergan 4. Toronto: University of Toronto, 1988.

———. "Natural Knowledge of God." In *A Second Collection*, 99–113. Edited by Robert M. Doran and John D. Dadosky. Collected Works of Lonergan 13. Toronto: University of Toronto Press, 2016.

———. "Natural Right and Historical Mindedness." In *A Third Collection*, –176. Edited by Robert M. Doran and John D. Dadosky. Collected Works of Bernard Lonergan 16. Toronto: University of Toronto Press, 2017.

———. *The Ontological and Psychological Constitution of Christ*. Translated by Michael Shields. Collected Works of Bernard Lonergan 7. Toronto: University of Toronto Press, 2002.

———. "The Origins of Christian Realism." In *A Second Collection*, 202–220. Edited by Robert M. Doran and John D. Dadosky. Collected Works of Lonergan 13. Toronto: University of Toronto Press, 2016.

———. "The Origins of Christian Realism (1961)." In *Philosophical and Theological Papers, 1958–1964*, 80–93. Edited by Robert C. Croken, Frederick Crowe, and Robert M. Doran. Collected Works of Bernard Lonergan 6. Toronto: University of Toronto, 1996.

———. "Philosophy and Theology." In *A Second Collection*, 163–175. Edited by Robert M. Doran and John D. Dadosky. Collected Works of Lonergan 13. Toronto: University of Toronto Press, 2016.

———. "Philosophy, God and Theology: Lecture I: Philosophy of God." In *Philosophical and Theological Papers, 1965–1980*, 162–178. Edited by Robert C. Croken and Robert M. Doran. Collected Works of Bernard Lonergan 17. Toronto: University of Toronto Press, 2004.

———. "A Post-Hegelian Philosophy of Religion." In *A Third Collection*, 194–213. Edited by Robert M. Doran and John D. Dadosky. Collected Works of Bernard Lonergan 16. Toronto: University of Toronto Press, 2017.

———. "Prolegomena to the Study of the Emerging Religious Consciousness of Our Time." In *A Third Collection*, 52–69. Edited by Robert M. Doran and John D. Dadosky. Collected Works of Bernard Lonergan 16. Toronto: University of Toronto Press, 2017.

———. "Questionaire on Philosophy: Response." In *Philosophical and Theological Papers 1965–1980*, 352–383. Edited by Robert C. Croken and Robert M. Doran. Collected Works of Bernard Lonergan 17. Toronto: University of Toronto Press, 2004.

———. "Religious Knowledge." In *A Third Collection*, 124–138. Edited by Robert M. Doran and John D. Dadosky. Collected Works of Bernard Lonergan 16. Toronto: University of Toronto Press, 2017.

———. "Revolution in Catholic Theology." In *A Second Collection*, 195–201. Edited by Robert M. Doran and John D. Dadosky. Collected Works of Bernard Lonergan 13. Toronto: University of Toronto Press, 2016.

———. "Sacralization and Secularization." In *Philosophical and Theological Papers, 1965–1980*, 259–281. Edited by Robert C. Croken and Robert M. Doran. Collected Works of Bernard Lonergan 17. Toronto: University of Toronto, 2004.

———. "The Scope of Renewal." In *Philosophical and Theological Papers, 1965–1980*, 282–300. Edited by Robert Croken and Robert Doran. Collected Works of Bernard Lonergan 17. Toronto: University of Toronto Press, 2004.

———. "Second Lecture: Religious Knowledge." In *A Third Collection*, 124–139. Edited by Robert M. Doran and John D. Dadosky. Collected Works of Bernard Lonergan 16. Toronto: University of Toronto Press, 2017.

———. "Self-Transcendence: Intellectual, Moral, Religious." In *Philosophical and Theological Papers, 1965–1980*, 313–331. Edited by Robert Croken and Robert Doran. Collected Works of Bernard Lonergan 17. Toronto: University of Toronto Press, 2004.

———. "The Subject." In *A Second Collection*, 60–74. Edited by Robert M. Doran and John D. Dadosky. Collected Works of Lonergan 13. Toronto: University of Toronto Press, 2016.

———. "The Supernatural Order." In *Early Latin Theology*, 562–665. Edited by Robert M. Doran and H. Daniel Monsour. Translated by Michael Shields. Collected Works of Bernard Lonergan 19. Toronto: University of Toronto Press, 2011.

———. "Supplementary Notes on Sanctifying Grace." In *Early Latin Theology*, 53–255. Edited by Robert Doran and H. Daniel Monsour. Translated by Michael Shields. Collected Works of Bernard Lonergan 19. Toronto: University of Toronto, 2011.

———. "The Syllogism." In *Shorter Papers*, 13–33. Edited by Robert C. Croken, Robert M. Doran, and H. Daniel Monsour. Collected Works of Lonergan 20. Toronto: University of Toronto Press, 2007.

———. "Theology and Man's Future." In *A Second Collection*, 114–126. Edited by Robert M. Doran and John D. Dadosky. Collected Works of Lonergan 13. Toronto: University of Toronto Press, 2016.

———. "Theology and Understanding." In *Collection*, 114–132. Edited by Frederick E. Crowe and Robert M. Doran. Collected Works of Bernard Lonergan 4. Toronto: University of Toronto, 1988.

———. "Theology as Christian Phenomenon." In *Philosophical and Theological Papers, 1958–1964*, 244–272. Edited by Robert C. Croken, Frederick Crowe, and Robert M. Doran. Collected Works of Bernard Lonergan 6. Toronto: University of Toronto, 1996.

———. "Theology in Its New Context." In *A Second Collection*, 48–59. Edited by Robert M. Doran and John D. Dadosky. Collected Works of Lonergan 13. Toronto: University of Toronto Press, 2016.

———. "Theories of Inquiry: Responses to a Symposium." In *A Second Collection*, 31–38. Edited by Robert M. Doran and John D. Dadosky. Collected Works of Lonergan 13. Toronto: University of Toronto Press, 2016.

———. "Third Lecture: The Ongoing Genesis of Methods." In *A Third Collection*, 140–160. Edited by Robert M. Doran and John D. Dadosky. Collected Works of Bernard Lonergan 16. Toronto: University of Toronto Press, 2017.

———. "Time and Meaning." In *Philosophical and Theological Papers, 1958–1964*, 94–121. Edited by Robert C. Croken, Frederick Crowe, and Robert M. Doran. Collected Works of Bernard Lonergan 6. Toronto: University of Toronto, 1996.

———. *Topics in Education: The Cincinnati Lectures of 1959 on the Philosophy of Education*. Edited by Robert Doran and Frederick E. Crowe. Collected Works of Bernard Lonergan 10. Toronto: University of Toronto Press, 1993.

———. "The Transition from a Classicist World-View to Historical-Mindedness." In *A Second Collection*, 3–10. Edited by Robert M. Doran and John D. Dadosky. Collected Works of Lonergan 13. Toronto: University of Toronto Press, 2016.

———. *The Triune God: Doctrines*. Edited by Robert M. Doran and H. Daniel Monsour. Translated by Michael Shields. Collected Works of Bernard Lonergan 11. Toronto: University of Toronto Press, 2009.

———. *The Triune God: Systematics*. Edited by Robert M. Doran and H. Daniel Monsour. Translated by Michael Shields. Collected Works of Bernard Lonergan 12. Toronto: University of Toronto Press, 2007.

———. "True Judgment and Science." In *Shorter Papers*, 34–44. Edited by Robert C. Croken, Robert M. Doran, and H. Daniel Monsour. Collected Works of Lonergan 20. Toronto: University of Toronto Press, 2007.

———. *Understanding and Being: The Halifax Lectures on "Insight."* Edited by Elizabeth Morelli and Mark Morelli. Second Edition. Revised by Frederick E. Crowe et al. Collected Works of Bernard Lonergan 5. Toronto: University of Toronto Press, 1990.

———. "Understanding and Method." In *Early Works on Theological Method 2*, 3–229. Edited by Robert M. Doran and H. Daniel Monsour. Translated by Michael G. Shields. Collected Works of Lonergan 23. Toronto: University of Toronto Press, 2013.

———. "Unity and Plurality: The Coherence of Christian Truth." In *A Third Collection*, 228–238. Edited by Robert M. Doran and John D. Dadosky. Collected Works of Bernard Lonergan 16. Toronto: University of Toronto Press, 2017.

———. *Verbum: Word and Idea in Aquinas*. Edited by Frederick Crowe and Robert Doran. Collected Works of Bernard Lonergan 2. Toronto: University of Toronto Press, 1997.

———. "What Are Judgments of Value?" In *Philosophical and Theological Papers, 1965–1980*, 149–156. Edited by Robert Croken and Robert M. Doran. Collected Works of Bernard Lonergan 17. Toronto: University of Toronto Press, 2004.

———. "The World Mediated by Meaning." In *Philosophical and Theological Papers, 1965–1980*, 107–118. Edited by Robert Croken and Robert M. Doran. Collected Works of Bernard Lonergan 17. Toronto: University of Toronto Press, 2004.

Long, D. Stephen. *The Perfectly Simply Triune God: Aquinas and His Legacy*. Minneapolis: Fortress Press, 2016.

Lubac, Henri de. *The Drama of Atheist Humanism*. Translated by Edith M. Riley, Anne Englund Nash, and Mark Sebanc. San Francisco: Ignatius Press, 1995.

Mabry, Eric. "*Inquantum est Temporaliter Homo Factum*: Background, Reception, Meaning, and Relevance of the Hypothesis of *esse secundarium* in the Christology of Thomas Aquinas." PhD Dissertation. University of St. Michael's College, 2018.

MacIntryre, Alasdair. *After Virtue: A Study in Moral Theory*. Third Edition. Notre Dame: University of Notre Dame Press, 2007.

———. *Three Rival Versions of Moral Enquiry*. Notre Dame: University of Notre Dame Press, 1990.

Marion, Jean-Luc. *God without Being: Hors Texte*. Second Edition. Translated by Thomas A. Carlson. Chicago and London: University of Chicago Press, 2012.

———. "Thomas Aquinas and Onto-theology." In *Mystics: Presence and Aporia*, 38–74, Edited by Michael Kessler and Christian Sheppard. London and Chicago: University of Chicago Press, 2003.

Martin, Jennifer Newsome. *Hans Urs von Balthasar and the Critical Appropriation of Russian Religious Thought*. Notre Dame: University of Notre Dame Press, 2015.

Massingale, Bryan. *Racial Justice and the Catholic Church*. Maryknoll, NY: Orbis, 2010.

Matava, J. R. *Divine Causality and Human Free Choice: Domingo Báñez, Physical Premotion and the Controversy de Auxiliis Revisited*. Brill Studies in Intellectual History 252. Leiden: Brill, 2016.

Matthews, William A. *Lonergan's Quest: A Study of Desire in the Authoring of Insight*. Toronto: University of Toronto Press, 2005.

Mealey, Mark T. "Lonergan's Notion of Speculative Theology in His Dissertation on *Gratia operans*, in Comparison with the Notions of Method in *Method in Theology*." *Method: Journal of Lonergan Studies* 19, no.1 (2001): 113–141.

Mencken, H. L. *Prejudices: Second Series*. London: J. Cape, 1921.

Mettepenningen, Jürgen. *Nouvelle Théologie: Inheritor to Modernism, Precursor to Vatican II*. London: T&T Clark, 2010.

Möhler, Johann Adam. *Unity in the Church, or the Principle of Catholicism: Presented in the Spirit of the Church Fathers of the First Three Centuries*. Translated by Peter C. Erb. Washington, DC: Catholic University of America Press, 2016.

Moltmann, Jürgen. *The Crucified God: The Cross of Christ as the Foundation and Criticism of Christian Theology.* Translated by R. A. Wilson and John Bowden. Minneapolis: Fortress Press, 1993.

———. *The Trinity and the Kingdom: The Doctrine of God.* Translated by Margaret Kohl. Minneapolis: Fortress Press, 1993.

Newman, John Henry. *An Essay in Aid of a Grammar of Ascent.* Notre Dame: University of Notre Dame Press, 1979.

———. *An Essay on the Development of Christian Doctrine.* Sixth Edition. Notre Dame, IN: University of Notre Dame Press, 1989.

Nichols, Aidan. *The Conversation of Faith and Reason: Modern Catholic Thought from Hermes to Benedict XVI.* Chicago: Liturgy Training Publications, 2011.

Novak, Michael. *Ascent of the Mountain, Flight of the Dove: An Invitation to Religious Studies.* New York and London: Harper & Row, 1971.

Oakes, Edward T., and David Moss, eds. *The Cambridge Companion to Hans Urs von Balthasar.* Cambridge: Cambridge University Press, 2004.

O'Regan, Cyril. *The Anatomy of Misremembering: Von Balthasar's Response to Philosophical Modernity, vol. 1: Hegel.* New York: Herder & Herder, 2014.

Orji, Cyril. *A Semiotic Approach to the Theology of Inculturation.* Eugene, OR: Pickwick Publications, 2015.

Ormerod, Neil. *The Trinity: Retrieving the Western Tradition.* Milwaukee: Marquette University Press, 2005.

Pannenberg, Wolfhart. *Systematic Theology, Volume 1.* Translated by Geoffrey W. Bromiley. Grand Rapids: Eerdmans, 1991.

Pelikan, Jaroslav. *Reformation of Church and Dogma (1300–1700).* The Christian Tradition: A History of the Development of Doctrine 4. Chicago and London: University of Chicago Press, 1984.

Pelster, Franz. "Die Bedeutung der Sentenzenvorlesung für die theologische Spekulation des Mittelalters. Ein Zeugnis aus der ältesten Oxforder Dominikanerschule." *Scholastik* (1927): 250–255.

Piaget, Jean. *The Psychology of Intelligence.* Translated by Malcolm Piercy and D. E. Berlyne. London: Routledge, 1950.

Pieper, Josef. *The Silence of St. Thomas.* Translated by John Murray and Daniel O'Connor. New York: Pantheon, 1957.

Pius XII. *Divino afflante Spiritu.* Accessed August 28, 2020. Vatican.va.

Przywara, Erich. *Analogia Entis: Original Structure and Universal Rhythm.* Translated by John R. Betz and David Bentley Hart. Grand Rapids, MI: Eerdmans, 2014.

Quantin, Jean-Louis. *Le catholicisme classique et les pères de l'église: Un retour au sources (1669–1713).* Paris: Ètudes augustiniennes, 1999.

Quinto, Riccardo. *Scholastica: Storia di un concetto.* Padua: Il Poligrafo, 2001.

Rabinow, Paul, and William M. Sullivan, eds. *Interpretive Social Science: A Second Look*, 82–140. Berkeley, Los Angeles, and London: University of California Press, 1987.

Rahner, Karl. *The Trinity.* Translated by Joseph Donceel. New York: Herder & Herder, 1970.

Reno, R. R. *Resurrecting the Idea of a Christian Society.* Washington, DC: Regnery Faith, 2016.

―――. *Return of the Strong Gods: Nationalism, Populism, and the Future of the West.* Washington, DC: Regnery Gateway, 2019.

Richardson, Alan. *History Sacred and Profane.* London: SCM Press, 1964.

Ricoeur, Paul. *Freud & Philosophy: An Essay on Interpretation.* Translated by Denis Savage. New Haven and London: Yale University Press, 1970.

―――. "Psychoanalysis and the Movement of Contemporary Culture." In *The Conflict of Interpretations: Essays in Hermeneutics*, 121–159. Edited by Don Ihde. Translated by Willis Domingo. Evanston, IL: Northwestern University Press, 1974.

Robin, Corey. *The Reactionary Mind: Conservatism from Edmund Burke to Donald Trump.* Second Edition. New York: Oxford University Press, 2018.

Rothacker, Erich. *Logik und Systematik der Geisteswissenschaften.* Second Edition. Bonn: H. Bouvier u. Co. Verlag, 1947.

Sadler, Gregory A., ed. and trans. *Reason Fulfilled by Revelation: The 1930s Christian Philosophy Debates in France.* Washington, DC: Catholic University of America Press, 2011.

Schussler Fiorenza, Francis, and John P. Galvin, eds. *Systematic Theology: Roman Catholic Perspectives.* Second Edition. Minneapolis: Fortress Press, 2011.

Smith, Gerald. *Freedom in Molina.* Chicago: University of Chicago Press, 1966.

Snell, Bruno. *The Discovery of Mind: The Greek Origins of European Thought.* Translated by T. G. Rosenmeyer. New York: Harper Torchbooks, 1960.

Sokolowski, Robert. *The God of Faith and Reason: Foundations of Christian Theology.* Reprint Edition. Washington, DC: Catholic University of America Press, 1995.

Sonderegger, Katherine. *Systematic Theology, Volume One: The Doctrine of God.* Minneapolis: Fortress Press, 2015.

―――. *Systematic Theology, Volume 2: The Doctrine of the Holy Trinity: Processions and Persons.* Minneapolis: Fortress Press, 2020.

Stebbins, J. Michael. *The Divine Initiative: Grace, World-Order, and Human Freedom in the Early Writings of Bernard Lonergan.* Toronto: University of Toronto Press, 1995.

Stegmüller, Friedrich. *Geschichte des Molinismus.* Münster: Aschendorff, 1935.

Tanenhaus, Sam. *The Death of Conservatism: A Movement and Its Consequences.* New York: Random House, 2010.

Tanner, Kathryn. *God and Creation in Christian Theology: Tyranny or Empowerment?* Minneapolis: Fortress Press, 2005.

Thomas Aquinas. *Basic Writings of St. Thomas Aquinas, Volume 1.* Edited by Anton C. Pegis. New York: Random House, 1945.

―――. *On Being and Essence.* Translated by Joseph Bobik. Notre Dame: University of Notre Dame Press, 1965.

―――. *On Evil.* Translated by John A. Oesterle and Jean T. Oesterle. Notre Dame: University of Notre Dame Press, 1995.

―――. *Summa Contra Gentiles.* Editio Leonina Manualis. Rome, 1934.

―――. *Summa Theologiae.* Editiones Paulinae. Rome, 1962.

Tracy, David. *Blessed Rage for Order: The New Pluralism in Theology*. New York: The Seabury Press, 1978.
Trilling, Lionel. *The Moral Obligation to Be Intelligent: Selected Essays*. Edited with an Introduction by Leon Wieseltier. New York: Farrar, Strauss and Giroux, 2000.
Vatican Council I. *Dei Filius*. Accessed August 28, 2020. Vatican.va.
Vatican Council II. *Dei Verbum*. Accessed August 28, 2020. Vatican.va.
———. *Sancrosanctum Concilium* Accessed August 28, 2020. Vatican.va.
Vermeule, Adrian. *Common Good Constitutionalism: Recovering the Classical Legal Tradition*. Cambridge and Medford, MA: Polity Press, 2022.
Voegelin, Eric. *Order and History, Vol. 1: Israel and Revelation*. Edited by Maurice P. Hogan. Collected Works of Eric Voegelin 14. Columbia and London: University of Missouri Press, 2001.
Ward, Graham. "*Allegoria Amoris*: A Christian Ethics." In *Christ and Culture*, 183–218. Challenges in Contemporary Theology. Oxford and Malden, MA: Blackwell, 2005.
Williams, Raymond. *Keywords: A Vocabulary of Culture and Society*. New Edition. Oxford: Oxford University Press, 2015.
Williams, Rowan. "Balthasar and the Trinity." In *Cambridge Companion to Hans Urs von Balthasar*, 37–50. Edited by Edward T. Oakes and David Moss. Cambridge: Cambridge University Press, 2004.
Wills, Garry. *Nixon Agonistes: The Crisis of the Self-Made Man*. New York: Signet, 1971.

# Subject Index

abstraction, 39, 58, 60–62, 64, 73, 76, 99, 131, 159, 160; abstractness, 26, 39; categories, 29; inquiry, 3; intelligence, 76; universals, 39; viewpoints, 57, 71
aesthetics: categories, 110, 111; and classicism, 6; pattern of experience, 40; theological, 145, 147, 148
*aggiornamento*, 14, 45
analogy, 12, 28, 98, 103, 124, 127, 130, 140, 142–144, 146, 153, 160; and dialectic, 3, 5; kenotic, 124, 130, 145, 149, 154; of habit, 109; of intelligible emanation, 37, 138; of proportion, 111; of science, 37. *See also* psychological analogy
analysis, 30, 32, 33, 50n65, 51n89, 66, 69, 71, 80, 91, 96, 100, 153; cultural, 70; empirical, 3, 61; formal, 111, 112; intentionality, 62; metaphysical, 20, 132; modern, 6, 57; philosophical, 28, 103; speculative, 110
authenticity, 57, 62, 72, 78–80, 89, 90

Bannezianism, 21, 47n14
being, 101–104, 129, 132, 147; cause of, 35; human beings, 31, 60, 62, 75, 91, 97–99, 115; idea of, 60; in the world, 7, 147; nominalist notions of, 10; question of, 3; proportionate, 91, 100, 109, 132; unrestricted, 34

Catholicism, 7; culture, 2, 5, 63; faith, 125, 129, 159; theology, 6, 8, 15n1, 16n8, 20, 21, 33, 38, 129, 130, 161
causality, 1, 3, 9, 21, 22, 35, 36, 38, 39, 44, 45, 60, 91–93, 95, 109, 115, 125, 126, 128, 129, 131, 140, 143, 145, 161
Christ, 55, 92, 96, 107, 113, 114, 133, 146–149; Christocentrism, 8; Christology, 8, 108, 117n5, 145, 151
classicism, 3, 7, 10, 57–59, 64–66, 69–74, 81, 86n71, 89, 91, 160
cognitional theory, 3, 33, 46, 52n90, 116, 139, 141
concreteness, 8, 69, 73, 76, 89
consciousness, 26, 32, 39, 41, 44, 55, 62, 64, 138, 140–144, 149, 150; differentiations of, 71, 79; duality of, 126; historical, 43, 45, 69, 70, 89, 91; intellectual, 38, 63, 132, 133, 160; polymorphism of, 57, 89; rational, 38, 40, 41, 63, 141
conversion, 40, 79, 87n87, 89, 126, 129, 133–135

## Subject Index

creation, 75, 76, 91, 92, 96, 100, 104–109, 116, 119n79, 128, 131, 146, 148, 149
culture, 3, 4, 7, 8, 10, 11, 56, 62, 64, 69, 70, 73, 75–77, 79, 87, 89, 112, 158; as empirical, 3, 45, 58, 63, 65, 70, 74, 87n88; as psychoanalysis, 68, 69; as semiotic, 66–68, 70

*de auxiliis*, 21, 47n14, 116
dialectic, 2, 5, 9, 13, 19, 23, 24, 27–31, 38, 41, 55, 58, 73, 74, 78–80, 82, 87n99, 89–93, 108, 111, 114–117, 123, 124, 126, 143, 144
distinction, 21, 26, 31, 32, 38, 41, 42, 52n92, 67, 68, 91, 93–97, 101–105, 107–109, 127, 131, 137
doctrine, 1, 5, 6, 8, 14, 19–23, 26, 27, 30, 32, 36, 40, 43, 57, 61, 62, 64, 73, 75, 77, 80–82, 91, 92, 94, 95, 99–102, 104–106, 108–111, 114, 116, 124, 126–129, 131, 139, 141, 143, 148, 155n27, 156n47
*Dramatics*, 145, 148

essence and existence, 38, 52n92, 101–104, 109
existentialism, 61–63, 103, 107, 117n5, 151, 159
extroversion, 101, 127, 135

faculty psychology, 62, 133, 139, 140

grace, 10, 13, 20–22, 25–27, 31, 34, 42, 91, 74, 91–101, 105, 112, 113, 117, 126, 131, 133, 137, 143, 144, 159

hermeneutics, 67, 68, 108

idealism, 1, 68, 126, 127
immediacy, 116, 126, 127, 138, 149, 159
incarnation, 75, 91, 92, 107, 108, 111, 113, 124, 146

insight, 21, 28, 33, 34, 37, 40, 64, 77, 80, 90–93, 98, 100, 104, 105, 112, 113, 123, 126, 129, 138, 140–142, 146
intellect, 7, 24, 25, 28, 59, 61, 76, 92, 93, 101, 128, 129, 132, 133, 138, 159
intelligibility, 25, 28, 39, 59, 61, 65, 69, 91, 95, 100, 102–104, 112–114, 124, 128, 129, 140, 146
intelligible emanation, 37, 129, 132–135, 138, 140, 142
integralism, 12, 160, 161
intentionality, 38, 62
intuition, 39, 138

judgment, 2, 10, 12, 32, 38–41, 43, 44, 63, 72, 80, 104, 133, 138, 141, 144, 151, 152

kenosis, 124, 129, 130, 144, 147–150, 152, 153
knowing, 1, 3, 7, 28, 32, 35, 36, 39, 59, 60, 75, 101, 103, 123, 136, 138, 139, 141
knowledge, 1, 3, 5, 7, 10, 22–24, 32, 34–36, 38, 40–42, 45, 59, 60, 62, 67, 69, 81, 93, 98, 99, 101, 102, 115, 126, 129, 136, 137, 139, 140

liberalism, 2, 3, 6, 9, 11–14, 161
logic, 29, 38, 42, 56, 60, 61, 97, 106, 159
love, 30, 71, 72, 79, 94, 98, 99, 134, 136, 138, 141, 142–144, 147–153

meaning, 14, 19, 24–26, 32, 33, 37–39, 45, 58–60, 62–64, 67–69, 72–76, 79, 81, 104, 106–108, 110, 124–127, 129, 133, 140, 143, 145, 146, 149
metaphysics, 12, 14, 20, 53, 56, 60, 64, 65, 69, 99, 103, 105, 106, 109, 110, 115, 132, 139, 143, 145, 153
method, ix, 1–4, 6–8, 14, 15, 21, 23, 28, 33, 34, 37, 38, 42, 45, 56, 57, 60–63,

## Subject Index

65, 69, 79, 81, 94–96, 99, 100, 106, 111–113, 115, 124, 159
mission, 124, 130, 133–135, 143–149, 152, 153
modernity, 4, 10, 11, 45, 57, 65, 66, 83n11
Molinism, 21
mystery, 24, 27, 30, 43, 65, 78, 80, 95–98, 109, 112, 116, 129, 130, 135, 136, 149

nature, 1, 12, 23, 24, 26, 28, 36, 42, 45, 55, 58, 60, 63–66, 68, 76, 78, 90–93, 97–99, 101, 102, 104–106, 109, 112, 113, 115, 116, 124, 131, 135, 137, 142, 143, 146
New Testament, 107, 133
Nicaea, council of, 107, 127
normativity, 58–61, 63, 65, 66, 72, 74, 78, 80, 81

order, 1, 3, 6, 8, 12–15, 20, 21, 23, 26, 28, 29, 31, 32, 34, 37, 41, 42, 55, 58–60, 68–72, 74, 77, 90, 92, 95–97, 99–101, 104, 105, 109, 112–114, 116, 117, 124, 135, 143, 144, 146, 150

person, 36, 37, 55, 75, 98, 125, 131, 133, 134, 137, 142, 144, 147, 151, 152
philosophy, 3, 5, 10, 12, 19, 28, 30, 39–41, 43, 46, 56, 58–61, 63–65, 70–72, 81, 91, 102, 105, 106, 123, 126, 159, 160
pluralism, 4, 20, 55–58, 73–75, 77–80, 82, 89, 90, 92, 108, 114, 116, 117, 124, 125, 128, 130, 133, 143, 153, 154, 159–161
postmodernism, 1, 26, 45, 57
potency, 30, 102–104, 133
procession, 37, 74, 124–126, 128, 129, 132–135, 138–140, 142, 144, 145, 148–150, 153, 160

psychological analogy, 113, 124, 130–133, 138, 139, 141–144, 146, 150–153, 155n27

realism, 63, 101, 126
*ressourcement*, 2, 5, 14, 18n52
revanchism, 2, 160
revelation, 5, 20, 22, 24, 31, 34, 37, 55, 61, 71, 72, 80, 92, 95, 108–111, 113, 128–130, 144–149, 152
revolution, 2, 3, 8, 10, 11, 13, 31, 45, 46, 57, 60–62, 70, 159

scholasticism, 15n1, 21, 26, 32, 33, 47n18, 55, 59, 63, 94, 98, 111, 131, 139, 141, 143, 159
science, 1–4, 21, 23, 32, 34–39, 41–43, 45, 57, 60–66, 68, 81, 105, 115, 159, 160
secularism, 1, 3, 6, 26, 42, 105
self-abandonment, 147, 148
self-appropriation, 124, 141, 142, 149
self-communication, 69, 93, 112, 128, 145, 146, 153
spirit, 4, 12, 44, 65, 70–72, 82, 110, 124, 125, 127, 128, 131, 133–136, 138–140, 143–152, 160
stages of meaning, 58
subject, 3, 8, 13, 34, 35, 40, 61, 62, 68, 74, 76, 77, 80, 89, 90, 109, 123, 141, 143, 144
syllogism, 34, 35, 50n65, 56

theology: dogmatic, 8, 61, 124; historical, 42, 115; moral, 73; positive, 5, 6, 15n2, 42–44; speculative, 2–9, 14, 15, 20, 22–25, 27–29, 31–33, 37, 42–46, 55–58, 60, 63, 64, 69, 72–82, 89–92, 96, 100, 110–116, 123–125, 131, 137, 143, 145, 146, 149, 150, 153, 159, 160; systematic, 7, 8, 16n8, 18n51, 23, 58, 78, 125
theorematic domains, 109–115, 125, 130, 132, 146, 153, 154

theorem of the supernatural, 21, 25, 80, 90–93, 97, 99, 100, 104, 105, 107–117, 124, 125, 128, 130, 143–146, 149, 153, 159

transcendence, 12, 71, 87n99, 95, 100–105, 106, 108, 115, 116, 117

transposition, 35, 91, 139, 143, 160

Trent, council of, 20

Trinity, 36, 37, 113, 125, 126, 129, 131, 135–137, 139, 141, 145, 148, 149, 151, 152

understanding, 5, 15, 21–28, 30–44, 55, 58, 60, 61, 63, 68–70, 74–80, 89–96, 98, 101, 104, 106–117, 125–133, 136–143, 146, 149, 151, 159–161; act of, 23, 28, 32–34, 38–40, 44, 49n54, 52n90, 80, 101, 129, 132, 133, 138, 140, 142, 151; flight from, 42, 160; unrestricted act of, 34

value, 3, 10, 44, 57, 59, 62, 63, 65, 66, 68–71, 74–80, 114, 133, 134, 138, 144, 151, 152

Vatican I, 32, 33, 49n55, 83n12, 95, 118n23

Vatican II, 5, 6, 15n2, 44, 63, 139

*via doctrinae*, 35, 36, 41

*via inventionis*, 35, 37, 57

wisdom, 12, 30, 44, 59, 62, 127

wonder, 30, 38, 95, 150

# Name Index

Ahmari, Sohrab, 12, 18n35, 36
Albert the Great, 21, 47n17
Anselm of Canterbury, 21, 47n17, 90, 94–96, 117n3
Aristotle, 25, 30, 35, 37, 38, 42, 50n68, 51n76, 52n90, 56, 63, 101, 102, 106
Augustine of Hippo, 2, 21, 33, 40, 47n17, 90, 93, 94, 113, 124, 133, 135–139, 143, 146, 153, 155n27, 156n47
Averroes, 102
Avicenna, 102, 103, 105, 132
Ayres, Lewis, 15n1, 19, 20, 46n2, 156n47

Balthasar, Hans Urs von, 6, 16n4, 16n8, 56, 114, 124, 129, 144–154
Barth, Karl, 8
Becker, Carl, 45, 69, 86n71
Beumer, Johannes, 32–34, 37, 41, 49n55
Blondel, Maurice, 23, 62, 69, 154n4
Bouillard, Henri, 6
Brague, Rémi, 11
Burrell, David, 26, 91, 103–106, 108, 111, 137, 138

Chenu, Marie-Dominique, 6
Coakley, Sarah, 7, 8, 57, 76
Congar, Yves, 5

Copeland, M. Shawn, 75, 87n88, 91
Cowell, F. R., 64

Daniélou, Jean, 6
Dawson, Christopher, 45, 58, 65, 69, 85n48
de Lubac, Henri, 5, 6, 26
Descartes, René, 10
Didion, Joan, 10
Doran, Robert, ix, 4n2, 18n51, 58, 70, 71, 73, 81, 82, 87n99, 109–112, 124, 143–145, 153
Duns Scotus, John, 10, 41

Eliot, T. S., 64

Freud, Sigmund, 68
Fukuyama, Francis, 14

Gadamer, Hans Georg, 45, 69, 70
Geertz, Clifford, 66, 67, 69, 85n55, 87n88
Gilson, Étienne, 16n7, 101, 102, 154n4
Grant, Sara, 104

Hegel, Georg Wilhelm Friedrich, 62, 101
Heidegger, Martin, 7, 17n16
Hofstadter, Richard, 9

Hunt, Anne, 113

Jacobs, Jane, ix, 1, 13
Johnson, Elizabeth, 77, 78
John XXIII, 14

Kant, Immanuel, 1, 7, 10, 26, 62
Kluckhohn, Clyde, 66
Kuhn, Thomas, 76, 84n28

Lacan, Jacques, 13
Langer, Susanne, 67–69, 85n55
Latour, Bruno, 66
Leo XIII, 83n12
Lilla, Mark, 10, 11, 13
Lombard, Peter, 15n1, 21, 25, 55, 96, 97
Lonergan, Bernard, 4, 6, 15, 16n8, 20–43, 45, 46, 51n89, 57, 59–63, 65, 68, 69, 73, 75, 76, 78, 79, 82n3, 87n99, 89–91, 93–99, 108, 109, 111–114, 117, 123–127, 131–135, 138–143, 146, 151–153, 154n4

Ma, Eric, 92, 117n5
MacI, Alasdair, 10, 11, 47n18
Maimonides, Moses, 105, 106
Marion, Jean-Luc, 16n10, 17n16
Mettepenningen, Jürgen, 6, 15n2
Moltmann, Jürgen, 131, 148, 152
Mondésert, Claude, 6

Newman, John Henry, 19, 23, 50n65
Nietzsche, Fredrich, 7, 10, 60
Nixon, Richard, 9
Novak, Michael, 77

Péguy, Charles, 5
Pelagius, 91
Pelikan, Jaroslav, 20
Philip the Chancellor, 21, 25, 93, 97–100, 105
Pieper, Josef, 105
Pius XII, 16n6, 83n12
Plato, 101, 102

Rahner, Karl, 8, 16n8, 129, 131, 139, 148, 149, 152, 155n26
Reno, R. R., 11, 12
Ricoeur, Paul, 68
Robin, Corey, 10

Socrates, 59, 111
Sokolowski, Robert, 91, 106–108
Sonderegger, Katherine, 7–8, 146, 157n70
Stebbins, Michael, 47n12, 94, 96, 98, 99
Strauss, Leo, 10

Tannenhaus, Sam, 11
Tanner, Kathryn, 47n14, 115, 116
Thomas Aquinas, 6, 16n16, 19, 20, 21, 25–27, 29, 33–37, 42, 43, 47n14, 49n41, 56, 58, 68, 90, 93, 105, 111, 112, 125, 128, 129, 131, 132, 137–141, 145, 152, 159, 160
Trilling, Lionel, 9

Vermeule, Adrian, 12
Voegelin, Eric, 10, 70, 81

Williams, Raymond, 64, 84n43
Wills, Garry, 9

# About the Author

**Ryan Hemmer** (PhD, Marquette University) is editor-in-chief of Fortress Press in Minneapolis, Minnesota. His writing has appeared in *The Lonergan Review*, *The Bulletin of the Colloquium on Violence and Religion*, *Syndicate Network*, and several edited volumes. He serves on the editorial council of Streets.mn, a transportation and land use news and information publication covering the Twin Cities metro and greater region. He lives in St. Paul, Minnesota.